ELEMENTARY SCHOOL INDUSTRIAL ARTS

classroom and laboratory

by

CARL GERBRACHT, PH.D.
STATE UNIVERSITY OF NEW YORK
COLLEGE OF ARTS AND SCIENCES, OSWEGO

and

ROBERT J. BABCOCK, ED.D.
WEST VIRGINIA UNIVERSITY
REHABILITATION RESEARCH AND
TRAINING CENTER, CHARLESTON

The Bruce Publishing Company, New York

Library of Congress Card Number: 76–92075
Copyright © 1969 The Bruce Publishing Company
Made in the United States of America

preface

Ten years (and some 20,000 copies) ago, *Industrial Arts for Grades K-6* was written. In the interval, the field of elementary school industrial arts has grown considerably, the Council for Elementary School Industrial Arts, a section of the American Industrial Arts Association, has come into being, and a rationale for the work has been formulated and articulated by the profession. It is time to take another look.

The new title, ELEMENTARY SCHOOL INDUSTRIAL ARTS, is meant to indicate that major changes have taken place. Most of the text is new. Chapter 1 still deals with "The Role of Industrial Arts in Elementary Education," but hopefully, it tells the story better and makes it more relevant to today's educational practices. Chapter 2 is entirely new, describing "Industrial Arts in Nontypical Programs," a subject too long neglected in the literature, though some very fine work has been done in the field. Chapter 3 has been greatly expanded and now deals effectively with the specialized industrial arts workshop or laboratory, as well as with the classroom work area. The chapter covers "Facilities, Equipment, Tools, and Supplies," in more detail. Chapter 4 on "Basic Skills," and Chapter 5 on "Projects and Activities," are better organized and more readable. The Appendix, addressed to the Industrial Arts Specialist-Consultant, has been retained, but streamlined. All of the chapters and the appendix are more fully illustrated because there are more things worth photographing in elementary "IA" today than there were ten years ago. The book now contains 268 illustrations, mostly photographs.

The underlying purpose of the book remains unchanged—to explain the role of industrial arts in elementary education and to suggest how the work may proceed.

We wish to thank the many publishers who have permitted portions of their works to be quoted, and the following persons and organizations for their counsel, advice, photographs, and many kindnesses: Brodhead-Garrett Company, Cleveland, Ohio; Dr. Merle E. Frampton, The New York Institute for the Education of the Blind, Bronx, New York; Dr. Harold Gilbert, Northern Illinois University, De Kalb, Illinois; Leonard Glismann, Salt Lake City Public Schools, Salt Lake City, Utah; Dr. Robert Hawlk, Ohio University, Athens, Ohio; Professor Robert Hostetter, State College, Millersville, Pennsylvania (and the Laboratory School of Millersville State College); Elizabeth Hunt, Department of Education, Trenton, New Jersey; Norman Martinus, Norwalk Public Schools, Norwalk, Connecticut; Professors Enzo Mazzer (Laboratory School) and Robert Cooksey, State University of New York College of Arts and Sciences, Oswego, New York; Charles McCabe, Great Neck Public Schools, Great Neck, New York; Dr. Howard F. Nelson, University of Minnesota, Minneapolis, Minnesota; Edward Niedzialek and Leonard Zwick, Rochester School for the Deaf, Rochester, New York; Frederick Noyes and Edward Jennings, Newark State School, Newark, New York; Herbert Siegel, New York Public Schools, New York City; Standard Pressed Steel Company (Hollowell School Shop Furniture), Jenkintown, Pennsylvania; Dr. Eberhardt Thieme, Robert DeLapp, Vincent Johnson, and Joseph Savino, Rochester Public Schools, Rochester, New York; Tolerton Company, Alliance, Ohio; and Professor Alvin E. Wutti, Wisconsin State University, Whitewater, Wisconsin.

September, 1969   CARL GERBRACHT
                                                      ROBERT J. BABCOCK

TABLE OF CONTENTS

5/ PROJECTS AND ACTIVITIES

Appendix/ THE INDUSTRIAL ARTS SPECIALIST-CONSULTANT

chapter 1 | THE ROLE OF INDUSTRIAL ARTS IN ELEMENTARY EDUCATION

A DEFINITION OF ELEMENTARY SCHOOL INDUSTRIAL ARTS

"You know, Mother, they really do get milk from cows!" This discovery, part of seven-year-old Mary Ann's enthusiastic report about the visit she made with her class that day to a farm, has a familiar ring; comments like it have been heard by every teacher. Learning begins with contact with the real world, and establishing that contact is a fundamental task of the elementary school. Attempts at learning without such contact result in children acquiring incorrect, inadequate, or "hollow" meanings. Mary had heard and read about cows giving milk, but the reality of such a thing was far beyond her comprehension. Her experience would not permit her to imagine it.

Some children, we know, come to school every day bubbling over with the stimulation provided by their environment—by travel, music, books, ideas, pets, toys. For others, life outside of school is bleak and void. The school must insure, at every level, that sufficient, appropriate, cultural contact takes place to permit meaningful learning of the subject matter of the curriculum.

What is the nature of this culture with which contact must be established? Obviously, it is tremendously complex. It includes people, things, natural phenomena, the fine arts, history, animals, the moon and stars, crime, language, and virtually everything else (Figure 1). The task of the curriculum builder is to catalogue this culture and to select from this vast

Figure 1. Modern, well equipped elementary schools provide for industrial arts activities.

store of knowledge that which is most necessary, pertinent, and appropriate for the learner.

One of the most necessary, pertinent, and appropriate areas for study in the elementary school involves man's industries: how he makes things and how he uses them. Today's industries affect our social organization, housing, transportation, communication, and food. Our industries produce the products we use, they employ our people, and they provide the means of our country's defense. They influence our language, science, history, and economics. Indeed, very little in our world is untouched by them. These industries should be reflected in the elementary school curriculum.

What should the child know about *industry?* He should know something of its *materials*, its *processes*, its *tools* and *machines*, its *workers* and *products*, and its *impact* on other aspects of living. This knowledge must, of course, be presented on a level that is comprehensible to the child.

How are these understandings to be achieved? The school should provide opportunity for firsthand contact with these elements—the materials and processes, the tools and machines, and the workers and products of industry —so that the impact may have meaning for the child. Contacts of this type are encompassed in the term "industrial arts."

Effects on Other Curriculum Areas

When children engage in industrial arts activities, it is sometimes difficult to separate the results which pertain solely to a study of industries from those which illuminate or support other subject matter fields, such as social studies, language arts, science, or mathematics. Suppose a class visits a construction site as a part of an industrial arts unit. The children put their senses to work. They watch the concrete truck deliver its load, they hear the sand and gravel scratching around in the mixing drum, they feel the rough steel of the reinforcing rods, and they smell the fir plywood as the whining power saw bites into it. In short, they are immersed in firsthand contact. In addition to having gained an increased understanding of certain industrial materials, processes, tools and machines, workers and products,

Figure 2. Real pulleys.

Figure 3. School should be fun.

the children have been in contact with many other things. They have seen how individuals in modern society specialize, and thereby contribute more efficiently to the common good. They have seen how cooperative effort increases man's accomplishments. They have seen how power is harnessed to multiply the capacity of human muscles. They have been exposed to sensory perceptions which, interpreted by a skillful teacher, can contribute to many of the school's goals.

Here is an example involving measurement. How long is "four feet long"? "Four feet long" is confusing if it is first encountered as a sentence in a book, but the question, and its answer, are completely intelligible to a child who has measured "four feet" on a stick to be used in a classroom project. The context provides an accurate meaning.

You might take any word and reflect on its meaning. Take the word "bend." Can you visualize some materials bending more easily than others? Do some things bend into smooth curves and others into sharp corners? Do some things remain in the shape into which they are bent and others spring back? Do some tend to break when they are bent? Do you see "bend" used figuratively? Where do these meanings come from? These meanings are all enriched by doing some "bending" for yourself.

If one accepts the notion that meaningful learning originates in contact with the real world, does this require that learners be forever dependent upon contact with physical things? Obviously not.

Less and less firsthand contact is required as learners gain a background of experience. There comes a time when the symbol, "chalk," is almost as useful as the material itself. True, one can never write with the symbol, but he can think with it, and he can use it to help him solve problems. He can even reject it in favor of another symbol, "typewriter," when the real thing to which "typewriter" refers is more suited to the task at hand. But notice that he can mentally select and reject *only when his symbols have accurate and useful meanings*. Those meanings, of course, must originate with firsthand contact. How can one know what chalk is until he has touched it and used it; how else can he know what a typewriter can do?

When a child is able to select or reject symbols for things, and no longer needs the objects themselves as aids to his thinking processes, he is operating on higher levels of abstraction. This is fine. Developing this ability to think abstractly is one of the goals of most schools. The starting point, however, is contact with *the things* for which the symbols stand. Without knowledge of the real things, the abstractions are meaningless.

These "cross over" contributions, which industrial arts activities can make to other subject matter areas, are in no sense "frosting on the cake." They are an essential part of the whole cake. If making a plant flat for an experiment with seeds generates an interest in science, then a substantive contribution has been made to the learning process. And if dividing a cork disk for a dart game helps to clarify the concept of fractional parts, the very substance of mathematics is being dealt with.

These "cross over" relationships are not to be left to chance. In a well-conceived program of elementary education they are built into the very fabric of the curriculum.

In summary, industrial arts activities appropriate for the elementary school serve two principal functions. First, they provide subject-matter content that helps a child to understand the industrial-technological nature of his world. Secondly, they provide firsthand, constructive, purposeful contact with material objects, and thereby enhance the total learning process.

Each of the following activities is an integral part of the school program: (1) constructing a model airport as part of a unit on transportation, (2) experimenting with the durability of textile materials as part of a unit on clothing, (3) visiting a home-building site as part of a unit on housing, (4) exploring a wooded area as part of a unit on nature's materials, (5) collecting and mounting samples of printing as part of a unit on communication, (6) making an abacus as part of a unit on numbers, (7) setting up a model power station as part of a unit on electricity, (8) building a castle as part of a unit on medieval history, (9) grinding corn meal as part of a unit on American Indians, and (10) observing an automobile assembly line as part of a unit on manufacturing. All of these industrial arts activities grow from the curriculum and enrich that curriculum.

HISTORICAL PERSPECTIVE

It is difficult to say exactly when the "practical arts" first became a concern of teachers. It seems reasonable to assume that they predate academic subject matter, since prehistoric man must have taught his children first what they needed to know for survival; then, what they needed to know for communication and self-expression; and, as time permitted, for leading the "good life" as it may have been defined at the time. As formal education developed, the teaching process was turned over to specialists. During the development of educational practices, the practical arts were sometimes popular, and sometimes less than popular, but they never disappeared for long. Evidently, there is something of timeless significance to the practical arts, for they appear in some form in nearly every era of educational history. It is worth noting that the cause of the practical arts inevitably is championed by the recognized thinkers who are in the forefront of each trend in the history of education.

Early Leaders in Educational Reforms

Rabelais (1483–1553) was one of the early French writers on the subject of educational reform. A physician and social philosopher, Rabelais was appalled by the formalistic education of his day. He had no quarrel with what the schools were trying to teach, but he felt that the schools actually made sense to few students and made life generally miserable for those who persisted in wanting to learn. In his *Gargantua*, he revealed his theories of good teaching. His students enjoyed school, for his lessons in "arithmetic, geometry, astronomy, and music . . . were learned by means of games with cards and dice." Furthermore, "On wet days he busied himself with carpentry, sculpture and other practical occupations, and visited the fencing school or some of the workshops in the town." [1]

Two centuries later, Rousseau (1712–1778), another French reformer, outlined his ideas for education in his classic *Emile*. Taking a good look at the nature of the learner, Rousseau prescribed learning through the hands as the gateway to the mind. He advocated that "a child should learn an industrial trade—not for any vocational purpose but because it was the best preparation for a well-born boy to understand social relationships. It also served to raise the pupil above any danger of becoming a human parasite and to discourage the tendency of despising those who must work with their hands." [2]

Another well-known name in educational history is Pestalozzi (1746–1827), one of the early advocates of education for all, poor as well as rich. Pestalozzi was so disturbed by the plight of vagrant urchins that he gathered a group of them in his home in Neuhof, Switzerland, and proceeded to teach school. There were few formal lessons; the educative process started with activities such as soil tilling, weaving, and domestic chores. These were things to talk about and think about, and under Pestalozzi's skillful guidance, the spoken and written language grew out of these experiences. The ill-mannered, undernourished, ignorant urchins became strong, alert, useful, music-loving people who worked successfully with their minds and their hands.

[1] William Boyd, *The History of Western Education* (London: Adam and Charles Black Ltd., 1961), p. 219.

[2] C. Atkinson and E. T. Maleska, *The Story of Education* (Philadelphia: Chilton Book Company, 1965), pp. 64–65.

Figure 4. Casting blocks for a house foundation.

In subsequent experiments at Stanz, Burdorf, and Yverdun, the Swiss pedagogue used similar techniques. Study always grew out of manual activities; the workshop was the classroom. "In addition to form study and drawing, Pestalozzi's students engaged in a great variety of activities, including spinning, weaving, farming, gardening, bookbinding, needlework, and cooking." [3]

Pestalozzi's work began with the belief that life-related education could reduce poverty (two and a half centuries before VISTA [4]), and the knowledge developed in his experiments contributed to the time-tested theories of learning accepted today. At the head of Pestalozzi's list of teaching methods was the use of concrete things and firsthand experience for instruction in the basic subjects.

Pestalozzi's most famous disciple, Froebel (1782–1852), is perhaps best known as the originator of the Kindergarten, which dates from 1839, in Blankenburg, Germany. Froebel used "gifts" and "occupations" as teaching tools. Balls, blocks, triangles, leaves, seeds, sticks, and similar objects were provided as playthings. Froebel demonstrated to the children that although the basic forms of these things could not be changed, they could be arranged and rearranged in many schemes, which he likened to many rigid aspects of society. The "occupations" included work with paper, wood, paint, clay, yarn, and cardboard. Froebel felt that modifying and controlling these materials provoked discovery, thought, and reasoning. Froebel believed that handwork stimulated all other learning, and that doing led to knowing.

[3] H. M. Byram and R. C. Wenrich, *Vocational Education and Practical Arts in the Community School* (New York: Macmillan Co., 1956), p. 135.

[4] Volunteers in Service to America (VISTA) was a part of the Great Society program of the Lyndon B. Johnson administration.

Although Pestalozzi had many followers, they did not all agree on his rationale. Herbart (1776–1841), for example, saw great value in handwork, but only as a device for teaching the regular school subjects; that is, he knew exactly where the handwork was supposed to lead. Froebel, on the other hand, provided the handwork opportunities and allowed them to lead where they would. Certainly, both approaches were Pestalozzian.

The Oswego Movement

The most successful importation of Pestalozzian methods to the United States was made by Sheldon (1823–1897). As Superintendent of Schools in Oswego, New York, Sheldon tutored his classroom teachers in Pestalozzi's object method and brought Pestalozzi's protégés from Europe. Sheldon became so excited about the process of teacher education in the object method, that in 1861 he founded, and became principal of, the State Normal and Training School at Oswego (now the State University of New York, College at Oswego), which included a school of practice. In the school of practice, Sheldon installed two workshops, one for the young children and one for the student teachers, where everyone worked with tools and materials. Learning blossomed from firsthand experience.

Sheldon's influence on elementary education spread; he traveled widely to speak of his experiences in teacher education, and thousands came to see his campus school in operation. Graduates of the Oswego Normal School were in great demand and held positions throughout the United States and abroad.

Manual Training

Thus far, the object teaching method was applied to what might be called general education as contrasted with vocational education or job training. In the late nineteenth century, there was, however, another branch of education in America, specifically, vocational training. Usually taught in the upper grades of elementary schools or in high schools, education of this type was first considered an adjunct of schooling rather than an integral part of the curriculum. It was designed to keep people (especially boys) in school, to provide vocational skills, and to develop leisure-time interests. The name usually applied to such activities was "manual (hand) training."

As teachers gained experience in manual training, they discovered that it had some important general educational (as well as vocational) values, and the two branches of manipulative work tended to merge. The work of Felix Adler (1851–1933) is an example of this merging.

Adler was one of the founders of the New York School for Ethical Culture. His interests centered around the children of the working classes. He wanted them to have schooling that would help them acquire the skills to earn a living, but he also wanted more. He wanted them to have the personal pride and dignity that comes with the deeper knowledge of "why" as well as "how." He wanted them to understand the principles involved in the use of tools, machines, and processes, and he wanted them to understand why certain tasks had to be performed. Then, he went one step further; he tried to relate the manipulative experiences of pupils "organically" to other school studies. He felt, for example, that aesthetic values and mathematical and physical principles would be better taught by working with material things.

Encouraged, no doubt, by Adler's broader point of view, leaders in industrial-vocational education began to take the position that manual activities were important regardless of the future vocation of a pupil. The notion that manual activities belong exclusively in vocational training programs gave way to the concept that these experiences have value for all.

As "shop" work tended towards general education rather than purely vocational education, and spread throughout the country, a significant change took place. Usually, early manual training work did not result in a useful product, but only in some sort of exercise, such as the making of a wood joint. Then, in an ever increasing number of school shops, interesting and useful articles began to appear, these helped shop work to gain in popularity. The objects produced were fairly small and usually arranged in a series; easily built projects were made first and succeeding projects were increasingly difficult. The fact that the finished products had utilitarian value made the entire manual training movement more attractive, and certainly more valuable from a pedagogical point of view.

During the period from 1890 to 1910, three main criticisms of manual training were voiced. One of these criticisms held that too much emphasis was placed on developing skills and not enough on providing information related to the skills. Another criticism was that little or no attention was given to the design of the articles. A third criticism was that no attention was given to relating construction activities to the rest of the curriculum, even where the connection was obvious. In other words, the shopwork idea spread, but the rationale was too often left behind.

As attempts were made to remedy the difficulties, the programs assumed a character best described by the term "manual arts," which gradually replaced "manual training" in the literature of the field. Some progress was made in upgrading instruction, to provide related information, and to stress good design, but little was done in those years to relate manual arts activities to the rest of the school program, except in isolated instances.

In the late nineteenth century, John Dewey entered the educational arena. In his University Elementary School in Chicago, he used "industrial occupations" as teaching methods for all subjects. In his *School and Society,* Dewey explained his industrial occupations as tasks that were characteristic of the adult world as well as the school world. He conceived industrial occupations as the very core of the school's program in the lower elementary grades. School experiences should start with real activities, and subject matter should be learned when and where it is needed. These needs become apparent in carrying out an activity.

Most educators who sought to interpret Dewey's point of view preferred to retain the logical subject-matter sequence in the school's curriculum. More and more, construction activities as a part of general education were expanded to include not only development of skills, but also appreciation and understanding of industry and (a fairly new idea at the time) intelligent selection and use of industry's products.

Once more, the term applied to construction activities—manual arts— was deemed inadequate because the products to be selected and wisely used were more and more the result of mechanical rather than manual processes. Since 1904, when it was first suggested, the new term "industrial arts" has gained wide acceptance as adequately describing the program.

Figure 5. Medieval castle.

Frederick Bonser of Teachers College, Columbia University, in *Industrial Arts for Elementary Schools*, combined many of the ideas thus far suggested, and included some new ones, in his philosophy of industrial arts. At that time, it should be remembered, two principal schools of thought existed regarding industrial arts in the elementary school. One conceived of industrial arts as a subject-matter field, valid for its own content, designed primarily to develop manipulative skills, and featuring information related to production. The other school conceived of industrial arts activities as a means or method of teaching standard subject matter, illustrative or motivational in character.

For Bonser, industrial arts included both content and method, but with a new perspective. According to him, the work of the elementary school should include "those elements of study which are of common value to all." He admitted the validity of such studies as science, mathematics, language, and social studies, but asked further: "Is there not also a body of experience and knowledge relative to the industrial arts which is of common value to all, regardless of sex or occupation?" [5]

Bonser suggested that attention be given to the study of foods, clothing, shelter, utensils, records, and tools and machines as vital concerns of everyone. He admonished, furthermore, that these studies are of value for their subject-matter content, not merely in order that manipulative skills might be developed. He then conceived these studies as means or method because of the various understandings and appreciations of the cultural heritage which would inevitably result.

Most of Bonser's content studies (food, clothing, shelter, etc.) have found their way into the curriculum of today, though not always under the name of industrial arts.

Principal Ideas Historically Guiding Elementary School Industrial Arts

These are the principal ideas that have guided elementary school industrial arts up to recent years:

European roots to the early nineteenth century
To provide lifelike experience with material things.
To train the mind through handwork.
To support understanding in the basic subject areas.

[5] Bonser and Mossman, *Industrial Arts for Elementary Schools* (New York: Macmillan Co., 1923).

Early and middle nineteenth century
>To develop tool skills basic to manual trades and occupations (home-making and industrial).
>To provide for constructive use of leisure time.

Late nineteenth century
>To develop vocational skills.
>To promote an appreciation of the dignity of labor through a broad knowledge of mechanical principles.
>To assist in the clarification of academic studies.

Turn of the century
>To develop an appreciation of good design.
>To provide knowledge related to industrial production, primarily for better orientation towards one's chosen vocation.
>To facilitate (through concrete experiences) the teaching of the common branches of study.

Early twentieth century
>To serve as "core" experiences upon which to build the curriculum in lower elementary grades.
>To develop an understanding and appreciation of industry as the concern of everyone in an increasingly industrialized society.
>To assist in the intelligent selection and use of industry's products.

Later twentieth century
>To provide experiences in practical, constructive activities (involving food, clothing, shelter, etc.) as necessary to the education of everyone, and through these experiences to develop understanding and appreciation of our cultural heritage.

The preceding outline is by no means all-inclusive, but it is a guide to the predominant thoughts regarding the nature and function of industrial arts activities during the last two centuries. Indeed, current statements on the place of industrial arts in elementary education include practically all of the earlier concepts with varying degrees of emphasis.

Mid-twentieth century

The writers of this book take the position that virtually all of the concepts outlined above have some grounds for validity today, making allowances for changes in word meanings which have evolved with time. The modern elementary school recognizes most of these concepts as worthy educational goals.

The 14th Yearbook of the American Council on Industrial Arts Teacher Education, a division of the American Industrial Arts Association (AIAA) and the National Education Association (NEA), states:

> There is little doubt that industrial arts at the elementary school level should emphasize the general development function of education. The age of the learners, in light of society's practices, precludes the need for the [vocational] development function. Industrial arts may serve to develop simple "skills" and the acquisition of additional knowledge of industry. However, such skills and knowledges should probably be thought of as contributing to the general development of the child and only incidentally, if at all, to his [vocational] development. Industrial arts can provide an initial and very elementary guidance function—largely information about the learner for future use. All areas of instruction should serve this function. It may also be safely assumed that industrial arts at the elementary level will prove to be as effective in recognizing the attitudes of the learner as will any other area and will provide the opportunity for the proper correction or change, as well as growth and development of such attitudes.[6]

The American Council of Industrial Arts Supervisors states:

> Industrial Arts in the elementary schools (kindergarten through grade six) is designed to further educational objectives and to enrich the experiences pupils have in attaining them. The activities in industrial arts place emphasis upon the planning and construction required in meeting needs that arise as pupils participate in social studies, science, mathematics, and language arts activities. Pupils enjoy greater satisfaction and understanding by actually producing objects which they have previously tried to visualize. Abstract concepts are made more meaningful with concrete evidence. The pupils make use of skills they have acquired in other phases of the construction program, acquire new skills, improve their ability to visualize, and in many other ways become increasingly proficient as individuals and as members of the groups to which they belong.[7]

CURRENT TERMINOLOGY

As is the case with many developing concepts in education, the search continues for the term that best describes the type of learning activity under consideration. The term "industrial arts" has been criticized by some

[6] *Approaches and Procedures in Industrial Arts*, 14th Yearbook, American Council on Industrial Arts Teacher Education, 1965, pp. 39–40.

[7] *Industrial Arts Education*, American Council of Industrial Arts Supervisors, 1963, p. 6.

people as having too narrow a scope (there are practical arts other than those related to industry). The term is disliked by some because its meaning when applied to junior or senior high school work is somewhat different and there is concern that secondary level procedures might unduly influence elementary level practice, which would be unfortunate. Other terms have been suggested and are sometimes used: "practical arts," "creative arts," "integrated handwork," "handcrafts," "arts and crafts," "construction arts," "industrial studies," and "technology" or "industrial technology."

Only time will tell which term can best convey the concept of purposeful, constructive activities suitable for the elementary school. "Industrial arts" is used in this book because it is, at present, the most widely accepted term, and because it indicates that the particular "arts" with which we are concerned are those involved in man's industries, that is, with his efforts to produce and use material things.[8]

CONTRIBUTIONS OF INDUSTRIAL ARTS TO ELEMENTARY EDUCATION

When people use the term "education" in reference to a child, they mean many things—motivating, guiding, helping, instructing, training, advising, molding, counseling, evaluating—all of which are in the interest of the child's total development. In the American society, the responsibility for some areas of the child's development is accepted by the home and family, some areas are the responsibility of the church or some other agency, and some are clearly the responsibility of the school, though the lines separating each sphere of influence are seldom drawn sharply. Listed in this section are those areas of human behavior in which the school plays a major role and to which the industrial arts can make a significant contribution.

Intellectual Development

Teachers should do all in their power to insure that adequate intellectual development takes place. Intellectual development is central in the school's purpose. Basic to a child's intellectual development is an adequate, accurate, understanding of things, places, people, ideas, and events. This understanding comes about through experience and contact with life to the fullest possible extent. Industrial arts activities provide much of that contact. The industrial arts provide the action through which the child senses, manipu-

[8] One section of the American Industrial Arts Association (NEA) is called the "American Council for Elementary School Industrial Arts."

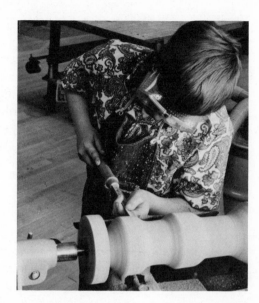

Figure 6. Fifth grader at work.

lates, and deals with the environment. The industrial arts provide a series of handles for the child to grasp. They help the child to come to know more fully that to which he is exposed. They give substance to the building blocks of knowledge.

Individual Differences

Teachers should recognize and make allowances for variations of learning capacities among students. No teacher can work with youngsters engaged in purposeful activities without becoming almost forcefully aware that individuals differ. When the results of work are readily observable, as in the field of construction activities, differences are obvious. Moreover, in the area of construction these differences can be accommodated. There may be only one way to spell a word, or only one acceptable answer to a problem in arithmetic, but there are many ways to make a gift for Mother's Day, and there are many alternatives in choosing what that gift shall be. Properly chosen projects can challenge superior students; other projects can provide successful experiences for slower learners. Often, a single group project involves tasks that cover a wide range—from the basic and easy, to the complex and difficult. The gifted child can proceed at a pace of which he is capable, and so can the slower child. Thus, the results of the work of each child can be satisfying to him.

Socializing Experiences

Socializing experiences should be provided. Social values such as those involved in sharing, respecting the efforts and property of others, accepting responsibility, appreciating the uniqueness of individuals, and understanding the purpose of economy in the use of materials, are among the generally accepted goals of education today. Contributions can be made to the development of these values when students participate in activities that involve tangible things (Figure 7). This is another way in which values can be taken from the realm of the abstract and reinforced as they function in the daily experience of each child.

Occupational Information

The school should provide the beginnings of occupational information. The decisions people make about their occupations have roots in their childhood experiences. School people are beginning to realize how important early experiences are in forming such decisions.[9] Specific choices are seldom made at the elementary school level, and it would be unfortunate if they were. At the same time, children need a chance to discover their talents and interests in various broad categories of work, of which the practical arts is certainly one.

Figure 7. Second graders making a house.

[9] See Virginia Bailard, "Vocational Guidance Begins in Elementary Grades," *The Clearing House*, Vol. 26 (April, 1952).

In discussing the rationale for occupational studies at the elementary school level, Hoppock mentions these objectives:

> To extend the occupational horizons of the child. To encourage wholesome attitudes toward all useful work. To begin developing a desirable approach to the process of occupational choice. To help students who are dropping out of school and going to work. To help students who face a choice between different high schools or high school programs. To show children who really need money how to get it without stealing.[10]

The foundations for occupational choice are strengthened in two ways through industrial arts. First, as children study about America's industries, they become aware of many kinds of occupations. The child who grows up without hearing about a quality control specialist, for example, is hardly likely to consider that field of work when he makes a vocational decision.

When one takes note of the enormous variety of occupations connected with industry he realizes that acquaintance with some of the major categories of work is essential to intelligent choices. Secondly, experience in some of the kinds of things done in industry naturally helps the children to discover whether or not they have the talents and interests required for success in one industrial field or another. There is of course a significant difference between using the small hand tools of an elementary school industrial arts shop and operating modern industrial machinery, but there are enough similarities to help a youngster begin to form important impressions. The work in both cases is manipulative, involving materials, requiring precision, and producing physical things. In short, it is one large, important category of human activity to be considered in choosing an occupation.

Satisfaction

Schooling should be fundamentally pleasant. Whatever else it may be, going to school should be fun. Over the long term, people do what gives them satisfaction, and if the school years make learning a pleasant process, one of the primary goals of education has been achieved.

Who are the school's failures? Mainly, they are the students whose school life has been unrewarding and generally frustrating. Industrial arts activities can save many of these people. For some, these activities may provide one of the few areas of success; for others, they may be one of the few areas

[10] Robert Hoppock, *Occupational Information* (New York: McGraw-Hill Co., 1957) pp. 344–46.

of school with relevance to real life. Properly exploited, the gateways to learning opened in this way could spell the difference between failure and vitality in the effort to learn.

Motivation

The teacher must be concerned with motivation. The opportunity to work with material things is not the only type of motivation the teacher can use, but it is a forceful one. The desire to work with tools to make things is strong in most children. These are the activities children talk about at home, and the products of their efforts are shown with pride. Areas of the curriculum that are generally uninteresting can take on a glamour that stimulates inquiry and learning. The "readiness" so important in the learning process can be created through projects intrinsically interesting to children. Making a model farm can be used to create the readiness necessary for a study of soil erosion and the means for its prevention. A simple woven mat can lead to a study of textiles and clothing.

Cultural Heritage

The curriculum should acquaint children with their cultural heritage. The cultural heritage of the human race involves manual and technological processes. It is impossible to appreciate the people of any age or any geographical region without understanding something of their handicrafts, or their industries and its products. Who could explain America without frequent references to its industries and what they have done for our culture? Everything we do is influenced by our extraordinary industrial system.

To make corn meal as the American Indian did is to develop a fuller understanding of the Indian's culture; to make adobe brick is to live with the people of Latin America; to weave grass mats is to understand one facet of Polynesian life. The same principles apply when one tries to understand contemporary American culture. Aluminum, plastics, and molded plywood are part of today's world, and to manipulate them is to experience contemporary America more fully.

Fundamental Skills

The school must teach fundamental skills. Number and word skills are fundamentals to learning, of course, and industrial arts activities help to develop them. There is, however, another kind of fundamental skill which

Figure 8. Making musical instruments.

is too often neglected in schools. It is manual and mechanical skill. "Do it yourself" is too ingrained in American life to be called a fad; it is part of our culture. We have surrounded ourselves with machines and gadgets which demand certain mechanical experiences, if they are to be used wisely. Every home is crammed with them: washers, dryers, ironers, and vacuum cleaners; television sets, radios, and record players; electric toothbrushes, knives, and pencil sharpeners; hairdryers and manicure sets; and on and· on. The garage or basement workshop houses another group of tools: lawnmowers, power saws and drills, sanders, hedge-trimmers, and snow-blowers. To move about we use automobiles, motorbikes, marine engines, and snowmobiles. The family helicopter is, perhaps, not far off.

There are skills and understanding that pertain to these objects and their intelligent use. Knowledge and skill are basic to their safe and efficient use. The handling of common household tools like hammers and screwdrivers, the operation of an automobile, and the piloting of a jet airliner —these kinds of skills have unique importance in our lives.

Industrial arts activities lay the foundation for manual and mechanical skills. Furthermore, they develop attitudes of respect for good workmanship and performance, and for the dignity of mechanical and technological pursuits.

These, then, are some of the values to be derived from elementary school industrial arts. In the final analysis, any measurement of the values accruing from the industrial arts activities must take into account the relative emphasis given to this type of work and the manner in which it is pursued.

CHARACTERISTICS OF CHILD DEVELOPMENT

Of vital concern is the child-person with whom we are to deal. He is neither a miniature adult nor a small adolescent. The makeup of each child is physically, intellectually, emotionally, and socially different from his peers and those of other age groups. Of even more importance from an educational point of view, children differ significantly from each other; they differ when they start school, and they develop at different rates. Still, in the developmental process, there are discernible patterns that provide guides to educational practice.

Physical Aspects

Muscle development and control is a regulating factor in the choice of industrial arts activities, since it determines the tools and materials with which a child can cope. Generally speaking, the large muscles of the limbs, shoulders, and back develop earlier in life than the small muscles of the fingers and eyes. Consequently, the big, sweeping motions needed to wield hammers and saws are possible for a child to handle, long before he can master the more exacting control needed for screwdrivers and knives. As physical development progresses, greater degrees of precision are possible, and more intricate tasks can be accomplished.

The process of physical development is slow and gradual, and little can be done to hasten it. Activities demanding coordination of which a learner is incapable are likely to result in frustration and a growing doubt in the child's mind about his own abilities. Self-confidence comes with achievement, not with failure and frustration. Furthermore, tasks beyond a child's capacities can be dangerous where sharp tools and power machines are involved.

Children are active, and they need to be active. Physical activity and movement are to be expected, and the industrial arts program should take this into account by providing the kinds of activities appropriate for each level of physical development. While engaged in industrial arts activities, the children should have relative freedom of movement; moving about the room to obtain needed tools and supplies, or by simply watching a classmate at work. Not only is such movement consistent with the physical needs of children, but it enriches the total educational experience, because children learn from what they see others do and from the total environment of a well-planned shop.

The following developmental characteristics are essentially physical:

a. Handedness is established by the time children start school.
b. Children tire easily; they are restless; activity appears in spurts. Rest periods are needed in the lower grades. As children mature, this activity moderates and becomes increasingly even and constant.
c. Children need between 10 and 12 hours of sleep at age six, and somewhat less sleep as they mature.
d. There is great susceptibility to communicable diseases, particularly in the lower elementary grades.
e. Hand-eye coordination and muscular (including eye) development is poor at the lower levels, but improves steadily. Primarily, large-muscle activity is appropriate in early years. Small-muscle skills generally can be expected to develop in nine- and ten-year olds, around Grade 4.
f. Children are active; their developmental characteristics call for many opportunities for manipulation, construction, and exploration.
g. In Grades 5 and 6, the onset of puberty contributes to a general upheaval in the life of the individual.
h. Children differ physically.

Intellectual Aspects

A vivid imagination and a flair for dramatic activity are characteristic of young children. They are not aware of their own limitations, and their interest span is short.

One of the teacher's goals should be to help the children to develop the ability to plan ahead realistically and to foresee outcomes. Industrial arts activities provide many such opportunities. Since planning does not develop spontaneously, the teacher must plan with the children at first, withdrawing more and more as the children gain experience. The choice of activities in early years should be closely circumscribed by the teacher, with greater freedom encouraged as the children mature.

The following developmental characteristics are essentially intellectual:

a. Interests grow from "home-centeredness" in the lower grades toward constantly expanding horizons.
b. At early levels children are interested primarily in an activity for its own sake; the product or result is of secondary importance.
c. Their span of attention is short, lengthening somewhat in the upper grades, but still limited.
d. Generally, children are not aware of their own limitations. This awareness develops with experience.

Figure 9. Bridge builders.

e. Children are aware of color, but they do not discriminate between shades of color at lower levels.
f. Imagination is vivid; realism and fantasy are almost indistinguishable in the early years. The importance of reality develops gradually. Dramatic activities are popular.
g. When judged by adult standards, children are hurried and careless, being relatively unable to foresee consequences.
h. Children should learn to foresee effects and consequences; that is, they should learn to plan.
i. Children are developing a sense of economics, but an understanding of the costs of materials cannot be assumed. The same is true of a sense of time.
j. In the intermediate grades, children are naturally competitive, and measure themselves against their peers.
k. Children shun decision-making in early grades, but seek opportunities for making decisions in the upper grades.
l. Ethical and moral values can be said to develop about Grade 2 and grow in strength with maturity.
m. Adaptiveness is developing, but in the lower grades the reassurance that comes with unvarying routines is essential.
n. Children differ intellectually.

Emotional Aspects

The enthusiasm with which children undertake a given activity is related to the satisfaction they receive from the activity. Children can learn to wait for deferred satisfaction, but in early years they will not wait too long. A given activity or project should require a short period of time, and the results should be apparent as work proceeds.

The praise and encouragement of the teacher is one form of satisfaction children need, and it should be freely given. Opportunities should be found to display the children's work. Fortunately, the field of industrial arts offers such a wide variety of opportunities that every child should be able to find satisfaction in some phase of the work. If the satisfaction is slow in coming, the teacher should quickly consider changes in the activity.

The following developmental characteristics are essentially emotional:

a. Enthusiasm for a given interest may appear boundless at one moment, but disappear shortly thereafter in favor of another interest.
b. Young children may cry easily and pout without being able to understand their own feelings.
c. Children need approval from adults: expressions of affection and love, praise, and encouragement; and a feeling of importance through expanding responsibilities and doing (and making) useful things.
d. In the intermediate years, children begin to seek peer approval.
e. Noise over long periods can be fatiguing.
f. In the upper grades, children seek independence.
g. Emotional disturbances can be expected at the onset of puberty.
h. Children differ emotionally.

Social Aspects

Some industrial arts activities should involve independent work and some should involve group effort. Obviously, the opportunity to develop social skills is one of the important values to be achieved. The ability to work together harmoniously and efficiently must be developed, and group projects afford excellent opportunities for this growth. The sharing of tools and

Figure 10. Working together.

shop facilities, cooperation in cleanup at the end of the period, delegation of responsibilities to complete a group project, and respect for the rights and property of others are some examples of the social values industrial arts activities can promote.

The following developmental characteristics are essentially social:

a. Children tend to be boastful.
b. A sense of ownership is established very early, and children should learn to share as they mature.
c. Children exhibit few inhibitions in early years.
d. Children are self-centered in early years; later they seek security in peer group associations and cliques.
e. In the early years, boys and girls associate freely, but beginning in Grades 2 and 3, they tend to associate primarily with members of their own sex.
f. Children exhibit little sense of group welfare in early years.
g. Children learn to work together (Figure 10); it cannot be assumed that this ability exists at the beginning of school.
h. Children like group activities.
i. Competitive spirit begins to be significant around Grade 3.
j. Children differ socially.

ORGANIZING AN INDUSTRIAL ARTS PROGRAM

When, where, and how should industrial arts activities be provided? In answering this question, one should keep in mind what is to be expected from the industrial arts work. To summarize the preceding material, at the elementary school level industrial arts activities help to:

a. Acquaint children with the industrial-technological aspects of their culture.
b. Reduce levels of abstraction, develop adequate meanings, and enrich the curriculum.
c. Provide for individual differences.
d. Provide socializing experiences.
e. Supply the beginnings of occupational information.
f. Make school and learning enjoyable.
g. Motivate learning.
h. Teach fundamental manual-mechanical skills.

With these ideas in mind, industrial arts activities should be provided whenever they can make significant contributions to the curriculum. An inflexible list of things to do would be impossible to justify, since curriculum patterns vary.

Scheduled or Unscheduled

There are two scheduling systems used in schools with successful industrial arts programs. One system sets aside a given number of periods each week,[11] during which the children engage in industrial arts work. The other system permits each classroom teacher to arrange time for industrial arts work as it seems to fit instructional needs. Where classroom teachers do not have the assistance of an industrial arts specialist-consultant, the latter system prevails. Where a specialist is provided, neither system seems to have great advantages over the other, provided the classroom teacher is involved in determining the class activities. This is an important point. The classroom teacher is the only person acquainted with both the curriculum material under consideration and the children in any particular group, and can best determine which industrial arts activities are most appropriate.

Where classroom teachers simply turn their classes over to industrial arts specialists for specific time periods, without regard for the relationships between the industrial arts work and the normal classroom work, much is lost. Under such conditions, the industrial arts work tends to become an "arts and crafts" activity and loses much of its potential relevance.

Ideally, the classroom teacher should be present when the industrial arts activities are going on. At the very least, the classroom teacher should know what is happening because he should consult frequently with the specialist about the work to be undertaken.

Where regular industrial arts periods are established, the industrial arts work tends to assume an independent character, with its own resource units. The following are examples of such units:

Manufacturing in Our City	Air Travel
Modern Means of Communication	Modern Waterways
Transportation, Past and Present	Minerals and Their Uses
Roads-Tunnels-Bridges	Fuels and Power
Mass Production in America	Modern Industrial Materials
Electricity as Power	Forest Products
Homes for Americans	Home Appliances and Their Care
Buildings for Work and Play	Maintaining the Home

There is no reason why such units cannot be connected to other classroom work, and they should be, for best results. The content of such units

[11] Anywhere from one period a week to one a day.

Figure 11. The industrial arts consultant is a helping-teacher and resource person.

should be appropriate to other classroom work, and the classroom teacher is the only person who can be sure that these appropriate relationships exist.

Where industrial arts periods are not rigidly established, but are arranged as a need in the classroom work makes them appropriate, there is likely to be a ready-made connection between classroom work and industrial arts activities. For example, a teacher whose class is working on medieval history may feel that the building of a model castle would be helpful. Thus, in consultation with the industrial arts specialist, such an activity is arranged. Or, as a part of the study of music, a classroom teacher may want the children to construct simple musical instruments. As a part of a science unit the teacher may feel the need for models to illustrate certain mechanical principles. Under such a system, the industrial arts consultant and classroom teacher jointly plan the required activity, the time it will take, the materials needed, and the methods of procedure. Further examples of industrial arts activities which grow out of the curriculum are given in Chapter 5.

Both scheduling systems are in successful operation in American schools. In general, the schools in larger metropolitan centers appear to favor the scheduled system, and the schools in smaller administrative units appear to favor the unscheduled system, though exceptions can be found.

Classroom or Shop?

In observing elementary school industrial arts activities around the country, one would see some work carried on in regular classrooms and some in separate shops or workrooms. Where regular classrooms are used, a corner is usually set aside for activities and modestly equipped with tools and materials. Sometimes tools and supplies are brought to the classroom by an industrial arts specialist on a portable cart, making it possible for a limited number of tools to serve several classrooms.

Using the regular classroom has some advantages. For one thing, it is possible for part of the class to be engaged in construction work while other children are doing other things; thus the entire class is under the teacher's control. For another, when construction facilities are present in the classroom, they are more likely to be used as spontaneous need for them develops, producing closer connections with the classroom studies. But there are disadvantages, too. Construction work involves noise, dust, and dirt, and occasionally spilled paint and glue, and construction work requires space which many classrooms cannot spare.

The separate industrial arts shop is considered by many people to be preferable. A shop can be equipped more fully than a classroom; indeed, it can be designed specifically for the work to be done. It can include storage space for a wider variety of materials and supplies than any one classroom can afford to stock, and it can provide work space and storage space for bulky projects. The shop can include machines that would be inappropriate in a classroom because of their cost, noise, and danger. Children of all grade levels enjoy coming to a shop to work. If it is equipped appropriately for the size and age of the children, even the very youngest can be accommodated safely. Finally, a separate shop demands a specialist, and this person should have the training to provide a superior program.

Figure 12. Industrial arts consultant-specialist in the shop.

The only significant disadvantage of a separate shop is the possibility that industrial arts work might deviate from the classroom curriculum, but this danger can be avoided through careful planning by conscientious teachers.

Perhaps the ideal arrangement would be a flexible system permitting the use of the shop for some activities, and regular classrooms for others. Some kinds of work are entirely portable and can be brought to the classroom, when circumstances indicate that this procedure is best. Some kinds of work are best conducted in the shop setting. There is no good reason why the choice between these alternatives cannot be made by the industrial arts specialist and classroom teacher, in the light of the conditions which prevail.

The Industrial Arts Specialist

Many fine programs of industrial arts activities are being carried on in elementary schools by classroom teachers working individually, on their own initiative or with minimum assistance. Unfortunately, too few classroom teachers have the time and skills to provide the wide variety of opportunities to which children are entitled. When one considers the breadth of competence expected of teachers in elementary schools, it hardly seems reasonable to add another field of work to an already heavy burden. More and more schools are recognizing the great value of specialist-consultants in guidance, music, art, home economics, science, industrial arts, and other curriculum areas. These specialists never replace classroom teachers in their control of the curriculum, but they can and should work with classroom teachers in the interest of improving the school program within their own special curriculum area. The classroom teacher remains "at the helm" when it comes to decisions affecting his class.

The primary function of the industrial arts specialist is that of a resource person. His special preparation has acquainted him with a large number of operations, processes, materials, projects, tools, machines, and various activities appropriate for the elementary school. He keeps in continual contact with classroom teachers, supplying information and offering suggestions. Furthermore, his specialized training and experience enable him to demonstrate procedures and methods with which teachers have not had an opportunity to become proficient or acquainted. Many industrial arts consultants conduct in-service classes and workshops for teachers, which have proved to be an effective way of helping teachers develop skills and obtain a background of related information in a variety of activity areas.

During industrial arts work periods, the specialist is usually in charge of the class, though preferably the regular classroom teacher is present as well. In any case, the work period should have been preceded by one or more planning conferences between the specialist-consultant and the classroom teacher. It is necessary that both have a clear understanding of the objectives and scope of the children's work and its relationship to other curriculum areas. Sometimes the idea for an activity originates with the classroom teacher, and sometimes it is suggested by the consultant after the classroom teacher has described the classroom curriculum. Usually, the details of each activity are worked out cooperatively.

If an industrial arts shop exists in the school, it serves as the consultant's headquarters. It includes storage facilities for tools, supplies, materials, and projects; a laboratory for in-service training; a conference room for consultations; and a work area for the children. In addition, such shops are sometimes used for adult education courses or other community activities. The cost of such installations must of course be weighed against the contribution that a well equipped shop can make to the school's goals.

TEACHER EDUCATION FOR CONSULTANTS AND CLASSROOM TEACHERS

With the growing popularity of industrial arts in elementary schools, teacher-training institutions are giving increased attention to the preparation of teachers qualified to guide these programs. There are two educational categories to be considered: one for students preparing to be specialist-consultants, and the other for students preparing to be classroom teachers. Both need industrial arts experience, but of different types.

Courses for Specialist-Consultants

In general, the people serving as industrial arts specialist-consultants are certified either in elementary education or in industrial arts education. Certification patterns vary from state to state, but in most states, a certificate in either field is adequate for legal purposes.

Those teachers whose major undergraduate concentration has been in industrial arts education are well prepared in manual and mechanical skills and related industrial information. However, the typical industrial arts teacher education program is geared primarily for the junior and senior high school level, with little attention to the elementary school, its curriculum, and young learners. Topics such as the following should be included in one or more special courses for industrial arts majors preparing to be elementary school specialist-consultants:

I. Understanding the elementary school child.
   A. What is he like?
   B. What does he need to learn?
   C. How does he learn?
II. Understanding the elementary school curriculum.
   A. What is the school's function?
   B. How is the school organized?
   C. What content and methods are appropriate?
   D. How is the educative process evaluated?
III. Understanding the part industrial arts should play.
   A. What approaches have been used in the past?
   B. What approach is appropriate now?
      1. What activities are appropriate?
      2. What methods are appropriate?
      3. How can the process be evaluated?
   C. How can the industrial arts "major" assist?
      1. As a specialist?
      2. As a consultant-coordinator?
      3. As an in-service educator for classroom teachers?
      4. As a protagonist?
   D. What is the function of teacher education institutions?
      1. In developing an understanding of content and method.
      2. In training in skills and specific knowledge.
IV. Understanding the physical requirements.
   A. Where should the work be done?
   B. What equipment is needed?
   C. What tools are needed?
   D. What supplies and materials are needed?
   E. How is storage provided?
      1. Tools.
      2. Materials and supplies.
      3. Pupils' work.
   F. What projects are appropriate?
   G. What reference material is appropriate?
   H. Model floor plans for classrooms and laboratories.

These courses should include extensive laboratory work and directed observation as well as student teaching at the elementary level, preferably under the supervision of an elementary school industrial arts consultant.

Directed observation of elementary school children is of paramount importance. Many industrial arts majors have initial difficulty in dealing with young children. Often they tend to assume too much experience on the part of the child, and their speech pattern includes such things as "16th's of an inch," "with the grain," "proper consistency," "inch brads," "oval-head, nickel-plated wood screws," and similar terms, or they tend to expect muscular coordination and skill beyond the capabilities of young children. Conversely, they sometimes overcompensate, and speak in "baby-talk."

Generally, industrial arts majors lack sufficient background and contact to understand the nature and capabilities of elementary school children. Extensive observation in classrooms and activity situations, together with opportunities to intellectualize their observations under the guidance of a specialist in child development or in elementary education, seems the best way of providing the necessary experience.

Special laboratory work, beyond the technical courses usually offered to industrial arts majors, should emphasize activities suitable for the elementary level and provide opportunities to develop and refine projects and activity ideas as well as resources to be applied. Laboratory activities should involve group planning and cooperative group activity, which is generally absent from technical courses for industrial arts majors. At the elementary level, the group problem-solving approach is the one most often used, and the prospective specialist-consultant needs experience in using this approach. Furthermore, the activities chosen should have variety in terms of the curriculum areas to which they connect, and in terms of all grade levels from kindergarten to sixth with distinctions among them. In addition, the laboratory work should include those areas of activity not usually found in the typical curriculum for industrial arts majors: food, clothing, household equipment, and general crafts.

In some schools, people with backgrounds in home economics, home and family living, or art are serving as industrial arts consultants. Their preparation for consultant work should be essentially the same as that of industrial arts majors with one important exception: they usually need much more laboratory experiences with tools and machines, if they are to become familiar with the many industrial processes and materials and develop the resources they will need as a consultant in this field.

Courses for Classroom Teachers

If classroom teachers are to be aware of the contributions of industrial arts activities in their teaching, it stands to reason that they must have an opportunity to become acquainted with the field. Classroom teachers usually

Figure 13. In-service course.

have a thorough understanding of child development and of the elementary school curriculum, so their industrial arts preparation needs to be different from that of industrial arts education majors. For classroom teachers, courses in industrial arts have two principal objectives. The first is to make clear the part which industrial arts can play in the total elementary school curriculum. Secondly, the necessary skills and knowledge in the use of tools, materials, and processes need to be developed. Again, laboratory work and directed observation are essential, together with student-teaching assignments in industrial arts activities.

The laboratory work should emphasize those activities which are appropriate to the elementary school, examples of which can be found throughout this book. The work should involve extensive group planning and group problem-solving. That is to say, the whole class or a group of the class might begin with a question like this: "What industrial arts activities could best contribute to an understanding of the concept of 'sets' in fifth grade mathematics?" The group should then analyze the problem and suggest solutions. The few most promising solutions should be carried through to completion and described in writing or sketches which can be used as resource material for actual classroom teaching. Some form of industrial arts resource notebook or folder should be prepared by each student, concentrating, if possible, on the grade levels for which the student is preparing.

As the course proceeds, the instructor should be sure that a variety of materials, tools, and processes are explored, and may want to keep a record of some sort to insure a variety of experience.[12] Specific instruction in tool

[12] Possibilities include lists of common tools with a place for each student to check his use of a tool, or some other modification of the familiar progress chart.

and machine techniques should be provided when appropriate. Using his own course outline, the instructor should insure that the minimum fundamentals in technical content are also identified and covered. Information concerning the procurement of materials is important too. Actual contact with modern industry by field trips, films, and other means should not be overlooked.

Throughout, the guiding thought should be that classroom teachers who are confident of their own ability to understand industrial arts procedures and to perform industrial arts activities are more likely to use those procedures and activities in their teaching than teachers who lack experience. Laboratory work should provide that confidence. Considering the important contributions to be made to elementary education by industrial arts work, some such laboratory experience should be provided for all prospective elementary classroom teachers.

For classroom teachers whose undergraduate preparation provided little or no industrial arts work, courses designed for in-service teachers generally are available. They take the form of workshops offered either by school districts or by colleges of education, in which case they usually carry undergraduate or graduate credit. These courses are always popular, and participants find that their enthusiasm grows as their confidence increases.

SELECTED REFERENCES

Approaches and Procedures in Industrial Arts, 14th Yearbook, American Council on Industrial Arts Teacher Education, 1965.

Babcock, Robert J., "Elementary School Industrial Arts," *Graduate Study in Industrial Arts,* 10th Yearbook, American Council on Industrial Arts Teacher Education, 1961.

Bennett, Charles A., *The Manual Arts* (Peoria, Ill.: Manual Arts Press, 1917).

———, *History of Manual and Industrial Education Up to 1870.* (Peoria, Ill.: Manual Arts Press, 1926).

———, *History of Manual and Industrial Education 1870 to 1917* (Peoria, Ill.: Manual Arts Press, 1937), Chapter 2.

Bonser, Frederick G. and Lois Coffey Mossman, *Industrial Arts for Elementary Schools* (New York: Macmillan Co., 1923), Part I and Chapter 13.

Brown, Mamie E., *Elementary Handcrafts for Elementary Schools* (Exposition Press, 1956), Chapters 1 and 9.

Byram, Harold M. and Ralph C. Wenrich, *Vocational Education and Practical Arts in the Community School* (New York: Macmillan Co., 1956), Chapters 9, 10, and 11.

Chamberlain, Duane G., "Practical Arts in the Elementary Classroom," *The Journal of Teacher Education*, Vol. 6 (September, 1955).

Conway, John O., "Industrial Arts for the Elementary Grades," *Teachers College Journal*, Vol. 31 (January, 1960).

Culpepper, Fred W., Jr., "The Elementary Industrial-Arts Experiment at Suffolk, Va.," *Industrial Arts and Vocational Education*, Vol. 41, (March, 1952).

Dawson, Kenneth E., et al., "Elementary School Industrial Arts," *National Education Association Journal*, Vol. 53 (January, 1964).

Ditzler, Walter E., "The American Industrial Arts Association Considers Industrial Arts in the Elementary School," *The Industrial Arts Teacher*, Vol. 14 (October, 1954).

Duncan, Glenn S., "Toward a Better Understanding of Industrial Arts in the Elementary Schools," *Industrial Arts and Vocational Education*, Vol. 52 (December, 1963).

Earl, Arthur W., "Industrial Arts for Every Child in Elementary School," *The Nation's Schools*, Vol. 47 (May, 1951).

Gerbracht, Carl and Harold Gilbert, "Industrial Arts for Grades K-6," *New York State Education*, Vol. 43 (June, 1956).

Gilbert, Harold G., "An Industrial Arts Teacher Education Program for Elementary Schools," (Ph.D. diss., Ohio State University, 1955).

———, *Children Study American Industry* (Dubuque, Iowa: William C. Brown, 1966).

Hanus, Paul H., *Beginnings in Industrial Education* (Boston: Houghton-Mifflin Co., 1908).

Hollis, Andrew P., *The Contribution of the Oswego Normal School* (Boston: D. C. Heath, 1898).

Holmes, F. A., "Industrial Arts for Elementary Grades," *The School Executive*, Vol. 74 (December, 1954).

Hunt, Elizabeth E., "ACESIA: How Can It Improve Elementary Industrial Arts? " *Industrial Arts and Vocational Education*, Vol. 52 (December, 1963).

———, *Industrial Arts Education*, Pamphlet, American Council of Industrial Arts Supervisors, 1963.

Ingram, Franklyn C., "The Effect of Elementary School Industrial Arts" (Ph.D. diss., The Pennsylvania State University, 1966).

Kazarian, Edward N., "Elementary Industrial Arts: Primer to Understanding," *Industrial Arts and Vocational Education*, Vol. 52 (December, 1963).

———, "K-6 Industrial Arts" (under "News of the Profession"), *Art Education*, Vol. 16 (January, 1963).

Klehm, Walter, "Handwork in the Elementary School," *Industrial Arts and Vocational Education*, Vol. 45 (September, 1956).

Kroh, Damon K., "The Four E's in Elementary School Industrial Arts," *Industrial Arts and Vocational Education*, Vol. 45 (December, 1956).

Leavitt, Jerome, "Interviews on Industrial Arts in the Elementary Schools," *Industrial Arts and Vocational Education*, Vol. 45 (February, 1956).

————, "Other Concerns Regarding Fine and Industrial Arts," *Education*, Vol. 75 (February, 1955).

Lux, Donald G., "The Emerging Nature of Industrial Arts in the Elementary School," *The Industrial Arts Teacher*, Vol. 17 (January–February, 1958).

McMullan, Mary, "Unified Arts in an Elementary School," *School Executive*, Vol. 79 (September, 1959).

McWhinnie, Harold J., "The Place of Industrial Arts in the Grades," *Industrial Arts and Vocational Education*, Vol. 51 (June, 1962).

Miller, W. R., "The Role of Industrial Arts in Elementary Education," *Industrial Arts Teacher*, Vol. 22 (September, 1962).

Moore, Frank C., Carl H. Hamburger, and Anna-Laura Kingzett, *Handcrafts for Elementary Schools* (Boston: D. C. Heath, 1953), Chapter 1.

Newkirk, Louis V., *Integrated Handwork for Elementary Schools* (Morristown, N.J.: Silver Burdett, 1940), Chapters 1 and 2.

————, and William H. Johnson, *The Industrial Arts Program* (New York: Macmillan Co., 1948), Chapters 2 and 3.

Nihart, Claude E., "Industrial Arts in the Elementary School," *Industrial Arts and Vocational Education*, Vol. 40 (October, 1951).

————, "Industrial Arts in the Elementary School—Grades 1–6," *The American School Board Journal*, Vol. 125 (September, 1952).

Petersen, Dorothy G., "Industrial Arts and the Elementary School Curriculum," *Journal of Industrial Arts Education*, Vol. 24 (March, 1965).

Phillips, Martin, "Industrial Arts for Youngest School Children Succeed," *New York State Education*, Vol. 47 (November, 1959).

Pollack, John M., "Industrial Arts in Nicaragua," *Journal of Industrial Arts Education*, Vol. 24 (November, 1965).

Robinson, Frank E., "Elementary School Industrial Arts," *School Shop*, Vol. 19 (December, 1959).

Ruley, M. J., "Elementary Industrial Arts in the Public Schools of Tulsa, Oklahoma," *Industrial Arts and Vocational Education*, Vol. 40 (September, 1951).

Schmitt, M. L. and W. D. Chismore, "Definitions for Industrial Arts," *Industrial Arts and Vocational Education*, Vol. 56 (March, 1967).

Scobey, Mary-Margaret, "Industrial Arts for Elementary Schools," *The Industrial Arts Teacher*, Vol. 13 (February, 1954).

————, "Introducing Children to Industrial Arts," *Journal of Industrial Arts Education*, Vol. 25 (March, 1966).

————, "Role of Industrial Arts in the Elementary School Program in Social Studies," *Elementary School Journal*, Vol. 55 (January, 1955).

————, "Trends in Industrial Arts in the Elementary Schools," *National Education Association Journal*, Vol. 44 (January, 1955).

Smith, Delite, "Elementary Industrial Arts on a Shoestring," *Industrial Arts and Vocational Education*, Vol. 54 (September, 1965).

Sredl, Henry J., "Industrial Arts in the 1920's," *Journal of Industrial Arts Education*, Vol. 25 (May, 1966).

U.S. Office of Education, *Industrial Arts—Its Interpretation in American Schools* (Washington, D.C.: U.S. Government Printing Office, 1938), Chapter 2.

Wiecking, Anna M., *Education Through Manual Activities* (Boston: Ginn and Company, 1928), Part III.

Williams, Walter R. III, "A Study of the Judgments of Experts and Practitioners Concerning Superior Practices in Elementary School Industrial Arts," (Ph.D. diss., University of Maryland, 1963).

————, "Elementary School Industrial Arts," *American Vocational Journal*, Vol. 39 (December, 1964).

————, "Studying Industry in the Grades," *Journal of Industrial Arts Education*, Vol. 24 (January, 1965).

Wonacott, Wayne A., et al., "Elementary School Industrial Arts," *Education Digest*, Vol. 29 (March, 1964).

"Woodwork and Metalwork," *The (London) Times Educational Supplement*, Vol. 2685 (November 4, 1966).

Wurzbacher, Frederick M., "Hobby Groups Introduce Industrial Arts," *New York State Education*, Vol. 39 (June, 1952).

Wutti, Alvin E., "Teacher Education Programs for Elementary School Industrial Arts," *Journal of Industrial Arts Education*, Vol. 24 (September, 1964).

Zimmerman, Theo. C., "Teaching Activities in Elementary I-A," *Industrial Arts and Vocational Education*, Vol. 52 (December, 1963).

See also contemporary books on principles, methods, and curriculum of elementary education.

Various state and local departments of education have produced instructional guides for industrial arts activities. These are not listed because they are often available only to teachers within their repective state or school systems. Departments of education should be consulted for lists of appropriate references.

chapter 2 / INDUSTRIAL ARTS IN NONTYPICAL PROGRAMS

The discussion in Chapter 1 focused primarily on the education of normal children in the usual elementary school setting. Industrial arts activities are found also in programs established for culturally disadvantaged children, for educationally exceptional children, and in rehabilitation therapy.

Education, an important ingredient in socio-economic development, is usually included in plans for economic assistance to developing countries. In our country too, special programs for the educationally disadvantaged have been initiated by federal, state, and local governments, demonstrating the importance of education in solving far-reaching social, political, and economic problems. And, in practically all educational programs related to developmental problems industrial arts can play a prominent part.

An area that is receiving more and more attention is the education of exceptional children: the mentally gifted, the mentally retarded, and children with handicaps involving sight or hearing; children with cerebral palsy, epilepsy, or orthopedic problems; and children with emotional disturbances, brain damage, and other physical impairments. Sometimes programs for exceptional children are conducted in residential schools, though there is a definite trend toward including more of these special programs in regular schools. Therefore, increasing numbers of teachers are coming into contact with these programs. Although many exceptional children come under the

Figure 14. Puppet maker; industrial arts programs play an important part in development of human resources.

care of teachers prepared in "special education," some children are placed in regular classes for all or part of the school day, and so all classroom teachers should know of methods appropriate for the education of these children.

Therapy is not *education,* but the two fields are often closely related. Frequently, a problem that therapy is designed to cure or alleviate constitutes a real obstacle to education. Since industrial arts activities are used so widely in many therapy programs, a section of this chapter is devoted to the subject.

CULTURALLY DISADVANTAGED

The terms, "culturally deprived," "culturally disadvantaged," and "culturally handicapped," have come into widespread usage recently, largely as a result of the attention called to the problem by the federal education programs of the mid-1960's, but these terms do not refer to a new phenomenon in public education. Every teacher knows that children vary widely in the background experiences they bring to school, and these variations are nowhere more striking than in the elementary grades. Any group of school children presents a continuum in the quality of the individual background experiences, richer at one end, poorer at the other, though in a normal or average group the low end does not represent deprivation.

To see what cultural deprivation means, one might look first at the out-of-school environment from which deprived children come, remembering that not all characteristics of the out-of-school life apply to all cases.

The pervasive factor in the environment is poverty. Annual family incomes are extremely low, $3000 a year, and often much less. Adult unemployment is high, and those adults who do have jobs earn low wages and often work irregularly. The salable skills of the adults are meager, and even then, they are not fully used. Sometimes, reliance on public assistance is part of the way of life.

Housing is poor and seldom owned by the occupants. Inadequate sanitary conditions are made worse by large families, and living space is crowded. Privacy is seldom found, quiet almost never.

The education level of adults is low, and although they are usually literate in a legal sense, they generally read little. There is virtual ignorance of "news," as defined by newspapers and magazines, and practically no interest in even the capsule news of radio and television. Radio and television are almost always available; however, they are regarded solely as entertainment and the choice of programs often indicates the lowest levels of taste.

Values, while deep-seated and inflexible, emphasize the immediate rather than the remote, and long-term consequences have little bearing on decisions regarding imminent actions. Crime and delinquency rates are high.

Illness and low energy levels accompany inadequate rest, poor nutrition, and marginal medical care. Emotional instability and even hostility result from the general inadequacy felt by most of the adults. Self-confidence and aspirations are low. A general attitude of cynicism, hopelessness, and despair prevails.

The children coming from such environments represent a big challenge to any teacher. And yet, where are schools and teachers needed more desperately than here?

Having scanned the environment, let us look now more closely at the child who emerges from this background. In the process, let us note especially positive features which might offer promise.

Above all, we should remember that there is a difference in meaning between the words "slow" and "stupid." When watching a child from a culturally deprived environment, one might easily confuse the two words. The child may be slow. The stimuli he has learned to cope with are far removed from schoolwork. Early in his childhood, he may have learned that an inquiring mind brings rebuke, and persistent questioning, a slap. He may

Figure 15. Making memo pads.

Figure 16. Children are delighted with the weather instruments they have made.

have learned that withdrawal is usually the safest course of action. He may have learned that enthusiasm brings ridicule; but given the conditions with which he has had to cope, he has learned his lessons well.

Even if we test the child, we must interpret the results with great care. The tests may not be valid in terms of the child's out-of-school learning. Riessman, referring to psychological studies on the testing of disadvantaged children, states:

> The Davis-Haggard investigators have two fundamental recommendations. One is the development of "culture fair" intelligence tests with questions equally applicable to all groups. There are problems in achieving this policy, however, and until it has been accomplished successfully, the best policy for school personnel would seem to be—teach! Don't use tests to tell you whether the children are teachable; make the assumption that they can learn, and push it to the limit.[1]

[1] Frank Riessman, *The Culturally Deprived Child* (New York: Harper and Row, 1962), p. 114. The reference is to the studies reported in "Social Status and Intelligence," *Genetic Psychology Monographs*, Vol. 49 (1954), pp. 141–186.

What approaches to teaching are most promising? Fundamental to success is the knowledge that deprived children are *physical* learners. They need intellectual achievement, and they need it badly, but they will get it through down-to-earth, act-it-out ways, using material things and firsthand involvement. Again, Riessman states:

> Abstract thinking is ultimately rooted in concrete sensory phenomena. But most of us in the course of educational experience have come to appreciate abstractions for their own sake. This is true whether we are talking about scientific theories or artistic-literary productions. We do not have to see the concrete applications or origins of Shakespeare in order to appreciate him. But deprived children have a very different attitude toward abstract concepts. They need to have the abstract constantly and intimately pinned to the immediate, the sensory, the topical. . . .[2]

If industrial arts work, with its emphasis on firsthand contact and constructive activities, is appropriate for the elementary education of children from normal backgrounds, how much more important it is for the disadvantaged child, whose experience is limited and whose cultural experiences are minimal.

Do the people of deprived areas value education? Definitely yes. They see it as the only hope of emancipation from poverty for their children. But they view education somewhat differently than most teachers. They are suspicious of the vague, generalized goals of liberal, nonspecific studies. To these people, education should be practical, and the sooner results can be seen, the better. They do not necessarily mean vocational education in the usual sense because they fear this will condemn their children to the bottom of the American labor force, but they do mean learning that can be put to immediate use and that has some readily visible consequences.

In this connection, industrial arts activities have a great deal to offer. Industrial arts studies involve the technology, which is visible. These studies start with the relatively familiar world of work, and usually result in something tangible. For the child and his parents, the approach makes sense; and for the teacher, the door is opened to achievements far beyond the activities and projects themselves.

One of the primary considerations in dealing with the culturally disadvantaged child is helping him to see how the school is relevant to him. The school must establish and maintain a correlation with life outside of school, which, as we have seen, is material-oriented and nonabstract. Industrial arts

[2] Riessman, p. 68.

activities deal with things that have practical meanings, things that can provide a common ground from which teacher and pupil start together, with common understandings and a common language.

A great deal has been said about the verbal ability, or inability, of culturally disadvantaged children, and indeed verbal ability and intellectual achievement are often closely related. However, we should not make the mistake of regarding these children as nonverbal, for they are often eloquent in the vernacular language they understand and use, though weak in formal language skills. Our first task, in this connection, is to encourage verbalizing itself, which is not an easy task, particularly if prior school experience has taught the child that his language patterns are unacceptable in school. The most promising approach is to provide something interesting to talk about. One way is to do something interesting. The absorbing activities of industrial arts can serve this end, providing a basis for the all too rare enthusiasm that cries out to be verbalized.

Another standard element in the lives of culturally disadvantaged children is the experience of failure. If teachers cannot do a great deal about life out of school, they can at least make the school the one bright spot in an otherwise bleak world. Construction activities can do much to provide satisfying experiences that result in success, the beginnings of pride, and the foundations of self-confidence and self-respect. Furthermore, those objects, made by the child and taken home, may open channels of communication with parents. The value of this communication far surpasses the value of the objects themselves.

We should not overlook the tool skills learned. Skills and understandings about common tools and household appliances may make a tangible contribution to the homes of culturally disadvantaged children, contributions that could very well improve the life-style of the family.

The child who engages in industrial arts activities gains valuable experience in the process of work itself. Habits of orderly work, systematic procedure, careful planning, problem solving, and care of tools and machines will make the child more efficient as a learner and subsequently more employable in whatever field of work he may choose. This is not vocational education in the narrow sense of developing tool-skill proficiency, but it certainly is prevocational in the broad sense of introducing the child to good work and behavior patterns, and possibly helping him to make wiser vocational choices in later years.

Finally, it should be remembered that intellectual values are the school's primary concern. The school can never abandon its responsibilities in this

Figur 17. Making a model of a kitchen.

area. And no part of the school's program can be permitted to oppose them. Properly conceived, industrial arts activities are in no sense anti-intellectual. On the contrary, they play an important role in the achievement of academic and intellectual values. Because industrial arts activities are closer to the out-of-school experiences of culturally disadvantaged children, they can and should be one of the principal paths leading to all that education has to offer.

The Educational Policies Commission of the National Education Association states:

> To achieve contact with each child, the school must make every effort to help him sense that the school is important to him. It must provide activities to which he can contribute, through which he can earn the respect of others, and in which he can improve his performance. His learning activities should be challenging, but if they are beyond what he can accomplish with reasonable effort, they become meaningless frustrations. Many of these experiences—including classroom activities, clubs, field trips, and sports—should be designed primarily to establish and strengthen contact between the school and the child, and to help him achieve the status he needs if he is to learn. Many children are not quick to develop motivation or ability in academic work. Intellectual development is of central importance, but some of the early steps along this road may not be directly concerned with it. The teacher must judge the need for such steps and must be free to provide a program based on his understanding of the pupil.[3]

[3] Educational Policies Commission, *Education and the Disadvantaged American,* National Education Association, 1962, p. 16.

INTELLECTUALLY EXCEPTIONAL CHILDREN

To their credit, members of the teaching profession, at least in the United States, are universally committed to the belief that each child should achieve as fully as his individual capacity will permit. When children are categorized according to intellectual variations, it is never to relegate some of them to an inferior education and favor others with a better education, but rather to seek the best education for all.

Intellectual Categories

The most common means of differentiating among learners by intellectual capacity is by intelligence quotient, or IQ. Whereas IQ measurement is subject to misinterpretation and requires a great deal of care in its application, it is a helpful tool when properly used. IQ is derived by dividing a learner's mental age (MA) by his chronological age (CA) and multiplying by 100. The formula is: $IQ = \dfrac{MA}{CA} \times 100$. Because the developmental period is regarded as the first sixteen years of life, 16 is the maximum number used for CA, even with older learners. Thus, a 10-year-old child with a mental age of 10 has an IQ of 100, which is considered normal.

Using the IQ yardstick, the range for normal children is between 80 and 120, with children who score at the lower end of the scale referred to as slow learners, and those at the upper end as rapid learners. Above the normal range, an IQ of 120 or above indicates superior; 135 or above denotes gifted, and above 170 denotes extremely gifted intelligence. Below the normal range, children with IQ's of 50 to 75 or 80 are called educable, those between 30 and 50 or 55 are called trainable, and those below 30 are referred to as custodial or dependent.

Figure 18. Repetitive tasks are sometimes appropriate.

The fact that authorities do not agree on the exact limits of these categories should alert us to the need for great caution in their use. (1) The measurement of intelligence is not precise, and variations of several points are possible with different tests administered at different times under varying conditions. (2) Factors other than IQ can play a significant part in intellectual achievement. (3) Children should be placed in various categories only after careful and expert analysis of test results and related factors.

Slow Learners

Children with IQ scores of 75 or 80 through 90 of the large normal group, do need special attention in some areas of school work, but are sufficiently intelligent to profit from regular school classes. Although they are seldom successful in college work, they are quite capable of finishing high school (though many do not), and of adapting as fully self-sufficient members of society. Sometimes such children are held back a grade or two, and where the practice of grouping children by their intellectual level is followed, they are usually found in one of the lower achievement groups. With relatively minor adjustments, slow learners are capable of succeeding in company with their average classmates.

In his book *Education for the Slow Learners,* Johnson states:

> The slow learners compose the largest group of mentally retarded persons. Among the general school population, 15 to 17 or 18 per cent of the children can be considered slow learners. Since they are a very large group and since they do not deviate as markedly from the average as do the other groups of mentally retarded children, special educational provisions have not been considered essential. They do provide one of the largest and most intense, continuing problems facing the general classroom teacher. They confront every teacher, with the possible exception of those teachers who instruct only advanced academic senior high school subjects. In an average community where the school serves children from all cultural, social, and economic levels, a class of 30 unselected children can be expected to contain 4 or 5 slow learners.
>
> These percentages and numbers are not true for all communities. Preferred suburban communities where executive and professional persons reside will have very few slow learners. In these communities it is not at all unusual for the mean or average IQ of the school children to be 110, 115, or even 120. The sub-cultural areas of large metropolitan communities where the children receive little psycho-social stimulation present quite a different picture. The mean IQ of the children attending some of these schools is 85 or 90. Fifty per cent or more of the children can appropriately be designated as slow learners.

The most obvious characteristic of the slow learners is their inability to "keep up" with the rest of the class in their rate of academic growth. For example, they learn to read approximately one year later than the majority of the children. Their rate of reading development is then about four-fifths to nine-tenths of a year during each succeeding school year. They start late and continue to fall farther and farther behind as they become older. What is true for reading is also true for other skill areas and the content areas as well. They grasp new skills and concepts more slowly than is expected for children in general. Their maximum mental growth ranges from 11 years to 13 years 6 months. They form the group of children who receive the majority of the grades in the lowest quartile. They often drop out of school before graduation. Deviate, anti-social, unacceptable behavior in the classroom and school is not rare.[4]

Mental Retardation

Sometimes the term, "mentally retarded," is used to include children in the lower ranges of the normal group. However, it is more commonly reserved for those whose IQ rating falls below 80. Taken as a total group, the children with IQ's below 80 comprise about three per cent of the school-age population.[5]

The following table shows the approximate percentages of the total school-age population found in the three categories of mental retardation.

Categories	IQ Range	Approximate per cent of school-age population
Educable (EMR)	50–75 (80)	2.40%
Trainable (TMR)	30–50	0.45%
Custodial (CMR)	Below 30	0.15%

Experience has proved conclusively that educable and trainable youngsters can profit from special education. Unfortunately, not all such youngsters have the opportunity. In 1963, a total of 393,430 mentally retarded children were enrolled in day classes in public school districts in the United States, and 38,640 were enrolled in public and private residential schools for a total of 432,070.[6] The total school-age population in 1963 was about 45 million,

[4] G. Orville Johnson, *Education for the Slow Learners* (Englewood Cliffs, N.J.: Prentice-Hall, Inc., 1963), p. 9.

[5] Thomas E. Jordan, *The Exceptional Child* (Columbus, O.: Charles E. Merrill Books, Inc., 1962), p. 162.

[6] *Statistical Abstract of the United States* (Washington, D.C.: U.S. Department of Commerce, Bureau of the Census, 1966), p. 120.

some one and one quarter million of whom were educable or trainable. This means that only about 35 per cent of educable and trainable youngsters were enrolled in special education classes.

The trend in special education enrollments, however, is very promising. In 1948, about 10 per cent of educable and trainable children were enrolled, and in 1958, about 20 per cent.[7] Put another way, although the total school-age population in the United States grew 54 per cent between 1948 and 1963, enrollment in special education for educable and trainable children grew 380 per cent.

Educable Mentally Retarded (EMR)

The largest of the groups below the normal range is composed of "educable" children, a useful term because it emphasizes what can be done rather than what cannot.

The children in the educable group are seldom able to profit from the usual elementary instruction program and must be placed in special classes for most of their school work. They are, however, capable of academic achievement when it is geared to their intellectual level. With the proper educational opportunities, these children are capable of social and occupational independence in adult life. The majority of these people eventually marry, usually to mates of somewhat higher intelligence, and they produce children whose IQ's are generally in the normal range.

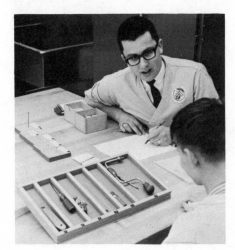

Figure 19. Recognizing and naming tools tests verbal ability.

[7] *Statistical Abstract*, p. 120.

The IQ range of educable retarded children is from 50 to 75 or 80, which means that they develop from one-half to three-fourths as rapidly as normal children. The academic work of which they are capable must then approximate the grade level for which their mental age is suitable. For example, a fifteen-year-old child with an IQ of 60 has a mental age of nine, and the appropriate level of work for him would be at about the fourth grade. Minimum literacy is possible for such a child, though it will be developed later and more slowly than for normal children. Academic achievement is generally confined to levels between the third and the seventh grades.

Trainable Mentally Retarded (TMR)

The lowest IQ group for which schools normally assume responsibility is made up of "trainable" children. The group is small, some 0.45 per cent (or less) of the school age population. IQ level ranges between 30 and 50.

Children in this category are handicapped by a rate of intellectual development, that is less than half that of normal children. Since the mental age of these children ranges from less than 5 years to a maximum of about 8 years, achievement is restricted to around the second grade level, at best. They are, therefore, incapable of literacy and related academic achievement.

In terms of what can be achieved, Dunn states:

> The trainable mentally retarded do have sufficient ability: (1) to develop self-care skills in dressing, toileting and eating; (2) to learn to talk and carry on a simple conversation though they will have little verbal communicative skill during pre-school years; (3) to guard themselves against common dangers in a protective environment or in familiar community settings; and (4) to perform simple chores in a sheltered environment in the home or community. As adults they will seldom be independent, socially or economically. Instead, they will need some care and supervision all of their lives. Thus, they seldom if ever marry, raise families, or set up independent living in their own homes. They usually continue to live with parents, relatives, or friends, or are cared for by some social agency which usually takes the form of a residential facility for the mentally retarded, but may be a halfway house or an independent living unit.[8]

Industrial Arts for Mentally Handicapped Children

It is evident that there could not be one uniform approach to instruction for children whose intellectual capacities range from "trainable"

[8] Lloyd M. Dunn, et al., *Exceptional Children in the Schools* (New York: Holt, Rinehart and Winston, 1963), p. 130.

Figure 20. Mechanical skills can be developed.

through "near-normal." In industrial arts activities, as in all school activities, the procedures used must be adapted to the characteristics of the learners.

When special education classes first began, many educators felt that retarded children should spend nearly all of their time at arts and crafts. Fortunately, it was soon recognized that such activities, while important, could not accomplish all that was possible or desirable.

The modern point of view recognizes industrial arts as one important curriculum area for children with less-than-normal intellectual ability, but insists that it be used in combination with, and related to the other curriculum areas.

What was said in an earlier section of this chapter about the importance of firsthand contact with the real world for normal children, applies with multiplied importance for children with learning difficulties. In general, these children have not had the range of experience of normal children, and secondly, because of their limitations, mentally handicapped children have generally learned less from the experiences they have had.

Speaking of the importance of activity in learning, Ingram states:

Learning, it is more and more being realized, occurs largely through concrete experiences that are a part of real life—going on excursions, for instance, or observing and handling such actualities as plants, animals, or specimens of any kind that can be brought into the classroom. Experience for the slow-learning child must also be kept on a concrete "doing" level through the use of materials, tools, apparatus, and machines. For him these facts are of special importance, since learning which depends only on narrated, described, and recorded experiences will always be more or less meaningless to him.[9]

[9] Christine P. Ingram, *Education of the Slow-Learning Child*, 3rd ed. (New York: The Ronald Press, 1960), p. 70.

In addition, the out-of-school world to which slow learners and retarded children are learning to adjust, is likely to be practical. The types of employment in which such children will engage do not emphasize the arts, the abstract, the professional, or the intellectual, but are oriented to repetitive tasks requiring unskilled or, at most, semi-skilled proficiency levels. Even these modest levels of achievement require that some groundwork be laid in the early years. Here, industrial arts can make a significant contribution.

> Above all, it is important that pupils develop good work habits and skills so they may be competitively employed in adulthood. The teacher of the retarded can do much to foster good work habits. First, the teacher's classroom management for many of the school activities should emphasize independent work. The teacher should set his standards for the pupils especially high in this regard. This probably deserves greater attention than the teaching of the 3 R's which traditionally has occupied a large proportion of the curriculum. Second, the practical arts can be important in developing good work habits and skills. However, arts and crafts should not be an end in themselves but a means of developing vocational, social, and personal adjustment. It is too late to wait until pupils enter vocational training or study-work programs in their youth before concentrating on the development of good, independent work habits.[10]

Furthermore, the joy of successful achievement is every bit as important to children of less-than-normal intelligence as it is to normal children, perhaps more; opportunities for successful experiences are obviously limited. Hobby and leisure-time pursuits can begin and develop in industrial arts activities. Indeed, it is essential that these pursuits begin early, as retarded rates of learning apply to this kind of activity, too, and interests and skills, which are not developed at an early age, may not be developed at all.

It is well known that children whose intellectual capacities are limited may not be as severely limited in other types of activity. Ingram states:

> The mentally retarded child approaches nearer to the average child in sensory acuity and motor ability than in more definitely intellectual processes. The majority approximate success at their chronological-age level most nearly in processes which call for eye-hand coordination and for motor response. The majority enjoy the manipulation of materials and the actual operations in the construction of any product, and can generally be taught to be proficient in hand skills. Practical arts and the "doing" experiences should, therefore, play a major part in their education.[11]

The exact kinds of things to be done in industrial arts must, obviously, vary widely, and perhaps the best guideline is to encourage children to

[10] Dunn, *Exceptional Children*, p. 91.
[11] Ingram, *Education of the Slow-Learning Child*, p. 62.

achieve to the maximum of their potential. For trainable youngsters, the activities will need to be highly repetitive and highly structured by the instructor. The details of each activity will have to be simple. For some children the process of sorting objects, sanding, or painting—tasks that require a minimum of dexterity—may be rewarding. Simple assembly tasks may be possible for some.

Educable children are capable of a modest degree of ingenuity and should be encouraged to put it to use where possible. Simple tasks, such as making toys, models, participating in mass-production processes, or even some creative work, may be possible. Sometimes, these children are placed in groups with normal children for industrial arts work, and the stimulation afforded by these contacts can result in surprising achievement for the retarded children. The social interaction experienced by the educable and the normal children should benefit both groups.

Usually, slow learners can do almost as well as normal children in constructive activities, and, in fact, they sometimes do better. The opportunities for developing a feeling of self-esteem are especially valuable to these children.

A large part of the work done in industrial arts by slow learners and retarded learners should be centered around home appliances, that is, in making and repairing things around the home, in sports and hobbies. These are the things that are most familiar to such children, and these familiar objects permit easy connections with life outside of school.

Although some extra precautions may be in order, retarded children often can use power tools without danger, particularly when operations are routine and closely supervised.

Considering the values to be achieved through the many activities available to a skilled, creative teacher, it is difficult to conceive of an educational program for intellectually handicapped children in which industrial arts activities are not included.

Above-Average Children

If opinions differ on the various degrees of low intelligence, they differ even more widely on the degree of high intelligence. There are a number of probable reasons for this, one of which is that bright people tend less to fit convenient patterns of behavior and to be more individualistic in their growth, and less predictable. In addition, when dealing with bright children, one is more likely to be concerned with originality and creativity, and similar attributes that are difficult to measure, or even to define.

There is a tendency to regard children with IQ's above 120 as superior, those above 135 or 140 as gifted, and those above 170 or 180 as extremely gifted. When these limits are used, the term, "superior," can be applied to from 5 to 10 per cent of the school-age population; "gifted" can be applied to 1 to 3 per cent; and "extremely gifted" to some 1/100 per cent or less.[12]

If an IQ of 135 is used as the starting point for intellectual giftedness, it appears that about 2.5 per cent of school-age children would fall into this category. Of the approximately 45 million school-age children in the United States in 1963, some 1.125 million could be regarded as "gifted." Of these, only 251,670 [13] or 19 per cent were enrolled in special education classes for gifted children. Although the percentage of gifted children who have the opportunity for special education is low, it is growing at a rapid rate, particularly in recent years. Between 1948 and 1963, the total school-age population increased 54 per cent. In that same period, enrollment in special education classes for gifted children rose 936 per cent.

The dramatic increase in special class enrollments for the gifted is an indication, at least in part, of the value society places on this human resource, and school people, in general, applaud the trend. Living patterns today, becoming increasingly complex, and requiring higher degrees of human competence, are not likely to reverse the trend. Even greater attention will be paid to the education of gifted children in the years ahead.

Practices in the special education of gifted children vary considerably from one community to another, but certain patterns are common. In a booklet for the National Education Association's Department of Classroom Teachers, Gallagher states:

> Each of the many programs designed to educate reasonably well-adjusted gifted children more effectively differ from each other in detail since they are tailored to local conditions. Actually, the similarities between programs usually outweigh the differences. The following are some characteristics common to almost all the programs:
> 1. Grouping of children with high intelligence for a part of the school day.
> 2. More responsibility given to pupils for planning of the program.
> 3. More emphasis on creative and interpretive activities and less time for memorization and routine practice of skills.
> 4. Smaller work groups.
> 5. More informality and less routine; less rigid time schedules.[14]

[12] W. Cruickshank, et al., *Education of Exceptional Children and Youth* (Englewood Cliffs, N.J.: Prentice-Hall, Inc., 1958), p. 149.

[13] *Statistical Abstract*, p. 120.

[14] James J. Gallagher, *The Gifted Child in the Elementary School*, National Education Association, Department of Classroom Teachers, 1959, p. 23.

Figure 21. Budding architect? There has been a dramatic increase in the enrollment of gifted children in industrial arts activities.

Industrial Arts for Above-Average Children

What is the role of industrial arts in the education of highly endowed children? Obviously, they have much less need for firsthand contact which is so important to children with less intelligence. These children have quick minds and are able to discern concepts and complex relationships, and to develop insights with a minimum of exposure to the material things involved. It is doubtful, for example, that such a child needs to see a model of a canal lock in order to grasp the principle which makes it work. He certainly does not need to cut up a disk of cardboard to see that $\frac{1}{4} + \frac{1}{4} = \frac{1}{2}$. In brief, the aspect of industrial arts that reduces levels of abstraction can be minimized when dealing with gifted children. Indeed, activities emphasizing that aspect of industrial arts would be generally inappropriate.

Yet, if one could identify the elementary schools with the liveliest, most comprehensive programs of industrial arts in the United States, a large number of them would be schools in economically favored communities where the mean intelligence level of children is the highest. Suburban communities and university campus schools, populated by the children of professional, executive, and managerial people, invariably use industrial arts activities in their instructional programs.

These are some of the contributions an appropriate industrial arts program can make to the education of gifted children:

1. Contact with children in the normal range of intelligence. Most special education programs for the gifted involve a degree of segregation or grouping. This procedure may be wise in terms of maximum intellectual growth; however, gifted children should not be segregated completely from their social contemporaries of normal intelligence, with whom they must learn to live. Activity areas, like industrial arts, provide one opportunity for re-integration where intellectual superiority is not as obvious and clear-cut as it is in most academic areas of the school.

2. Wide ranges of interest can be accommodated. The interests of gifted children are widely varied, and industrial arts activities can be individualized to permit independent work more easily than can many school subjects. In his industrial arts work, each child can devote his time to an activity which is largely independent, and tailored to his interests and capacities.

3. Experimentation and discovery can be emphasized. It is not unusual for gifted children, when given the opportunity, to develop rather sophisticated devices, particularly of a mechanical or electronic nature, and thereby to test theories and strengthen interests. It would be unfortunate if gifted children came to regard the material world beneath their dignity. Some of these children have potential to become the scientists, architects, designers, and engineers of tomorrow, and in these areas the theoretical must be tested in material and practical terms.

4. Leisure-time skills are important. Often, the importance of being a well-rounded person has been abused to the detriment of valuable talent; nevertheless, it is a factor to be considered in the education of the gifted. Most children find satisfaction in some area of constructive endeavor, and they should have the opportunity to experiment to see what some of the possibilities of this kind of work may be. Skills developed in childhood may lay the groundwork for leisure-time activities which will give life-long satisfaction and pleasure.

5. Work and dignity can go together. Among the values which contribute to the strength of American society is the high regard placed on honest work. Gifted children are seldom destined for the ranks of production workers or skilled labor, but it would be unfortunate if they regarded people engaged in such work with disdain. Certainly they need to learn to respect their fellow human beings, regardless of their place in society. In large measure, attitudes of respect for human dignity have many roots in the knowledge of the life-style and the work of others. Some contact with the mainstream of workers and work is important for all citizens, gifted or otherwise.

Teachers responsible for industrial arts activities for intellectually superior and gifted children might consider the following suggestions:

a. Safety instruction and supervision should be provided for gifted children as they are for all others.

b. Considerable freedom of choice should be permitted in determining activities.

c. Children should be encouraged to plan their work, attempting to foresee consequences, but should be permitted to revise their plans as experience is accumulated.

d. Independent work should be emphasized, particularly that which involves problem solving and research.

e. When group work is undertaken, the children should participate actively in planning for cooperative achievement.

f. Opportunity should be provided for the children to explain and demonstrate their work to others.

g. New ways of doing things and novel designs should be encouraged.

h. Cooperative effort should be enforced in necessary routine tasks, such as shop cleanup, careful use of tools, and returning supplies to their proper places.

Figure 22. Learning to work together.

CHILDREN WITH SIGHT AND HEARING HANDICAPS

Among the cherished values of American democracy is the belief that all children, normal and exceptional, should have the opportunity to profit as fully as possible from education. The challenge facing teachers is to find and employ the means to provide that opportunity. Fortunately, the means are largely available today.

Although the special needs of children with sight and hearing handicaps certainly require changes in some of the procedures of education, they do not require an educational system essentially different from that of normal children at the elementary level. The broad goals of education for democratic living, after all, apply for handicapped children as well as for normal children.

Sight Problems

How extensive are sight problems among school children? The prevalence of visual handicaps varies considerably from community to community in the United States, but on the average about 80 per cent of school children have normal vision, and another 19.75 per cent have vision that can be corrected (usually with glasses) to the normal range.[15]

Vision is extremely complicated and involves many technical variables, but the factor most commonly measured is acuity. By the use of the familiar Snellen eye chart, containing letters or symbols in sequence from large to small, it is possible to determine how acutely one person sees as compared with others. If, for example, a child sees at 20 feet what someone with perfect vision sees at 40 feet, that child's visual acuity is said to be 20/40. By this measurement, 20/20 is considered perfect vision. The term, "normal," is applied for educational purposes to vision correctible in at least one eye to the range of 20/20 to 20/70. Some 99.75 per cent of children have vision within this range.

The next category for educational purposes includes those children whose vision, with the best possible correction, falls between 20/70 and 20/200. These children are called "partially sighted," and they make up about 0.20 per cent of the school-age population. Most of these children are capable of learning in a regular school environment, though some provisions, such as preferential seating in the classroom, are usually necessary. About one child in 30, at the low end of the partially sighted group, requires special education.[16]

[15] Harry J. Baker, *Exceptional Children*, 3rd ed. (New York: Macmillan Co., 1959), p. 297.
[16] Dunn, *Exceptional Children*, p. 424.

Children in the category called "legally blind," have vision rated at 20/200 or less in the better eye with the best possible correction, and these make up some 0.03 per cent of the school-age population. It should be noted that about 4 out of 10 of these children use their eyes for reading, though special educational facilities are required for the entire group.[17]

All of the children in the legally blind category, added to those at the low end of the partially sighted group, make up some 0.09 per cent of the school-age population for whom special education provisions should be made. In 1963, this group totalled some 40,500 children in the United States, but only 21,520 were enrolled in special education programs for the visually handicapped in residential and public day schools.[18] A large number of the handicapped children were enrolled in regular classes, where they pursued their schooling at a distinct disadvantage.

In keeping with the belief that handicapped children should do things as much like normal children as possible, there is a definite trend to enroll blind and partially sighted children in regular schools wherever the necessary special education provisions can be made. As school systems grow in size, this becomes increasingly feasible, and many authorities feel that social and emotional development is generally better when visually handicapped children are not segregated completely from children with normal vision (obviously, however, some circumstances still require segregation). When regular schools assume responsibility for the special education of visually handicapped children, the arrangements most commonly found are either the "cooperative" plan or the "integrated" plan. In the cooperative plan, the homeroom is the place where the necessary special education is provided, and in the integrated plan the handicapped children are enrolled in a regular homeroom, but use a resource room for their special education. In both plans, the handicapped children are placed with their normally sighted classmates as much as possible, and they use the special education facilities only for areas where their handicaps prevent them from learning.

Industrial Arts for Sight Handicapped Children

Unless one has had experience with blind and partially sighted children, his first reaction might be that work with tools and machines is too dangerous. Although some special provisions for safety are needed, most of the typical industrial arts activities are well within the capabilities of even those who are totally blind.[19]

[17] Dunn, *Exceptional Children*, p. 424.
[18] *Statistical Abstract*, p. 120.
[19] See *Industrial Arts for Blind Students*, American Foundation for the Blind, 1960.

What are the educational values of industrial arts work for children with visual problems?

1. Concept formation depends more on the tactual (touch) sense for these children than for those with normal sight, and the impressions gained through working with material things add to their depth of understanding.

2. Except for the most severely handicapped, who require the full and constant attention of the teacher, visually handicapped children can be placed with children of normal vision in industrial arts work.

3. The development of manipulative skills is as important for handicapped children as for the normal children, and probably more so, and foundations in manipulative skills must be laid early.

4. Self-confidence and greater independence is acquired as children discover what they can do. A sense of achievement is vital for everyone, and achievement is possible in industrial arts.

5. Authorities agree that residual vision should be used as fully as possible, and activities interesting to children encourage its use.

6. If constructive hobby interests are important to normal children, it hardly need be stated that the child whose handicap prevents him from some activities should have the opportunity to develop interests and talents in those fields which are within his capabilities.

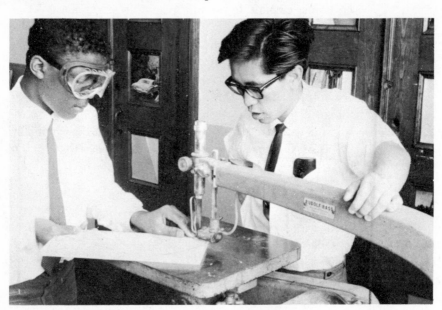

Figure 23. Special fixture enables a blind student to use a jig saw safely.

Figure 24. Blind student uses his fingers to "see" the shape of a bowl he is making in ceramics shop.

Hearing Problems

Most people with normal use of all five senses tend to regard sight as the most important and precious. From the viewpoint of the education of very young children, however, this is not necessarily the case. The child born without the sense of hearing, or the child who loses his hearing at an early age, is under a handicap at least as severe as the visually handicapped child. This becomes apparent as one considers how preschool learning takes place. It depends primarily on the process of communication and language. The child with severe hearing problems is denied these in large measure, and his early education suffers as a result.[20]

As with all types of handicap, the degree of difficulty in dealing with the problem varies with its severity. The most common measurement of hearing loss uses the symbol "db" (for decibels), and refers to the intensity level of sound at which a person begins to hear. If, for example, one has a 25 db hearing loss, this means that sounds of less than 25 decibels intensity cannot be heard. Since sound varies in frequency (or pitch) as well as intensity, the measurement is usually made in the so-called speech range, at least for education purposes.[21]

[20] It should be noted that the number of blind students doing college-level work is many times greater than the number of deaf students, though in the general population the totally deaf outnumber the totally blind by about three-to-one.

[21] The speech range is generally considered to be from 512 to 2048 cycles per second.

Figure 25. Student and teacher communicate through the use of finger spelling.

It is estimated that about 5 per cent of the school-age population have some hearing difficulty, ranging from "mild" to "profound." From 0.5 to 1.0 per cent of all school children have hearing losses so severe that special education is required, and about 0.1 per cent are totally deaf.[22]

In categories which have much meaning from an educational point of view, Streng identifies five classes of difficulty:

Class 1. They are the children with *mild* losses (20–25 db in the better ear in the speech range). They learn speech by ear and are on the borderline between the normally hearing and those with significant defective hearing.

Class 2. They are the children with *marginal* losses (30–40 db). They have difficulty in understanding speech by ear at a distance of more than a few feet and in following group conversation.

Class 3. They are the children with *moderate* losses (40–60 db). They have enough hearing to learn language and speech through the ear when sound is amplified for them and when the auditory sense is aided by the visual.

The children in these first three categories may be considered as being hard of hearing.

Class 4. They are the children with *severe* losses (60–75 db). They have trainable residual hearing, but their language and speech will not develop spontaneously, so they must learn to communicate through the use of specialized techniques. They are on the borderline between the hard of hearing and the deaf, and may be considered the "educationally deaf" or partially deaf.

[22] Richard Silverman, "Education of the Deaf," *Handbook of Speech Pathology* (New York: Appleton-Century-Crofts, 1957), p. 393.

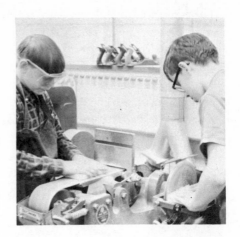

Figure 26. Deaf children can use power tools safely.

Class 5. They are the children with *profound* losses (greater than 75 db). They cannot learn to understand language by ear alone, even with amplification of sound.[23]

There are three identifiable trends in the education of partially-hearing and deaf children. First, with the improvement in recent years of hearing aids, it has become possible to place more and more hearing-handicapped children in regular schools. Secondly, as the school systems have grown in size, it has become possible for more regular schools to offer the special education necessary for children with severe hearing difficulties. Thirdly, it has become widely accepted that the education of children with hearing handicaps should not be essentially different from the education of children with normal hearing.

Kirk states:

Hard-of-hearing children . . . are not very different from their classmates. Except in speech, language, and reading they are not seriously retarded academically. Special classes are provided for those with marked variation or with variations in many areas, but when a discrepancy occurs in only one or two remediable areas, it is advisable to keep the child in the regular grades and allow him to leave the class for short periods for specific tutoring in his regions of difficulty. For this reason, special classes for the hard of hearing are decreasing in school systems.[24]

[23] Alice Streng, *Hearing Therapy for Children* (New York: Grune and Stratton, 1955), pp. 164–65.
[24] Samuel A. Kirk, *Educating Exceptional Children* (Boston: Houghton-Mifflin Co., 1962), p. 169.

The education of children with hearing difficulties makes full use of what hearing ability exists. The teachers speak to the children, making use of sound amplification devices where they are useful, and they encourage the children to talk. Where appropriate, lip-reading is taught in combination with whatever sound can be heard. Children whose hearing loss requires it are taught finger spelling [25] where each letter of the alphabet is represented by finger positions (Figure 27). The combination of these methods usually can be relied on to develop considerable communication ability (Figure 25).

Once the basic concepts of language are grasped by hearing-handicapped children, the development of language skills proceeds rapidly, though obviously not as rapidly as with normal children. Special books are not used; texts are chosen in terms of the reading level appropriate for the learners.

As the children with hearing handicaps become adults, they are able to lead lives not too different from those whose hearing is normal. Even the totally deaf person can perform a wide variety of tasks, with the exception of those requiring high levels of skill in oral communication.

Industrial Arts for Hearing Handicapped Children

Assuming that a teacher can communicate with the children, there is no reason why industrial arts activities for children with hearing handicaps should be different from those for children with normal hearing in any important respect.

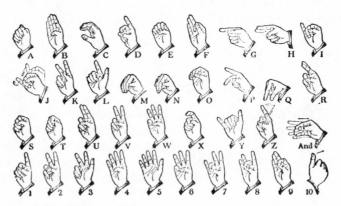

Figure 27. Finger spelling positions.

[25] Finger spelling is not to be confused with the cruder "sign language," which is not generally encouraged for children because it is less useful educationally.

Many of the values of an industrial arts program for visually handicapped children apply to those with hearing handicaps:

1. The tactual sense should be developed.
2. Integration with normal-hearing classmates is possible (except in special cases).
3. The development of manipulative skills is important, since the majority of deaf adults are employed in manipulative occupations.
4. Self-confidence and independence can be enhanced.
5. What hearing ability does exist should be used in a variety of situations.
6. Varied interests and talents should be accommodated.

INDUSTRIAL ARTS AS THERAPY

Therapy is defined as treatment for illness, abnormality, or maladjustment. It is not education, but where children are involved, therapy and education are closely related. A child suffering from cerebral palsy, for example, is a special individual whose educational development is inevitably influenced by his handicap. The same is true of children with emotional problems, hearing difficulties, and a wide range of physical impairments.

The principal concern of this book is the role industrial arts plays in education, but the use of industrial arts activities in certain kinds of therapy is growing. Though this work is usually referred to as "manual arts therapy." the content is very similar to that found in industrial arts. Most of the people working as manual arts therapists are graduates of industrial arts teacher education programs.

It is important to keep in mind that the objective of industrial arts therapy is curative rather than educational, and one would expect the activities to vary somewhat from those in a usual school program. In therapy, the industrial arts work is prescribed by the attending physician, along with diet, medicines, and other types of treatment.

For example, a physician may prescribe light mechanics to increase the finger dexterity of an injured hand, or heavier work to improve weak arm muscles. Intricate work, such as in weaving or electronics, may be recommended to build up tolerance for work and concentration. Sketching may be prescribed as part of a psychiatric testing sequence. Assembly of parts or model building may be used to enforce concentration. Work in ceramics can provide a sense of achievement. Work in sheet metal may encourage a form of emotional release. The type of work to be done is prescribed according to the needs of each patient.

Industrial arts therapists work as members of the paramedical profession. In consultation with attending physicians and colleagues in related fields such as psychology, social work, or physical therapy, an industrial arts therapist provides clinical treatment for patients and participates in evaluation of patient progress. Under the auspices of the American Association for Rehabilitation Therapy [26] the therapist may secure official certification as a Registered Rehabilitation Therapist (R.R.T.).

A FINAL WORD

Every elementary teacher has at least one primary obligation with regard to exceptionality in children. That obligation is the recognition of behavior which may denote any type of exceptionality. Although teachers are not expected to diagnose specialized difficulties, their observations of children in school situations are often helpful in prescribing the best possible educational procedures. Frequently, their observations can contribute to the early discovery of handicaps, which in turn can make profound differences in the lives of exceptional children.

SELECTED REFERENCES

Baker, Harry J., *Exceptional Children*, 3rd ed. (New York: Macmillan Co., 1959).
Baumgartner, Bernice B., *Helping the Trainable Mentally Retarded Child* (New York: Bureau of Publications, Teachers College, Columbia University, 1960).
Beck, J. M. and R. W. Saxe, eds., *Teaching the Culturally Disadvantaged Pupil* (Springfield, Ill.: Charles C. Thomas, Publisher, 1965).
Betando, Donald J., "Industrial Arts Activities in the Rehabilitation of the Handicapped," *Industrial Arts and Vocational Education*, Vol. 52 (April, 1963).
Crow, Lester D., et al., *Educating the Culturally Disadvantaged Child* (New York: David McKay, 1966).
Cruickshank, W. M., et al., *Education of Exceptional Children and Youth* (Englewood Cliffs, N.J.: Prentice-Hall, Inc., 1958).
Devilbiss, Joseph M., "The Mentally Retarded: Old Problem or New Challenge?" *Journal of Industrial Arts Education*, Vol. 24 (September, 1964).
Dunn, Lloyd M., ed., *Exceptional Children in the Schools* (New York: Holt, Rinehart and Winston, 1963).
Educational Policies Commission, *Education and the Disadvantaged American* (National Education Association, 1962).

[26] American Association for Rehabilitation Therapy, Inc., North Little Rock, Arkansas 72116.

Foote, F. M., "Classrooms for Partially-Seeing Children," *Exceptional Children*, Vol. 22 (1956).

Frost, Joe L., and Glenn R. Hawkes, eds., *The Disadvantaged Child* (Boston: Houghton-Mifflin Co., 1966).

Gallagher, James J., *The Gifted Child in the Elementary School* (Washington, D.C.: National Education Association, Department of Classroom Teachers, 1959).

Industrial Arts for Blind Students, American Foundation for the Blind, 1960.

Ingram, Christine P., *Education of the Slow-Learning Child*, 3rd ed. (New York: Ronald Press Co., 1960).

Itinerant Teaching Services for Blind Children, American Federation of the Blind, 1957.

Johnson, G. Orville, *Education for the Slow Learners* (Englewood Cliffs, N.J.: Prentice-Hall, Inc., 1963).

Jones, John W., *Blind Children: Degree of Vision, Mode of Reading* (Washington, D.C.: Government Printing Office, 1961).

———, "The Blind Child in School," *School Life*, Vol. 43 (March, 1961).

Jordan, Thomas E., *The Exceptional Child* (Columbus, O.: Charles E. Merrill Books, Inc., 1962).

Kirk, Samuel A., *Educating Exceptional Children* (Boston: Houghton-Mifflin Co., 1962).

Loretan, J. O. and S. Vmans, *Teaching the Disadvantaged* (New York: Bureau of Publications, Teachers College, Columbia University, 1966).

McNeice, W. C. and K. R. Benson, *Crafts for Retarded* (Bloomington, Ill.: McKnight and McKnight, 1964).

National Society for the Study of Education, *The Education of Exceptional Children*, 49th Yearbook, Part II (Chicago: The University of Chicago Press, 1950).

Nelson, Hilding E., "Slow Learners, A Challenge for Industrial Arts Education," *American Vocational Journal*, Vol. 39 (October, 1964).

Orr, K. N., *Cardinal Objectives in Teaching the Educable Mentally Retarded* (Terra Haute: Indiana State College, 1962).

Riessman, Frank, *The Culturally Deprived Child* (New York: Harper and Row, 1962).

Sharkey, F. E. and C. B. Porter, "Industrial Arts for the Mental Retardate," *American Vocational Journal*, Vol. 39 (May, 1964).

Silverman, Richard, "Education of the Deaf," *Handbook of Speech Pathology* (New York: Appleton-Century-Crofts, 1957).

Smith, Robert M., "Industrial Arts Activities for Children with Individual Differences," *Journal of Industrial Arts Education*, Vol. 23 (May, 1964).

Smith, R. W. and W. J. Tisdall, "Working with the Retarded Pupil in Industrial Arts and Vocational Education," *School Shop*, Vol. 24 (April, 1965).

Streng, Alice, *Hearing Therapy for Children* (New York: Grune and Stratton, 1955).

U.S. Department of Health, Education, and Welfare, Office of Education, *Teachers of Children Who Are Mentally Retarded* (Washington, D.C.: U.S. Government Printing Office, 1957), Bulletin No. 3.

Viggiani, James C., "Industrial Arts for Exceptional Children," *School Shop,* Vol. 24 (March, 1965).

Willey, R. D. and K. B. Waite, *The Mentally Retarded Child* (Springfield, Ill.: Charles C. Thomas, Publisher, 1964).

chapter 3 / FACILITIES, EQUIPMENT, TOOLS, AND SUPPLIES

Many teachers conduct modest industrial arts programs in their regular classrooms at little or no cost, often using borrowed tools and donated supplies. Although some valuable experiences can be provided for children under such conditions, a program adequately funded and properly organized is more likely to achieve its purposes. The cost of activity programs varies widely, depending on a number of factors. Given some idea of the number of classes and numbers of children involved, however, an industrial arts specialist could estimate costs rather closely.

In regard to costs, one point needs emphasis: Activity areas, such as industrial arts, require consumable supplies. Therefore, a sum of money must be allocated annually to support the program. A substantial investment in permanent equipment and tools would be a foolish gesture if consumable supplies were not also provided. Multiply a money factor (x dollars) by the number of children to be served by the industrial arts program, adjusting the money factor (the value of x) from time to time as conditions warrant.

A PLACE TO WORK

A suitable work area is of primary concern. The following are possibilities:

1. A workroom adjoining the classroom.
2. An area of the classroom permanently set aside for this type of work (Figure 29).

Figure 28. Group house-building project; work is done in the classroom.

3. A shop or workroom reserved exclusively for the industrial arts activities of elementary school pupils.
4. An area of the classroom that serves multiple purposes, one of which is construction.
5. The junior-senior high school shop.

In addition to the features which every good schoolroom should have, such as adequate light, ventilation, and safety exits, the three requirements which follow are essential when choosing or designing an area suitable for industrial arts work:

1. It should be possible for the teacher to oversee the work constantly and easily. In the interests of child safety and good administration, the area should be free of pillars and stored materials which could obstruct vision. A clear view of all parts of the room or work area should be possible from any point.
2. The area must be large enough and so arranged as to permit efficient and safe working conditions. Work benches should be far enough apart to prevent interference among the children, and aisles of traffic should be wide enough to permit free movement. Potentially dangerous machines, electric power panels, and heat producing devices like melting furnaces and kilns, should be "pocketed" away from traffic aisles.
3. There should be a minimum of disturbance and distraction for pupils engaged in other school work. Sound absorbent walls and ceilings are desirable and, where possible, doors should be closed to contain the noise in the work area. Where a separate shop or workroom is used, it should be located in an area of the school near other noise producing activities and away from classrooms.

Various arrangements can be used to obtain industrial arts areas with the features listed. One plan is to have *a workroom adjoining the classroom* (Figure 29). The room should be soundproof and separated from the classroom by a glass partition. The glass wall permits the teacher to monitor both the classroom and the workroom simultaneously, while the soundproofing makes it possible to carry on reading, discussion, or other activities in the classroom.

A more commonly found arrangement is *an area of the classroom that is used only for construction work.* This is preferable to a multi-purpose area, since the children look upon it as a place where only certain types of work

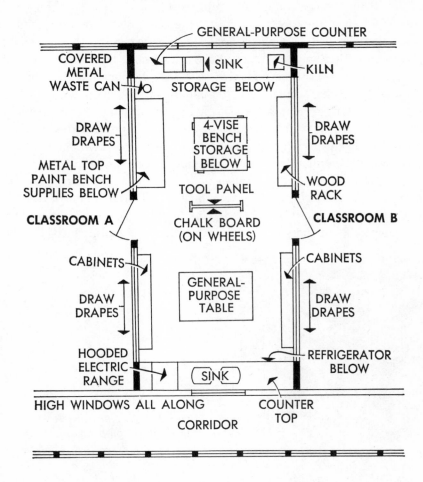

Figure 29. Practical arts area adjoining two classrooms.

are to be done. Further, hammering, sawing, painting, and other forms of construction work can easily result in damage to bookcases with glass doors or to finely finished school furniture located in a multi-purpose area. This problem is minimized, if not eliminated, when one corner of the room is devoted to construction work and the tools and supplies have permanent storage places.

A *shop or workroom completely apart from the classroom* is perhaps the best arrangement. If this alternative is chosen, the room should be *reserved for the exclusive use of the elementary grades.* Only in this way can suitable equipment, tools, and supplies be provided for the children of the lower grades. If the room was originally designed for older students, the benches will be too high, the tools too big, and the needs of the younger children, who are smaller, will be slighted in many other ways. A special advantage of this setup is that only one room in the school need be equipped for construction work. If classes are properly scheduled, this one room can be used by all of the grades, keeping costs to a minimum. The one serious disadvantage of this arrangement is the danger that construction work done away from the classroom will have little or no relationship to activities of the classroom. The danger can be minimized by frequent consultation between the specialist-consultant and the classroom teacher.

The fourth alternative is *an area of the classroom that serves multiple purposes, one of which is construction.* Such an arrangement might be necessary where space is severely limited. The disadvantages of the arrangement are comparable to those of many combination-type tools, which do many

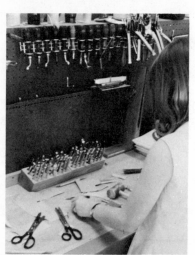

Figure 30. A specialized workroom can be fully equipped.

jobs in a halfway manner, but which do nothing well. When it is necessary to move a lot of things around before industrial arts work can take place, there is the danger that the work will never be done. Of course, even this type of work space is preferable to none.

A final alternative, as a place to work, is the *junior-senior high school shop*. The principal disadvantage of this possibility is that the equipment is not child-size. The pupil is handicapped by benches that are too high, tools that are out-of-reach, and machines that he will not be permitted to use. He will be frustrated by man-size implements in his child-size hands. The resourceful teacher, of course, can do much to minimize these disadvantages. If space and fund limitations demand it, this alternative can be considered until more appropriate facilities become available.

In the most effective industrial arts programs today, both classroom facilities and special elementary shops or workrooms are provided. Some of the work is carried on in the classroom and some in the shop, under the supervision of an industrial arts consultant.

A suitable and attractive place to work is important to a successful industrial arts activity program. Naturally, one should strive for an ideal arrangement. If a compromise with the ideal is necessary, however, the activities should be provided.

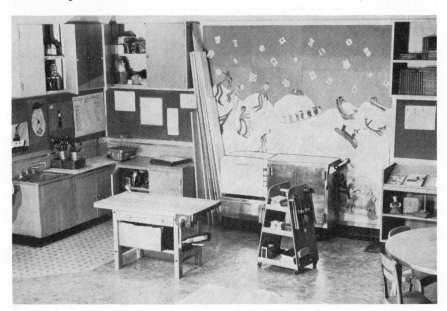

Figure 31. Classroom industrial arts area.

CLASSROOM WORK AREAS

The arrangement of furniture and equipment in an industrial arts area must be done in terms of the requirements of the individual situation. Such factors as the following should be considered:

Space available In a classroom work area, it would be unusual for an entire class to be engaged in construction work at one time. The space required to accommodate an entire class is seldom available. The usual classroom work area accommodates eight to ten pupils, and requires about 200 square feet of floor space. When the area is not in use, pushing portable equipment against walls adds from 50 to 100 square feet of space.

Equipment inventory and the extent of the program Some teachers make use of industrial arts activities rather regularly and others rarely. The amount of money to be invested in equipment, and the space devoted to the storage and use of the equipment, should be in proportion to the frequency of its use. For occasional use, portable equipment stored somewhere other than the classroom might be considered.

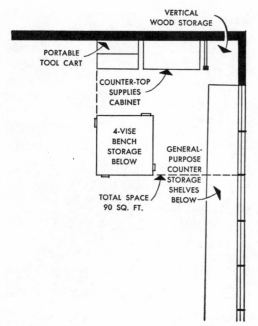

Figure 32. Classroom industrial arts area.

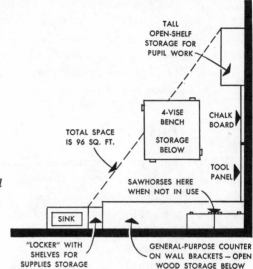

Figure 33. Classroom industrial arts area.

Accessibility of utilities One or more electrical outlets will be needed, as will a sink, preferably stainless steel. For easy access, it would be desirable to have these utilities located in the work area. The flooring around sinks should be made of ceramic tile or some other material impervious to water. Walls near sinks should not be easily damaged by splashing water.

Storage Quantities of materials and supplies required in any one classroom are rather limited, but some space will be necessary for their storage. Wood should be stored where it will not be exposed to heat, cold, or moisture.

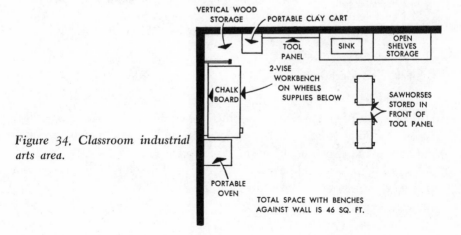

Figure 34. Classroom industrial arts area.

Where possible, boards should be stood on end, and secured by a chain to prevent them from falling. A box should be provided for small pieces of wood. Additional space is required for small supplies, and a series of shelves or racks are necessary for the objects on which the children are working.

Figures 32 to 34 show possible ways of arranging equipment to provide efficient classroom work areas.

SPECIALIZED INDUSTRIAL ARTS SHOPS

When designing an elementary school shop, consideration should be given to the purposes to be achieved, the educational program to be carried out, and the total local situation—architectural policies, existing facilities, probable future needs, funds available, and other similar considerations. It is not possible to prescribe a shop plan that would be applicable everywhere. Plans must vary, and they should vary. It is possible, however, to make some suggestions that ought to be considered in the planning, indicating what might be included by way of equipment, and showing possible floor layouts.

Laboratory planning assistance is available from city and state departments of education (bureaus of school buildings and grounds, and bureaus of industrial arts education), colleges of education, shop equipment manufacturers, and publications on the subject.

An elementary school industrial arts workshop can be put to these uses:

1. Headquarters and conference room for industrial arts consultant.
2. Workroom for projects beyond the scope of the classroom.
3. Storeroom for supplies, materials, and tools.
4. Machine-equipped workshop for supplying specific needs of classrooms.
5. Classroom-laboratory for in-service shop courses for classroom teachers.
6. Classroom-laboratory for adult education and recreation programs.

General Considerations

The general shape of the laboratory should be square or almost square, in the interest of an efficient arrangement of equipment and adequate supervision. A compromise with this general principle may often be required, but one should strive for the ideal.

The laboratory should be at ground level, and it should have a large outside door and an access to a driveway for the delivery of equipment and supplies.

Figure 35. Specialist-consultant and classroom teacher are partners.

Total space requirements vary. Some specialists favor a laboratory small enough to discourage its use for large classes. Others feel that larger laboratories are more useful because they are more flexible. Opinions regarding optimum size vary from 750 (25 feet x 30 feet) to 1600 (40 feet x 40 feet) square feet or more. Utilities to be considered for workrooms include:

1. *Water*—hot and cold, for drinking fountains, washing hands, toilet facilities, cleaning paint brushes, and working with ceramics.
2. *Drainage*—in addition to standard facilities, one sink should be equipped with a clay trap to prevent clogging the drainage system.
3. *Gas*—useful for metal-melting furnaces, soldering furnaces, and small heat sources such as Bunsen burners.
4. *Electric power*—110-volt alternating current generally is sufficient to operate small machines, though some specialists prefer 220-volt current for kilns, electric furnaces, and heavier machines.
5. *Heat*—as provided in regular classrooms, but thermostat controlled locally.
6. *Ventilation*—as provided in regular classrooms, but at least one exhaust fan should be installed.
7. *Compressed air*—may be considered either as permanent installation or as supplied by small portable unit.
8. *Vacuum exhaust*—may be considered as one manner of cleaning the shop, as an exhaust is necessary where toxic fumes (such as in certain paints) may be present.

Wall, ceiling and floor treatments, windows, lighting, heating, and ventilation should follow good shop design practices; provisions should be made for safety, rapid exit, and fire prevention and control.

Major Work Areas

After consideration of the purposes a shop is to serve and the program of activities to be conducted, the next step is the listing of principal work areas to be included in the room, and the preparation of a work area plan. These are the work areas most commonly included in industrial arts shops in elementary schools:

1. Woods
2. Metals
3. Ceramics
4. Textiles
5. Electricity
6. Graphic arts
7. Crafts
8. Large project assembly
9. Demonstrating-teaching
10. Display
11. Consultation office
12. Library and planning
13. Finishing
14. Storage—materials, supplies and pupils' work

Specialist-consultants may wish to modify the list of work areas to meet the requirements of specific programs and schools.

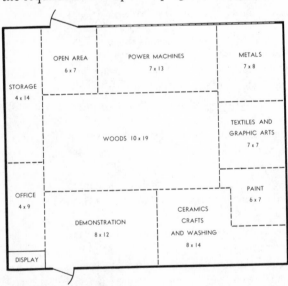

Figure 36. Area plan for a 750 square-foot shop.

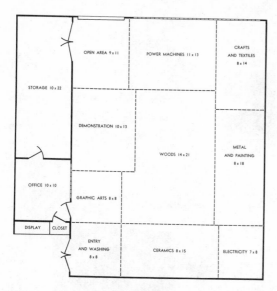

Figure 37. Area plan for a 1600 square-foot shop.

Some of the areas require more floor space than others, depending mainly on the way they are to be equipped. Obviously, the total space available will have some bearing on the number of work areas to be included, and the space to be allocated to each area. Figures 36 and 37 are examples of two work area plans, one for a modest shop of 750 square feet (25 feet x 30 feet) and the other for a rather complete shop of some 1600 square feet (40 feet x 40 feet).

EQUIPMENT AND ITS ARRANGEMENT

Among the most important pieces of equipment in the classroom work area or the shop are the workbenches. The following are the criteria that should be applied to their selection:

1. They must be sturdy.
2. They should provide a sufficient number of work stations.
3. They must be of a height that permits comfortable use by pupils.
4. They should use available space efficiently.
5. They must be equipped to hold wood and other materials securely while work is being done.
6. They should provide storage space as well as a working surface.

Figure 38. General-purpose bench. Courtesy: Brodhead-Garrett Company.

Figure 39. General purpose bench with storage. Courtesy: Brodhead-Garrett Company.

Figure 40. Portable bench with tool panels and storage space. Courtesy: Brodhead-Garrett Company.

Figure 41. Collapsible and portable bench. Courtesy: Brodhead-Garrett Company.

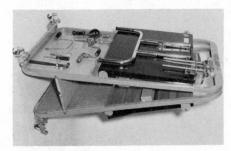

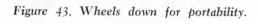

Figure 42. Home-made bench and tool carrier.

Figure 43. Wheels down for portability.

Figure 44. Tool carrier shown open.

For many years the only benches commercially available were designed for older students and adults, and consequently were too high and too large for most elementary pupils. Now a number of commercially manufactured benches are available, especially designed for the elementary grades, which is testimony to the growing popularity of work on this level. Figures 38 through 41 show some of these.

Experience has shown that the following bench heights are practical for use by elementary pupils: 24 inches for kindergarten and grade one; 26 inches for grades two and three; and 28 inches for grades four through six. The practice of standing on boxes or other objects to reach working surfaces should be discouraged, since it adds unnecessary risks of accidents.

If it is impossible to purchase benches especially designed for elementary pupils, it may be possible to obtain adult-size benches and cut them down to an appropriate size. If the benches meet the other criteria, they will serve well.

Figure 45. Working at a home-made workbench.

Figure 46. Using a sawhorse workbench.

In the event that commercially produced benches cannot be secured, the teacher can make one, or have one made in the high school shop or at the local lumber mill. The construction of a serviceable bench is not difficult, nor is the material unduly expensive. Such benches are shown in Figures 42 and 45. Construction details for the bench in Figure 45 are in Chapter 5.

If space is extremely limited a type of workbench (really a sawhorse), like that shown in Figure 46, may have to serve. This style of bench has been fairly satisfactory, but there must be a number of them, since not more than two children can work on each one. The design is such that the benches can be stacked when not in use. Furthermore, this type of bench can be made easily and cheaply, and will serve as a temporary expedient while permanent benches are being made or bought. A use can always be found for a bench similar to the one shown. One serious deficiency is the lack of a vise. The bench is too small and light for one. The use of a C-clamp to hold materials has been found to be satisfactory.

Last in the list of workbench possibilities are a number of miscellaneous makeshift arrangements such as library tables, boxes, sawhorses with planks, and other items which may have to do temporarily. The disadvantages to these makeshift arrangements are apparent, and they should be discarded as soon as possible.

There are many kinds of vises (holding devices) available. The two most common types are the woodworker's vise (Figure 47) and the machinist's vise (Figure 48). Both types will be useful in industrial arts work.

Figure 47. Woodworker's vise

Figure 48. Machinist's vise.

One version of the woodworker's vise has a feature called "rapid action." This is not recommended for the elementary level because children have difficulty in using it. The standard, continuous-screw type vise is preferable. In general, there should be enough vises in a work area or shop to accommodate one-fourth of the students who will be working there at any one time. Some vises require holes in bench tops for bolts; others can be clamped to bench tops and easily removed when desired (Figure 49).

Equipment included in industrial arts areas of classrooms varies, quite naturally, with the scope of programs. When programs are in the beginning stages, equipment may consist only of a workbench or sawhorse. As programs develop and as budgets permit, other pieces of equipment are added. These are some of the items more commonly found:

1. Workbench and vises
2. Tool panel or cabinet (Figure 50)
3. Sawhorse
4. Supplies cabinet
5. Clay cart or crock
6. Sink with hot and cold mixer-type faucets
7. Paper towel dispenser
8. Scrap woodbox
9. Counter brush
10. Dustpan
11. Drop cloth

The items listed below are often added as programs develop:

1. Wood storage rack (Figure 51)
2. Metal-covered waste can
3. Small loom(s)
4. Portable sewing machine
5. Ceramics kiln
6. Storage shelves for pupil work
7. Paint cabinet

Figure 49. Clamp-in vise. Courtesy: Brodhead-Garrett Company.

Figure 50. Tool storage cabinet. Courtesy: Hollowell School Shop Furniture.

Figure 51. Lumber storage rack. Courtesy: Hollowell School Shop Furniture.

Specialized workrooms obviously require more equipment than do the industrial arts areas of classrooms. Equipment appropriate for industrial arts shops is listed below with suggested sizes. The two columns to the right of the equipment show the number of items that might be provided for shops of two typical sizes:

	1600 SQUARE FOOT SHOP	750 SQUARE FOOT SHOP
1. GENERAL ITEMS		
a. Galvanized cans (20 gal)	2	1
b. Wall tool panels (4′ x 8′)	2	1
c. Bulletin boards (3′ x 4′)	2	1
		use ceramic
d. Wash sink, drinking fountain	1	sink
e. Push brooms	4	2
f. Fire extinguishers	3	2
g. First aid kit	1	1
h. Counter brushes	12	8

	1600 SQUARE FOOT SHOP	750 SQUARE FOOT SHOP
2. WOODS AREA		
a. Four-place benches with vises and storage below (4½′ x 5′)	4	2
b. Reciprocating jig or scroll saws (26″) .	2	1
c. Vibrating jig saws	2	1
d. Table saw (10″ tilting arbor)	1	1
e. Band saw (12″–14″)	1	0
f. Drill press (14″–15″)	1	0
g. Portable power drill (¼″)	1	1
h. Jointer (6″–8″)	1	1
i. Grinder, with oil stone bench	1	1
j. Wood lathe (12″ x 36″)	1	0
k. Sawhorses	2	2
3. METALS AREA		
a. Workbench with machinist's vises, stakes, and storage below (3′ x 5′) ..	1	1
		use grinder
b. Buffing head	1	
c. Bench top furnace and melting pot ..	1	0
d. Scroll bender	1	0
4. CERAMICS AREA		
a. Absorptive type counter with storage below (2½′ x 5′)	1	0
b. Sink with clay trap	1	1
c. Drying cabinet	2	1
d. Damp cabinet	1	0
e. Electric potter's wheel	1	0
f. Electric kiln with pyrometer (14″ x 14″ x 14″)	1	1
g. Electric kiln with pyrometer (8″ x 8″ x 8″)	1	0
h. Clay crocks or carts	4	2
5. ELECTRICITY AREA		
a. Test panel and workbench (2½′ x 4′)	1	0
b. Cabinet for experiment equipment ..	1	0
6. TEXTILES AREA		
a. Work tables (3′ x 5′)	2	1
b. Four-harness looms (20″)	2	0
c. Four-harness looms (8″)	2	2
d. Electric sewing machine, simple	1	0

	1600 SQUARE FOOT SHOP	750 SQUARE FOOT SHOP
7. GRAPHIC ARTS AREA		
a. Stencil duplicator, hand operated ...	1	1
b. Rubber stamp machine	1	0
c. Etching press (8" x 10")	1	1
d. Platen press (6½" x 10")	1	0
8. CRAFTS AREA		
a. Leather-working bench with storage below (2½' x 4')	1	0
b. All-purpose table, round (4' diameter)	1	0
9. DEMONSTRATION AREA		
a. Chalkboard (4' x 8')	1	1
b. Small stools	25	12
c. Movie sound projector and screen ...	1	1
d. Slide-strip projector	1	1
e. Tape recorder	1	1
f. Overhead transparency projector	1	1
10. DISPLAY AREA		
a. In-wall showcase	1	1
b. High shelves in shop	16'	8'
11. CONSULTANT-SPECIALIST'S OFFICE AREA		
a. Desk and chair	one set	one set
b. Other chairs	2	1
c. Four-drawer file cabinets	2	2
d. Book case	1	1

Figure 52. Display case for elementary school industrial arts projects.

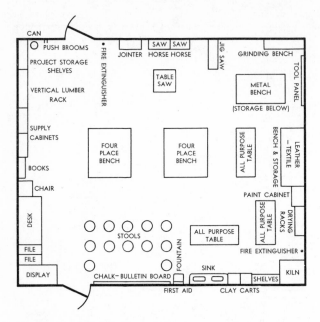

Figure 53. Layout for a 750 square-foot shop.

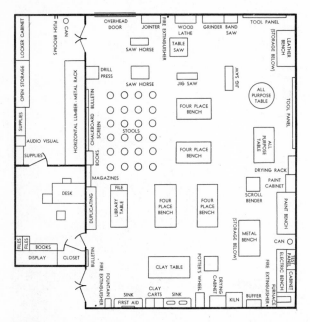

Figure 54. Layout for a 1600 square-foot shop.

	1600 SQUARE FOOT SHOP	750 SQUARE FOOT SHOP
12. LIBRARY AND PLANNING AREA		
a. Bookshelves	1	0
b. Library table	1	0
c. File cabinet	1	0
d. Magazine rack	1	0
13. FINISHING AREA		
a. Stainless-steel-top bench with storage below (2½' x 4')	1	0
b. Paint cabinet	1	1
14. STORAGE AREA		
a. General supplies cabinet	2	1
b. Locker cabinet for student work	1	0
c. Lumber rack	1	1
d. Metals rack	1	0
e. Open area for crates and boxes	yes	yes

NOTE: Blades, cutters, and accessories should be purchased for machines to suit program needs.

Figures 36 and 37 presented shop work area plans, indicating spaces allotted to areas, but not showing equipment arrangement. The next step in planning the shop is an actual equipment layout drawn to scale. Working from area plans and equipment lists, industrial arts specialists usually proceed by cutting cardboard shapes to rough scale and moving them about, on room plans drawn to the same scale, until a good equipment layout is achieved. The cardboard silhouettes are then traced, and the result is the shop layout. Examples of layouts, and the equipment lists in the preceding pages, are shown in Figures 53 and 54.

BASIC TOOLS FOR USE IN A CLASSROOM

It would be difficult to overemphasize the importance of choosing the appropriate tools and keeping them in good condition. Everyone has had the experience of trying to do something with an implement not suited to the task. Furthermore, whether it be a carving knife, a pair of scissors, or an auger bit, if the implement is not in good condition, the difficulty of the task is increased. Children have enough to concentrate on when conditions are ideal. The wrong tool, or even the right one in poor condition, introduces unnecessary difficulty and frustration.

The teacher usually finds that he has considerable latitude in making up a list of required tools. What criteria, then, can be used in selecting tools for an elementary industrial arts program?

1. There should be enough tools for the work to be done.
2. Tools should be suited to the physical capacities of the children.
3. The most essential tools should be purchased first, if all the tools cannot be obtained at the same time.
4. A few tools of various kinds are to be preferred to a large number of one kind of tool.
5. Tools should not be toys, but should be substantially constructed so as to take the inevitable rough handling they will receive.
6. Tools should be in serviceable condition at all times.

Some teachers make the mistake of buying inexpensive tools to keep costs down. They believe that since children will mishandle tools and replacement will be necessary, the tools do not have to be of the best quality. This is faulty reasoning. Good tools are sturdily constructed; they will take the punishment that inexperienced hands give them; they will outlast inferior tools many times over; and most important, they will work well. It is strongly recommended that tools of good quality be purchased.

If the services of an industrial arts specialist-consultant are available, he will either be responsible for all the tools to be used or be able to provide guidance in tool selection for classroom teachers. Where such services are not available, classroom teachers will find the following suggestions helpful.

The number of tools suggested here is suitable for about eight workers at one time in a classroom industrial arts area, not for a shop. It is recommended that the following tools be purchased first, even if the number of workers is to be greater than eight. The teacher can observe the frequency with which tools are used and buy additional tools where necessary.

Vibrating jig saw (Figure 55) The jig saw is the only power tool that is recommended for classrooms, but it should be given high priority. One machine should be adequate. Various models of this machine can be purchased at very reasonable prices. The vibrating type jig saw is recommended because there is practically no danger connected with its use. Since the blade moves only a short distance, it is not likely to cut the skin even if fingers accidentally touch it. Care must be taken to purchase blades that fit the machine.

Panel saws (Figure 56) Two panel saws are recommended for the classroom. These should be crosscut saws of about 10 points per inch (nine teeth to the inch), and the blades should be about 20 inches long. A rip saw is not needed; for the few occasions when ripping (sawing with the grain) is to be done, the crosscut saw will serve fairly well. A saw of good quality steel is the only type worth considering. Cheap saws become dull after being used a short time, and are practically worthless.

It might be added, parenthetically, that most saws are spoken of as having so many "points" per inch, rather than teeth. There is a minor difference, and it need not concern us here. The number stamped on a saw blade, near the handle, refers to points per inch.

Compass saw (Figure 57) One compass saw should be sufficient for the classroom. The blade should be from 10 to 12 inches long and should have from 10 to 14 points per inch. Saws with a relatively large number of points per inch have smaller teeth, cut with less effort, and produce a smoother cut. This type of saw is suitable for sawing holes in thick materials or in cutting holes in large pieces which cannot be cut with the vibrating jig saw or coping saw. The compass saw can also be used to saw gradual curves in thick material or to cut in hard-to-reach places.

Figure 55. Vibrating jig saw.

Figure 56. Panel saw.

Figure 57. Compass saw.

Backsaw (Figure 58) One backsaw is adequate. The backsaw also is quite popular with children because it is small and comparatively easy to handle. Because it is of sturdy construction, it will not buckle or bend. A blade with about 12 to 14 points per inch and not longer than 12 inches in length is recommended.

Coping saws (Figure 59) Two coping saws are adequate. These popular tools do the same type of work as the vibrating jig saw. They are used primarily to cut curves in thin wood. Coping saw frames, which permit the blades to be turned, are preferable to the rigid type. Coping saws with screw-type handles, the blades of which are replaced by turning the handle, are better than those which must be sprung to release and insert blades. Be sure that the blades procured fit the saw frames, since there are different sizes and styles available.

Try square (Figure 60) One try square will do. Try squares come in various styles and blade lengths. If only one is to be procured, an 8-inch blade should be chosen. If a second try square is needed, a 6-inch blade will be practical. The all-metal type of try square is to be preferred because of its rugged construction. Aluminum alloys are desirable for these tools because of their rust-resisting qualities.

Straight rules Two straight rules are recommended. These should also be metal rules. Aluminum alloys are preferred, but steel is acceptable. For elementary industrial arts, straight rules should be 24 inches long and an inch or so wide. Free or inexpensive wood yardsticks are usable substitutes, but they frequently break and are attractive to children as construction lumber. Some measuring devices are necessary even if the best available are only common desk rulers.

C-clamps (Figure 61) Two C-clamps will be needed. These holding devices should open to a distance of 4 inches. The movable screw part should not wobble, but should fit snugly.

Tin snips (Figure 62) One pair will do. Tin snips are seldom used by children in the lower grades, but the teacher will have occasional use for them in cutting metal, screen wire, and similar materials. Straight, right-handed, 10-inch snips are recommended.

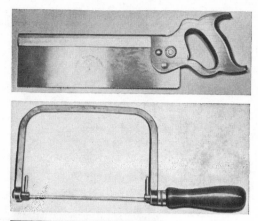

Figure 58. Back saw.

Figure 59. Coping saw.

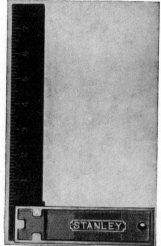

Figure 60. Try square.

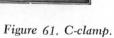

Figure 61. C-clamp.

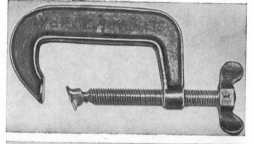

Figure 62. Tin snips.

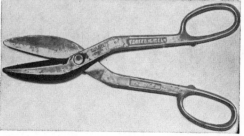

Pliers (Figure 63)   Two pairs of pliers will be needed. One pair should be side-cutting pliers for cutting the heads off nails and for cutting wire, and the other pair should be combination pliers for which the teacher will find many uses.

Hand drill (Figure 64)   One hand drill should be sufficient. When selecting a hand drill, one should be especially careful to obtain a quality tool. Cheap hand drills are available, but they will not prove serviceable, since they have a tendency to bind and turn hard. There should be two small gears (pinions) on the shaft of the tool, rather than just one. Also, one should look for a relatively large cranking wheel (speed gear), since it provides a better driving power. On some hand drills, the gears are enclosed. These are excellent for children in the lower grades, and provide an extra measure of safety.

Twist-drill bits (Figure 65)   A few carbon-steel twist-drill bits should be procured for use with the hand drill. Since children may break these bits frequently, six each of the following sizes should be procured: ⅛, 5⁄32, and 3⁄16 inches.

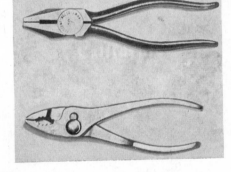

Figure 63. Pliers. Above: side-cutting; below: combination.

Figure 64. Hand drill.

Figure 65. Twist-drill bit.

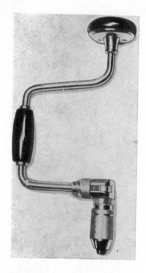

Figure 66. Ratchet bit brace.

Figure 67. Auger bit.

Figure 68. Brace countersink.

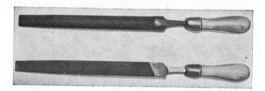

Figure 69. Files. Above: half-round cabinet; below: second-cut mill.

Ratchet bit brace (Figure 66) One ratchet bit brace is adequate. This tool is used to bore holes larger than those which can be drilled with the hand drill. The brace should have a 6 to 8-inch sweep, since braces with smaller sweeps require more strength than children have.

Auger bits (Figure 67) Four bits, which are used with the brace, should be provided. They should be of the following sizes: ¼, ⅜, ½, and 1 inch. It may be desirable to secure more sizes later, but these four will serve as a starting set.

Brace countersink (Figure 68) One, also used with the brace, should be provided to recess screw heads.

Files (Figure 69) Three files are needed. Two files should be half-round cabinet wood files, and the third should be a second-cut mill file. All should be 8 inches long and should have handles. A **file card (Figure 70)** should be provided for cleaning files.

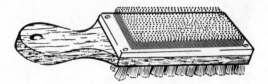

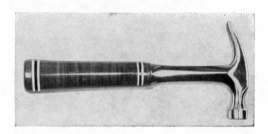

Figure 70. File card.

Figure 72. Screw driver.

Figure 71. Claw hammer.

Claw hammers (Figure 71) Two claw hammers should be sufficient. Claw hammers are ordered according to the weight of the metal head. For general purposes, 12 or 13-ounce hammers are best. Lighter hammers cannot be used successfully by children, because they do not have the weight necessary to drive nails. There should not be even the slightest amount of looseness where the hammer head joins the handle. The newer, one-piece, metal-alloy hammers, with leather, cork, or rubber grips are excellent.

Screw drivers (Figure 72) Two screw drivers should be adequate. Of the great variety of screw drivers available, the plastic-handle type is recommended. One should have a 4-inch blade and the other, a 6-inch blade. These will not serve all purposes, but they should do for most work requiring a screw driver.

Safety eye shields Two shields should be available. Eye protective devices should be worn when the jig saw is used, and whenever there might be danger from flying chips. In addition, one should check on eye safety regulations to be followed in the school system.

A separate category The following tools, though highly desirable and useful, are somewhat less essential than those listed previously:

Wrench, one, adjustable, 10 inch (Figure 73)
Block plane, one (Figure 74)
Nail set, one, $\frac{3}{32}$ inch (Figure 75)
Scratch awl, one, wooden handle (Figure 76)
Push-pull rule, one, 8 feet long (Figure 77)

This completes the list of classroom tools; it by no means exhausts all possibilities. Hundreds of tools are available, some of which might be useful in elementary grades. However, if one has all or most of the tools listed, he will have an excellent assortment available and will be able to provide for a wide variety of construction activities. The following is a list of recommended tools, with space to list the prices of various brands or sources for comparison.

Figure 73. Adjustable wrench.

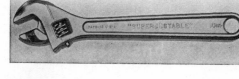

Figure 74. Block plane.

Figure 75. Nail set.

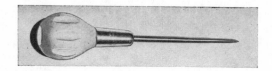

Figure 76. Scratch awl.

Figure 77. Push-pull rule.

Tools for Classroom Use	Prices for Comparison		
1. One vibrating jig saw, electrically operated 110–120 volt, 60-cycle, a.c.	_____	_____	_____
One gross blades to fit machine	_____	_____	_____
2. Two panel saws, crosscut, 20″, 10 pts. . . .	_____	_____	_____
3. One compass saw, 10–12″, 10–14 pts.	_____	_____	_____
4. One backsaw, 10–12″, 12–14 pts.	_____	_____	_____
5. Two coping saw frames, adjustable for turning blades, screw-type handles for changing blades	_____	_____	_____
One gross blades, to fit frames, 16–18 teeth per inch	_____	_____	_____
6. One try square, 8″ blade, all-metal	_____	_____	_____
7. Two straight rules, metal, 24″ by 1″ . .	_____	_____	_____
8. Two C-clamps, 4″ opening	_____	_____	_____
9. One pair of tin snips, straight, right-handed, 10″	_____	_____	_____
10. Two pairs of pliers, one side-cutting, one combination	_____	_____	_____
11. One hand drill	_____	_____	_____
Six of each size, carbon-steel drill bits, ⅛″, ⁵⁄₃₂″, ³⁄₁₆″	_____	_____	_____
12. One ratchet bit brace, 6″–8″ sweep	_____	_____	_____
Four auger bits, ¼″, ⅜″, ½″, 1″	_____	_____	_____
One brace countersink	_____	_____	_____
13. Three files, two half-round, cabinet wood; one second-cut mill, all 8″, all with handles	_____	_____	_____
One file card	_____	_____	_____
14. Two claw hammers, 12–13 oz., one-piece, metal-alloy, rubber grips	_____	_____	_____
15. Two screw drivers, one 4″, one 6″, both with plastic handles	_____	_____	_____
16. Two safety eye shields	_____	_____	_____
17. Separate category			
One adjustable wrench, 10″	_____	_____	_____
One block plane, 6″	_____	_____	_____
One nail set, ³⁄₃₂″	_____	_____	_____
One scratch awl, wooden handle	_____	_____	_____
One push-pull rule, 8′	_____	_____	_____
Totals	_____	_____	_____

For advice on particular brands of tools, industrial arts consultants, shop instructors, school purchasing agents, and hardware store suppliers and merchants can make suggestions valuable to a classroom teacher who is not familiar with tools.

The maintenance of equipment is an important responsibility at all educational levels, though most of the tools listed here will require little care. This is true of the C-clamps, claw hammers, try squares, straight rules, coping saw frames, hand drills, ratchet bit braces, brace countersinks, pliers, files, file cards, tin snips, adjustable wrenches, nail sets, and push-pull rules. However, an occasional drop of light oil on the moving parts of these tools will keep them working well. If hammer heads become loose, or if other serious trouble develops with these tools, they should be turned over to a mechanic for repair. Other than that, cleaning the tools and wiping steel parts with a lightly oiled rag before putting them away for summer storage is all that is needed. The children can share in this maintenance task.

The manufacturer's directions should be followed for the maintenance of the vibrating jig saw. Jig saw blades and coping saw blades should be discarded when they break or become dull.

Some tools require maintenance beyond that which the classroom teacher can be expected to provide. Of these, compass saws, panel saws, and backsaws should be sent to a saw fitter when they become dull. Carbon-steel drill bits rarely need attention when they are used in soft wood, but if they do become dull, they can be reground. Auger bits can be filed when they become dull. Screw drivers, the cutter from the block plane, and the scratch awl become dull, worn, or nicked in the course of their use. These can be reconditioned readily by someone who has the necessary skill and equipment. The maintenance of the tools mentioned in this paragraph, should not, however, be the responsibility of the classroom teacher, except for storing them with reasonable care.

Probably the teacher's major responsibility is to see that dull tools are sharpened or replaced. Dull tools are hard to work with and often cause injuries. The maintenance, repair, and replacement of tools should be provided for when the school budget is prepared, because these are valid educational expenses.

It is just as important that tools be stored correctly as it is that they be carefully maintained. Tools can become damaged or lost through improper storage practices. The following points are suggested as principles for the development of a classroom tool storage system:

1. Tools should be protected from damage.
2. Tools should be easy to remove from their storage places, with no chance of injury to the worker selecting them.

3. Storage facilities should be designed so that a rapid check can be made to see that all tools have been put away properly.
4. There should be a definite place for every tool.
5. When tools are to be used in different places, the tools should be easy to move all at once.

In view of the preceding points, some type of portable tool panel is indicated. The one shown in Figure 78 has been found highly satisfactory. It is not difficult to construct, and the materials required are inexpensive. Furthermore, it is about the right size for storing the tools listed earlier in this chapter. The greatest advantage of the portable panel is that two or more grades can use the same set of tools. When necessary, this reduces costs.

Some of the newer workbenches (Figures 39 and 40) include space for tool storage, and these work very well.

Another possibility, if space permits, is a tool panel fastened permanently to the wall (Figure 79), and located low enough to be within the reach of the children. Three-quarter-inch plywood makes an excellent panel, as does pegboard.

When planning the layout of a tool panel, the following procedures will be found helpful: Using chalk, draw a rectangle the exact size of the panel on the floor. Arrange the tools on the board, moving them around until the best arrangement is discovered. Be sure to keep safety in mind when positioning these tools. The teeth of saws, for example, should be turned in the safest direction. The possibility of youngsters bumping into the tool panel also must be considered.

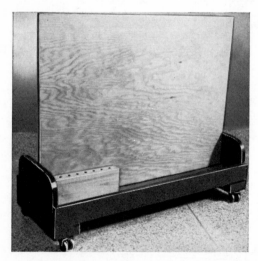

Figure 78. Home-made portable tool panel.

Figure 79. Tool panel.

Some tools can be conveniently stored by inserting them in holes which have been bored in wooden blocks attached to the tool board. Such tools are the screw driver, auger bit, scratch awl, brace countersink, and drill bit. Other tools can be hung on shoulder-screw hooks (sometimes called "square-bent" screw hooks). These are L-shaped hooks with threads on one end, similar to those on a screw. The length of the hook will depend on what it is to hold. When purchasing hooks, it should be understood that the threaded part is not included in the length. A two-inch hook will be longer than two inches, if the length of the threaded end is included in the measurement. For the tools listed previously, the following shoulder-screw hooks will be adequate: two dozen, 1¼ inches long; and one half dozen, 2½ inches long. The longer hooks are used for the panel saws, coping saws, and C-clamps, since two of each of these tools are recommended, and they can be hung on top of each other. Extra coping and jig saw blades can be kept in a small box or can.

If peg board is used for the tool panel, special hangers are available to fit the holes. These hangers can be purchased in hardware departments and from dealers in building materials.

Children are more likely to return tools to their proper places when a silhouette of each tool is painted on the panel indicating the proper place. A label giving the correct name of each tool, and glued onto the panel above each tool silhouette, will also assist in tool recognition and will provide an application of a meaningful reading experience.

The last possibility for tool storage is some kind of cabinet or chest of drawers. This is not very satisfactory because the tools bump and rub against each other and are hard to find, but it may have to serve as a temporary expedient. If you use this method, unusual care must be taken to protect the tools, and to prevent cuts and scratches when tools are removed and returned.

BASIC TOOLS FOR INDUSTRIAL ARTS WORKROOMS

The tools necessary in a specialized elementary school industrial arts shop depend, of course, on the nature of the work to be done and the ages of the children to be served. There is no such thing as a standard list, but the following will serve as a starting point with modifications to be made to suit local situations.

Tools For Industrial Arts Workroom Use

TOOL	NUMBER NEEDED	COMPARISON PRICES
Awls, scratch, 6″	4	
Bits		
Auger, set of (No. 4–No. 16)	1	
Twist drill, set (³⁄₃₂″–³⁄₈″)	1	
Blades		
Coping saw, pin end, 15 teeth	100	
Coping saw, pin end, 10 teeth	100	
Hack saw, 10″, 24 teeth	12	
Brace, bit, 8″ sweep	1	
Calipers		
Outside, 4″	1	
Outside, 6″	1	
Carving tools (leather), set	1	
Carving tools (wood), small, medium	2	
Card, for file cleaning	2	
Chisels		
Cold, ½″	1	
Cold, ¾″	1	
Wood, ¼″, ⅜″, ½″, ⅝″, ¾″, 1″, one each	6	
Woodturning, set of 8, for lathe	1	

Clamps
    C-clamps, 4" .... 6 ____ ____ ____
    C-clamps, 6" .... 6 ____ ____ ____
    C-clamps, 8" .... 6 ____ ____ ____
    Bar, 4' .... 2 ____ ____ ____
Dividers, 6" .... 1 ____ ____ ____
Drills
    Hand, ¼" .... 2 ____ ____ ____
    Electric, ¼" .... 1 ____ ____ ____
Files, with handles
    Half-round, wood, 10" .... 4 ____ ____ ____
    Flat, wood, 10" .... 2 ____ ____ ____
    Mill, 2nd cut, 8", 10", one each 2 ____ ____ ____
    Auger bit .... 1 ____ ____ ____
Gauges
    Wire, American standard ...... 1 ____ ____ ____
    Sheet metal, U.S. standard .... 1 ____ ____ ____
    Marking, 6" .... 2 ____ ____ ____
Glass cutter, common .... 2 ____ ____ ____
Goggles, safety, adjustable ...... 24 ____ ____ ____
Hammers
    Claw, 7 ounce .... 2 ____ ____ ____
    Claw, 13 ounce .... 6 ____ ____ ____
    Claw, 16 ounce .... 6 ____ ____ ____
    Ball peen, 4, 8, 12 ounce, one each 3 ____ ____ ____
    Riveting, 8, 12 ounce, one each . 2 ____ ____ ____
    Soft face, 8, 16 ounce, one each . 2 ____ ____ ____
Knives
    Putty .... 2 ____ ____ ____
    Exacto .... 2 ____ ____ ____
    Sloyd .... 2 ____ ____ ____
Level, aluminum, 24" .... 1 ____ ____ ____
Mallets, tinners .... 2 ____ ____ ____
Mitre box and saw, 24" .... 1 ____ ____ ____
Modeling tools
    Ceramics assortment .... 1 ____ ____ ____
    Leather assortment .... 1 ____ ____ ____
Nail sets, ³⁄₃₂" .... 2 ____ ____ ____
Oil cans
    Bench oilers, rigid spout .... 2 ____ ____ ____
    Bench oiler, flexible spout ...... 1 ____ ____ ____
    Oiler, pump type .... 1 ____ ____ ____

Oil stones, combination	2			
Planes				
Block	6			
Jack	1			
Smooth	2			
Pliers				
Side-cutting, 6½"	2			
Diagonal cutting, 5"	1			
Needle-nose, 5"	1			
Utility (water pump), 10"	1			
Combination, 6"	2			
Combination, 8"	2			
Punches				
Revolving, for leather	1			
Center, 4"	2			
Prick, 4"	2			
Rasps, with handles				
Round wood, 10"	2			
Cabinet, 10"	2			
Rivet sets, No.'s 5, 6, 7, 8, one each	4			
Rules				
Aluminum or steel, 24"	6			
Push-pull, 8'	2			
Saws				
Hand, panel, 20", 10 pt.	6			
Hand, panel, 26", 10 pt.	1			
Hand, rip, 26", 5½ pt.	1			
Compass, 12"	1			
Coping, 6½" pin end	8			
Hack, adjustable	1			
Back, 10"–12", 12–14 pt.	4			
Scissors				
Round tip, 6"	4			
Trimming, 8"	2			
Screw drivers				
Phillips, points No.'s 2, 3, one each	2			
Straight, 2", 4", 6", 8", one each	4			
Snap fastener set for leather	1			
Snips				
Tin, straight, right-hand, 11"–12"	2			
Pattern, 7"–8"	2			
Aviation, combination, 10"	2			

Soldering devices
    Gun, electric   1   _____ _____ _____
    Irons, electric   2   _____ _____ _____
Squares
    Try, 6"   2   _____ _____ _____
    Try, 8"   4   _____ _____ _____
    Combination, 12"   1   _____ _____ _____
    T-bevel, 8"   1   _____ _____ _____
    Framing, 16" x 24" aluminum ..   1   _____ _____ _____
Tape measure, 50', steel   1   _____ _____ _____
Tapewriter, ⅜"–½"   1   _____ _____ _____
Wire nippers, 10"   1   _____ _____ _____
Wrenches
    Adjustable, 6", 8", 10", 12", one
       each   4   _____ _____ _____
    Pipe, 10", 12", one each   2   _____ _____ _____
Yardsticks, common   24   _____ _____ _____

BASIC SUPPLIES FOR INDUSTRIAL ARTS PROGRAMS

These are some of the materials commonly used in elementary school industrial arts programs.

Cardboard

Large boxes, such as those used for packaging household appliances, provide cardboard in varying thicknesses and sizes. Obtainable at no cost, the cardboard has many uses. The boxes themselves can be used as various items of furniture, sometimes simply by cutting out parts and painting the cardboard. Where more strength is required, pieces of wood can be fastened to the boxes to provide reinforcements. Again, the boxes can be cut apart and the cardboard used to make stage scenery or other large, flat surfaces. The cardboard can be cut and folded with relative ease, and it takes water-based paints very well.

Wood

Although wood is used less in modern packaging than it once was, occasionally crates and packing cases do become available. Some containers are made of thin, flimsy wood that warps easily. These are of little value as construction lumber. On the other hand, some boxes and crates contain clean, straight lumber which is very useful in elementary industrial arts programs. After a little experience with these types of materials, the teacher will be able to recognize the kinds of wood with which it is best to work. (See page 162 for a description of the process of taking boxes apart.)

Of the many kinds of lumber which can be purchased, white pine probably is best for general use in activity programs. It is soft, straight-grained, light, and worked easily. When properly selected, it is free from knots and other defects. Where it is available, basswood is also very popular.

Lumber is sold in standard grades and sizes. The best grade of lumber usually should be purchased. Further, standard size lumber should be used whenever possible.

Dealers will deliver lumber of almost any size specified, but when it is necessary for them to supply wood in special sizes, it will cost more. The most useful of the standard sizes of lumber for the elementary grades are 1″ x 6″ and 1″ x 8″. For the construction of workbenches and other heavier pieces, 2″ x 6″ lumber will be needed. In each case, the first numeral refers to thickness and the second to the width of boards (Figure 80). One may specify length to suit his purposes, but this, too, is standard: 8′, 10′, 12′, and so forth.

The nominal size of lumber is slightly different from its actual size, but there is a logical explanation for this fact. When a 1″ x 6″ board is cut from a log, it actually measures 1″ x 6″, but it is rough from the coarse saw. To make the board smooth, some of the wood must be removed, thereby reducing its size. Therefore, the actual size is somewhat less than nominal size in standard lumber. Lumber is ordered and paid for according to its nominal size.

As stated previously, it is most economical to purchase lumber in standard sizes, but occasionally odd thicknesses and widths will be needed. For example, ½″ pine boards may be wanted. If there are no machines available in the school to cut lumber to this size, they usually can be procured directly from the lumber dealer. The additional machine work will, of course, increase the lumber cost.

Another often used product obtainable from the lumber dealer is fir plywood. This is the product that looks like a wood sandwich, made of

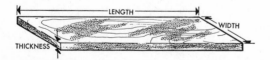

Figure 80. Lumber terms.

thin layers of wood. For a given thickness, plywood, because of its construction, is stronger and less likely to crack or warp than a solid board. It will prove satisfactory wherever thin material is needed, as in some toys, easels, and flannelboards. Plywood can be bought in various thicknesses, with ¼" material most commonly used in the elementary grades. Other types of panel material are also very useful. Materials such as fiber wallboards and hard wallboards which are sold under trade names like Homosote, Masonite, and Upson board, can be used in place of thin wood.

Broomsticks and other round sticks of varying diameters should be collected and stored. When these are not available, wooden dowels, which are approximately the same thing, can be purchased from lumber dealers.

Metal

Although used less frequently than wood, metal does play a part in industrial arts programs. It is relatively expensive and its sharp edges can be dangerous, but there are some purposes for which no adequate substitute exists. Also, it is an extremely important material in our society, and the children should have some experience in using it.

Discarded food containers are one source of sheet metal. Lids should be removed with can openers which do not leave jagged edges. Where desired, both ends of a can can be removed; then, the metal cylinder can be cut apart with tin snips and flattened out with rubber or wooden mallets.

If desired, new tin plate (the material from which tin cans are made) can be purchased in varying sizes. A thickness of about .012 of an inch is good, and sheet sizes of about 20" x 28" are easy to handle and store.

Aluminum in sheet form sometimes is useful. For specific purposes, aluminum is available in a wide range of specifications. For general use, "soft temper" aluminum is best, in about .025 of an inch thickness, and sheets about 24" x 48".

For copper tooling, .005 of an inch thick copper is available in rolls 12 inches wide and in varying lengths.

Metal or plastic screening often is useful for building pet cages. It comes in standard width rolls (24 to 48 inches wide) and in varying lengths and mesh, or openings per inch. Chicken wire or poultry netting is most often purchased in 36 inch rolls, with 1 inch hexagon mesh and No. 20 wire, in varying lengths.

Finally, band iron finds a number of uses in industrial arts programs. Two useful sizes are 1/16" x 1/2" and 1/8" x 5/8" in 8 foot lengths.

Finishes

The use of paints and other finishing materials is one of the chief sources of interest and satisfaction for pupils. The materials most commonly used are water colors, shellac, oil paints, enamels, lacquers, and water-soluble, latex-base paints.

Water colors can be used on wood and most other materials if a coat of shellac or clear lacquer is applied over the water colors to protect them.

Shellac is a transparent finishing material that can be used not only over water colors, but also for a natural finish on clean surfaces, and it can be used as a good base coat or sealer under oil paint. White shellac should be purchased in metal containers, preferably in the ½ gallon size. Denatured alcohol, in quart cans, will be necessary because alcohol is used to thin out shellac that has become too thick, and also to clean the brushes used to apply shellac.

Some opaque finishing materials also are desirable. These may be either wall paints, enamels, or lacquers. The variety of colors to be used can be determined by the teacher. It is not necessary to requisition all of these—paints, enamels, and lacquers—since they will serve approximately the same purpose. Paints are the least expensive, but they are not as glossy as enamels and lacquers, and they may take a day or more to dry. Enamels and lacquers produce a shinier finish and dry faster, but they are more expensive. Whichever is chosen, half-pint, pint, or quart cans are desirable sizes. Paints and finishing materials in larger containers often dry out or become dirty before they can be used. Smaller cans are easier for children to handle, and they are more economical in the long run.

Figure 81. Painters at work.

If paints or enamels are used, turpentine will be needed as a thinner and brush cleaner. If lacquers are used, either clear transparent lacquers or colored lacquers, lacquer thinner must be used as a thinner and brush cleaner.

Solvents, thinners, and brush cleaners cannot be used interchangeably. The following table may be helpful:

FINISH	SOLVENTS, THINNERS, AND BRUSH CLEANERS
Water colors	Water
Shellac	Alcohol
Oil paints	Turpentine
Enamel	Turpentine
Varnish	Turpentine
Lacquer (dopes)	Lacquer thinner
Water-soluble, rubber-base paints	Water

Working with many of the finishing materials described here is not without problems. First, some of these materials constitute a fire hazard; secondly, many children find it difficult to clean brushes properly. If the brushes used to apply shellac, oil paints, enamels, and lacquers are not thoroughly cleaned, they become useless. When the possibility of damage to clothing, floors, and school furniture is added to the difficulties already listed, many teachers decide to do without these finishes altogether.

Some of the problems can be minimized by purchasing paints, enamels, and lacquers in spray cans, and by following the directions printed on the containers. Solvents are still needed for clean-up chores.

Fortunately, a finishing product that reduces or eliminates all the hazards associated with the more familiar finishes is available. It is water-soluble, latex-base paint, and it is available at most paint and hardware stores. This type of paint was developed for both indoor and outdoor use. It dries rapidly; it is thinned with plain water, and brushes are easily cleaned with ordinary soap and water. In view of its advantages, including the elimination of a variety of thinners and brush cleaners, it is not surprising that many teachers use water-soluble paints exclusively.

Care must still be taken to keep water-soluble paints away from clothing and to wipe up spills and drippings when they occur. When latex paint dries, it is difficult to remove.

A supply of cotton rags will be needed to wipe hands and clean up drips, and large pieces of a light canvas can be used as drop cloths to protect flooring from paint.

Textile Materials

Textile materials used most frequently are unbleached muslin, flannel, colored rug yarns, and roving. Unbleached muslin is used as a light, inexpensive covering over wood frames for stage scenery, puppet stages, store fronts, and similar projects. Flannel is used for flannelboards and display boards. Both of these are purchased by the yard.

Rug yarns are highly desirable for elementary weaving. They are fairly thick, easy to use, and produce pleasing results. These rug yarns are available in a wide variety of colors and are purchased by the ball or skein, or in larger quantities. Roving is much like rug yarn, but it is thicker, particularly the multiple-ply types. Often it is used in the lower grades for simple weaving projects, and it is purchased usually by the ball, the skein, or the pound.

Miscellaneous Supplies

Of the many kinds of coated abrasives (often called sandpaper) available, flint paper probably is best for classroom use. It should be purchased by the full sheet, 9" x 10", in packages of 50 or 100 sheets. Flint paper is available in many grits, ranging from very coarse to very fine, and designated either by a name such as "medium," or by a number. As the numbers become larger, the grit becomes coarser, so that No. 2 paper is coarser than No. ½; No. 0 paper is coarser than No. 00, and so on. Two grits will probably be sufficient—No. ½ for smoothing wood, and No. 00 (sometimes written No. 2/0) for rubbing finishes between coats. In the interest of simplicity, many teachers find "medium" sandpaper satisfactory for all purposes.

Garnet paper is much more durable than flint paper, but it is more expensive. If used, it should be bought in 9" x 11" sheets, in No. 0 grit.

Brushes for applying finishes should be available in at least two sizes, ½" and 1½" (measured across the width of the bristles). They should be of good quality, with the bristles held firmly in place so they will not come out and spoil a finished surface. Smaller artists' brushes also should be available.

Nails are designated by type and by length (Figure 82). The three basic varieties of nails are "common," "box," and "finishing." Common nails and box nails are similar, except that box nails are somewhat thinner and less likely to crack thin wood. Both have flat heads. Finishing nails have smaller heads and are used when it is undesirable to have the heads show.

The size of nails is designated by the term "penny," which is the same as the symbol "d." A 2d nail is 1 inch long. When the digit by the "d" in-

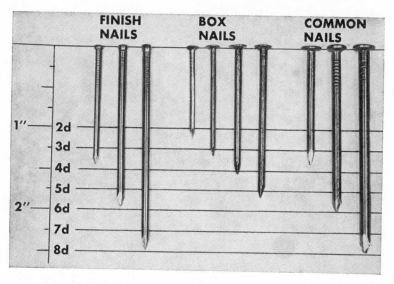

Figure 82. Nail chart; chart is slightly smaller than actual size.

creases, the nail becomes ¼ inch longer, thus a 3d nail is 1¼ inches long, a 4d nail is 1½ inches long, and so forth. This is not uniformly true above 8d, but little use will be found for nails longer than this (2½ inches).

It is difficult to specify the sizes or kinds of nails needed until the program is known. However, a box or two of assorted small nails, such as those purchased in hardware and variety stores, certainly will be useful for small work. Two other kinds that are certain to be needed are 4d (4-penny) box nails and 6d finishing nails. A small box of 1″, No. 18, wire brads (small finishing nails) also will be useful.

Wood screws vary widely in styles. The three basic types are known as "flat-head" (F.H.), "round-head" (R.H.), and "oval-head" (O.H.) (Figure 83). Wood screws are made of various metals, such as steel, brass, blue steel, nickel-plate, and so on. Screws are designated according to their length and diameter, for example, 1″, No. 10; 1¼″, No. 12. The number refers to the diameter of the screw, and as the number increases the thickness of the screw increases.

Unless specified, wood screws have a standard slot for which standard screw drivers are designed. Phillips-head screws have a recess shaped like a plus sign (+) in the head, requiring a Phillips screw driver. In general, Phillips-head screws require more coordination than young pupils possess, and use of such screws should be discouraged.

Glue is a very useful material. A wide variety of glues are available for specialized jobs, but the kind recommended for most of the work to be done in elementary grades is all-purpose polyvinyl resin glue. This is available in plastic squeeze bottles, which not only reduce spoilage but also eliminate the danger of broken jars.

Other small supplies frequently used are pictured in Figure 84.

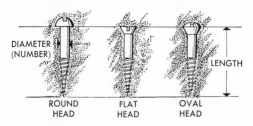

Figure 83. Common wood screws.

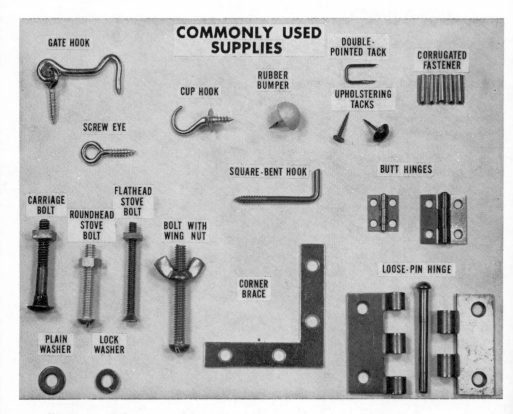

Figure 84. Other frequently used supplies.

SUPPLIES FOR A TYPICAL INDUSTRIAL ARTS CLASSROOM PROGRAM

The quantities listed here are suitable for a single classroom. They are not sufficient to stock a shop to be used by a number of classes. Even in a single classroom, these supplies will need to be augmented and replenished from time to time. As a program develops, a simple supplies inventory system should be started to help maintain adequate stocks of materials.

Supplies for Classroom Use

1. Large sturdy cardboard boxes as available.
2. White pine (or basswood), best grade, selected for straight clear stock, 1″ x 6″ x 8′, 80 lineal feet (40 board feet).[1]
3. White pine (or basswood), best grade, selected for straight clear stock, 1″ x 2″ x 8′ (ripped from wider stock and jointed), 192 lineal feet (approximately 40 board feet).
4. White pine (or basswood), best grade, selected for straight clear stock, ½″ x 8″ x 8′ (planed), 48 lineal feet (approximately 32 board feet).
5. Pine or poplar or birch dowels, ¼″ x 3′, ½″ x 3′, 1″ x 3′, 9 lineal feet of each.
6. Discarded broom handles and round sticks, as available.
7. Plywood, fir, ¼″, marine, good both sides, 2 sheets 4′ x 8′ as follows: one sheet cut to six pieces approximating 24″ x 32″; and one sheet ripped into two pieces approximately 12″ x 8′ and four pieces approximating 6″ x 8′.
8. Fiber wallboard, unfinished, ½″, 2 sheets 4′ x 8′ cut same as plywood above.
9. Optional: additional lumber as required for special projects, such as workbenches, tool panels, and easels.
10. Optional: balsa wood as desired.
11. Optional: various small sizes and shapes of soft wood, usually considered waste by lumber yards and shops.
12. Discarded containers (tin cans) as available.
13. Water-soluble, latex-base paints, assorted colors, 8 quart-size cans.
14. Paint brushes, ½″, (six); 1½″, (six); artists' brushes, assorted sizes, (twelve).
15. Optional: shellac, white 4-pound cut, in metal can, ½ gallon; and denatured alcohol in metal can, 1 quart.
16. Optional: inside paint, assorted colors, 8 pint-sized cans or spray cans; and turpentine, in metal can, 2 quart-size cans.
17. Assorted cotton paint rags.

[1] A "board foot" is equal to 144 cubic inches measured on the nominal size of lumber. Thus, a board 1″ x 12″ x 10′ would contain 10 board feet, and a 2″ x 6″ x 10′ would also contain 10 board feet. Lumber prices can be quoted either by board feet or lineal feet.

18. Light canvas drop cloth, approximately 4' x 8', (one).
19. Unbleached muslin 35"–38" width, 10 yards.
20. Colored rug yarns, roving, assorted colors, 1-ounce balls, 1 dozen balls.
21. To suit program, purchase as needed: sheet metals, poultry netting, band iron, wire screening, and flannel.
22. Flint abrasive sandpaper, No. ½ (medium), 9" x 10" sheets, 50 sheets.
23. Nails, assorted, small, 1 box; 4-penny, box, 1 pound; 6-penny, finish (or casing), 1 pound; 2-penny, finish (or casing), 1 pound (same as 1" brads).
24. Wood screws, O.H. brass, ¾", No. 6; F.H. steel 1¼", No. 8; R.H. bright, 1½", No. 10, 1 gross of each.
25. Glue, all-purpose polyvinyl resin in plastic squeeze bottle, 8-fluid-ounce size, 2 bottles.

It often is feasible to have pupils, or the parents of pupils, furnish some of their own materials and supplies. The shopping experiences are valuable to children, and it is unnecessary to stock items whch are used infrequently.

CLASSROOM STORAGE FACILITIES

The quantities of supplies required in any one classroom are limited; therefore, storage is not a great problem.

Cardboard and lumber should be stored where they will not be exposed to heat, cold, or moisture. Cardboard should be laid flat. Lumber should be stacked to minimize bending or warping. Neat piles of lumber in the corner of a work area are not objectionable, and if space is a factor, boards can be stood on end *and secured with a chain to prevent them from falling*. To facilitate storage, lengths of boards should not exceed 8 feet. A box for short pieces of wood should be provided.

Most of the other supplies can be kept in the drawers or on the shelves of almost any type of cabinet. *Inflammable paint and solvents should be kept in a metal cabinet with a well-fitting door.*

Shellac, if used frequently, can be kept in a pint fruit jar, with the brush suspended in the shellac by means of a rubber cap made especially for the purpose (Figure 85). The shellac must cover the major portion of the bristles. Otherwise, the bristles will stiffen as the shellac dries. This device makes it unnecessary to clean shellac brushes after each use. It is not recommended for other finishing materials because of their drying characteristics, and the fact that any one color will probably be infrequently used. The shellac jar then should be stored in the metal cabinet used to store paint.

An all-metal, covered can should be provided as a container for discarded paint rags and paper which would otherwise be a fire hazard.

Metal clothing lockers can serve as storage cabinets with a little modification (Figure 86). Shelves can be cut from ½" fir plywood or from 1" pine,

Figure 85. Shellac brush on a rubber brush cap.

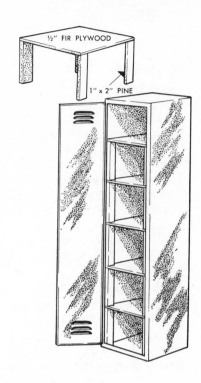

Figure 86. Locker storage cabinet.

and fastened in place with wood screws placed through holes drilled in the sides of the metal cabinet. If it is impractical to punch or drill holes in the cabinet, wood spacers can be cut to serve as legs for the shelves. The legs can be fastened to each shelf with two 4d box nails, and each shelf can stand on the one below it, making the shelves adjustable.

SUPPLIES FOR INDUSTRIAL ARTS WORKROOM

Until he establishes his own inventory checklist of supplies, the specialist-consultant may find the following helpful. Quantities must be determined according to the extent of the local program.

Checklist for Industrial Arts Workroom Supplies

ITEM	UNIT	PRICE	ON HAND	TO ORDER
Abrasives, coated, 9″ x 10″ (or 11″) sheets				
Emery cloth, fine, 50 sheet ..	package			
Emery cloth, medium, 50 sheet	package			
Flint paper, fine, 100 sheet ...	package			

ITEM	UNIT	PRICE	ON HAND	TO ORDER
Flint paper, medium, 100 sheet	package	_____	_____	_____
Garnet paper, No. 00, 100 sheet	package	_____	_____	_____
Garnet paper, No. ½, 100 sheet	package	_____	_____	_____
Garnet paper, No. 1, 50 sheet .	package	_____	_____	_____
Cement				
Asbestos, 50 pound	bag	_____	_____	_____
Mortar-mix, 70 pound	bag	_____	_____	_____
Perf-a-Tape, U.S. Gypsum, 25 pound	box	_____	_____	_____
Portland, 90 pound	bag	_____	_____	_____
Fasteners				
Bolts, carriage, with nuts				
¼″ x 2″	dozen	_____	_____	_____
¼″ x 2½″	dozen	_____	_____	_____
5⁄16″ x 3″	dozen	_____	_____	_____
5⁄16″ x 4″	dozen	_____	_____	_____
Bolts, machine, RH brass, with nuts				
No. 8 x ½″	gross	_____	_____	_____
No. 12 x ¾″	gross	_____	_____	_____
¼″ x 1″	gross	_____	_____	_____
¼″ x 1½″	gross	_____	_____	_____
Bolts, stove, RH steel, with nuts, 100/box				
⅛″ x ½″	box	_____	_____	_____
⅛″ x 1″	box	_____	_____	_____
⅛″ x 1½″	box	_____	_____	_____
3⁄16″ x ¾″	box	_____	_____	_____
3⁄16″ x 1″	box	_____	_____	_____
3⁄16″ x 2″	box	_____	_____	_____
¼″ x 1″	box	_____	_____	_____
¼″ x 2″	box	_____	_____	_____
¼″ x 3″	box	_____	_____	_____
Escutcheon pins, RH brass				
⅜″, No. 20	pound	_____	_____	_____
5⁄8″, No. 18	pound	_____	_____	_____
⅞″, No. 16	pound	_____	_____	_____

ITEM	UNIT	PRICE	ON HAND	TO ORDER
Gate hooks and eyes, bright steel				
1½″	dozen			
2½″	dozen			
Nails, wire				
Brads, ¾″, No. 18	pound			
Box, 3d	pound			
Box, 4d	pound			
Box, 6d	pound			
Common, 6d	pound			
Common, 8d	pound			
Finish, 2d (or 1″ brads)	pound			
Finish, 4d	pound			
Finish, 6d	pound			
Rivets				
Aluminum, RH, ⅛″ x ¼″	pound			
Aluminum, RH, ⅛″ x ⅜″	pound			
Tinners, black iron, No. 1, box/1000	box			
Tinners, black iron, No. 1½, box/1000	box			
Screws, wood, standard slot				
½″, No. 2, FH, brass	gross			
⅝″, No. 4, RH, brass	gross			
¾″, No. 6, RH, brass	gross			
⅝″, No. 4, FH, bright	gross			
¾″, No. 6, FH, bright	gross			
1″, No. 8, FH, bright	gross			
1¼″, No. 8, FH, bright	gross			
1½″, No. 10, FH, bright	gross			
¾″, No. 6, RH, blue	gross			
1″, No. 8, RH, blue	gross			
1½″, No. 10, RH, blue	gross			
¾″, No. 6, OH, bright	gross			
1″, No. 8, OH, bright	gross			
Tacks				
Blind staples, ⅜″	pound			
Blind staples, ½″	pound			
Double pointed, ¼″ x ¹⁵⁄₃₂″	pound			
Upholsterer's, ⅜″, No. 3	pound			

ITEM	UNIT	PRICE	ON HAND	TO ORDER
Upholsterer's, ½″, No. 6 ...	pound			
Upholsterer's, ⅝″, No. 10 ..	pound			
Washers				
Brass, plain, No. 8	gross			
Brass, plain, No. 12	gross			
Brass, plain, ¼″	gross			
Lock, steel, ⅛″	dozen			
Lock, steel, ³⁄₁₆″	dozen			
Lock, steel, ¼″	dozen			
Lock, steel, ⁵⁄₁₆″	dozen			
Steel, plain, ⅛″	dozen			
Steel, plain, ³⁄₁₆″	dozen			
Steel, plain, ¼″	dozen			
Steel, plain, ⁵⁄₁₆″	dozen			
Wood fasteners				
Chevrons, ⅜″	100			
Corrugated, ⅜″ x 4″ (quarters)	100			
Corrugated, ½″ x 5″ (quarters)	100			
Glue				
Casein, waterproof, powder ..	pound			
Du Pont DUCO cement, 1¾ ounce tube	each			
Epoxy, double tube set	set			
Paper paste, 8 oz. jar	jar			
Polyvinyl resin, plastic container (and half-pint plastic bottles)	gallon each			
Hardware Accessories				
Bolts, eye, with wing nuts				
¼″ x 1″	dozen			
¼″ x 2″	dozen			
¼″ x 3″	dozen			
(see also fasteners, washers)				
Cotter pin assortment, 1000 cotters	set			
Cup hooks, brass				
1⅜″	dozen			

ITEM	UNIT	PRICE	ON HAND	TO ORDER
2¾″	dozen	_____	_____	_____
Screw eyes, bright wire				
No. 214	100	_____	_____	_____
No. 208	100	_____	_____	_____
Square bent screw hooks				
1⅜″	dozen	_____	_____	_____
2¼″	dozen	_____	_____	_____
Wire				
Galvanized, soft, No. 16, 100 foot	coil	_____	_____	_____
Galvanized, soft, No. 12, 100 foot	coil	_____	_____	_____
Copper, soft, No. 18, ¼ pound	coil	_____	_____	_____
Stove pipe, 5 pound	coil	_____	_____	_____
(see also Lamp Cord)				
Hinges				
Box, brass plated, ¾″ x ⅝″ ...	pair	_____	_____	_____
Butt, steel, fast pin				
1″ x 2″	pair	_____	_____	_____
1½″ x 2¾″	pair	_____	_____	_____
Cabinet, steel, loose pin				
1″ x 1″	pair	_____	_____	_____
1½″ x 1⅞₆″	pair	_____	_____	_____
2″ x 1⁹⁄₁₆″	pair	_____	_____	_____
Cabinet, strap, steel				
1″ x 4″	pair	_____	_____	_____
1³⁄₃₂″ x 6″	pair	_____	_____	_____
T-hinge, steel				
2″ x 2″	pair	_____	_____	_____
3″ x 2⅜″	pair	_____	_____	_____
Lamp Cord				
Rubber, white, No. 18	100 feet	_____	_____	_____
Rubber, brown, No. 18	100 feet	_____	_____	_____
Metal				
Aluminum insect screening, 24″ wide	foot	_____	_____	_____
Aluminum, soft, .025″ x 24″ x 72″	sheet	_____	_____	_____

ITEM	UNIT	PRICE	ON HAND	TO ORDER
Band iron (mild steel)				
1/16" x 1/2"	foot			
1/8" x 5/8"	foot			
1/8" x 1"	foot			
Brass tubing, 1/8", 12 foot lengths	length			
Copper, .005" x 12" (roll)	foot			
Discarded containers	each			
Galvanized steel, 26 gauge, 24" x 96"	sheet			
Hardware cloth, 1/4" mesh, 24" width	foot			
Hardware cloth, 1/2" mesh, 30" width	foot			
Poultry netting, 1" mesh, 36" width	foot			
Tin plate, .012" x 20" x 28"	sheet			
Non-Skid Floor Fabric (with adhesive)	various			
Oil, lubricating				
3-In-One, 8 oz.	can			
Engine, S.A.E. No. 10, quart	can			
Machine, medium, quart	can			
Paints and Finishing Materials				
Alcohol, denatured	gallon			
Brushes, artists', camel's hair				
No. 4	dozen			
No. 6	dozen			
Brushes, paint, Nylon bristles				
1/2"	dozen			
1"	dozen			
1 1/2"	dozen			
2"	dozen			
Drop cloth, light canvas, 4' x 8'	each			
Enamel, 16 ounce spray cans, assorted	can			
Glass fruit jars, screw cap, pint size	each			

ITEM	UNIT	PRICE	ON HAND	TO ORDER
Lacquers, pint size, assorted colors	can			
Lacquer thinner	quart			
Latex paints, water soluble, assorted	quart			
Mineral spirits paint thinner ..	gallon			
Rags, cotton	each			
Rubber brush caps, holders ..	each			
Scouring pads	each			
Shellac, white, 4 pound cut ..	gallon			
Turpentine	gallon			
(see also Abrasives, coated)				
Panel Wallboard				
Homosote, ½″ x 4′ x 8′	sheet			
Masonite, soft, ³⁄₁₆″ x 4′ x 8′ ..	sheet			
Masonite, perforated, ⅛″ x 4′ x 8′	sheet			
(tool hangers to fit perforaations)				
Masonite, tempered, ¼″ x 4′ x 8′	sheet			
Upson board, ⅛″ x 4′ x 8′	sheet			
Upson board, ³⁄₁₆″ x 4′ x 8′ ...	sheet			
Paper and Cardboard				
Brown wrapping, 40 pound, 30″ width	roll			
(with appropriate holding frame)				
Carbon, noncurling, 8½″ x 11″	100			
Cardboard boxes	each			
Cross-section bond, ⅛″ squares, 9″ x 12″	ream			
Cross-section bond, ¼″ squares, 9″ x 12″	ream			
Easel, newsprint, 24″ x 36″ ..	ream			
Poster, 9″ x 12″, assorted colors	ream			
Tracing, 8½″ x 11″	ream			
White cardboard, 6 ply, 22″ x 28″	100			

ITEM	UNIT	PRICE	ON HAND	TO ORDER
Safety Signs and Panels, assorted	each	————	————	————
Solder				
Rosin core, 1 pound spool	each	————	————	————
Wire, plumber's	pound	————	————	————
Tape				
Friction, black, ¾", 8 ounce ..	roll	————	————	————
Rubber, black, ¾", 8 ounce ..	roll	————	————	————
Masking, 1", 60 yard	roll	————	————	————
Transparent, ⅝"	roll	————	————	————
Textile Materials				
Flannel, 9–11 ounce	yard	————	————	————
Muslin, unbleached, 35"–38" width	yard	————	————	————
Roving, assorted colors, 3 ply, 1 pound	hank	————	————	————
Rug yarns, assorted, 1-ounce ball or tube	each	————	————	————
Twine				
Hemp, upholstery, 100 yard ..	ball	————	————	————
White cotton, No. 16, ½ pound	ball	————	————	————
Wood				
Balsa, "A" grade, rough				
1"x 3" x 3' or larger	board foot	————	————	————
2" x 2" x 3' or larger	board foot	————	————	————
3" x 3" x 4' or larger	board foot	————	————	————
Basswood, "FAS," S2S				
¼" x 6" x 8'	board foot	————	————	————
⅜" x 8" x 8'	board foot	————	————	————
½" x 10" x 8'	board foot	————	————	————
¾" x 8" x 8'	board foot	————	————	————
Dowel rods, birch, 3' lengths				
⅛"	length	————	————	————
¼"	length	————	————	————
⅜"	length	————	————	————
½"	length	————	————	————
¾"	length	————	————	————

ITEM	UNIT	PRICE	ON HAND	TO ORDER
Fir plywood, exterior				
⅜″ x 4′ x 8′, A-D	sheet			
½″ x 4′ x 8′, A-D	sheet			
Fir plywood, interior				
¼″ x 4′ x 8′, A-A	sheet			
¼″ x 4′ x 8′, A-C	sheet			
⅜″ x 4′ x 8′, A-A	sheet			
⅜″ x 4′ x 8′, A-C	sheet			
½″ x 4′ x 8′, A-C	sheet			
¾″ x 4′ x 8′, A-C	sheet			
Pine, No. 1, clear, selected				
½″ x 10″ x 8′	board foot			
1″ x 6″ x 8′	board foot			
1″ x 8″ x 8′	board foot			
1″ x 12″ x 8′	board foot			
2″ x 4″ x 12′	board foot			
1½″ diameter clothes pole .	lineal foot			
¼″ x 1⅝″ x 8′, lattice	lineal foot			

NOTE: Not listed here are supplies for the areas of ceramics, the graphic arts, electricity, leather, and plastics. These areas are not always included in elementary industrial arts programs, and when they are included, activities vary so widely that standardized supplies are difficult to identify.

SELECTED REFERENCES

American Council on Industrial Arts Teacher Education, *Planning Industrial Arts Facilities*, 8th Yearbook (Bloomington, Ill.: McKnight and McKnight, 1959).

Amon, Martha R. and Ruth H. Rawson, *Handcrafts Simplified* (Bloomington, Ill.: McKnight and McKnight, 1961).

Association for Childhood Education International, *Recommended Equipment and Supplies*, Bulletin No. 39, 1953.

Barr, George S., "Mechanic's Corner," *The Instructor*, Vol. 65 (February, 1956), No. 6.

Basilone, James, "Modern Elementary Industrial Arts Room," *Industrial Arts and Vocational Education*, Vol. 55 (March, 1966), No. 3.

Culpepper, Fred W., Jr., "The Elementary Industrial-Arts Experiment at Suffolk, Va.," *Industrial Arts and Vocational Education*, Vol. 41 (March, 1952), No. 3.

Ericson, Emanuel E., *Teaching the Industrial Arts* (Peoria, Ill.: Chas. A. Bennett Co., 1960), Chapter XIV.

Fortin, John E., "The New Riverdahl (Rockford, Ill.) Elementary School," *Industrial Arts and Vocational Education,* Vol. 43 (March, 1954), No. 3.

Kazarian, Edward N., "Elementary Industrial Arts: Primer to Understanding," *Industrial Arts and Vocational Education,* Vol. 52 (December, 1963), No. 10.

Klehm, Walter, "Handwork in the Elementary School," *Industrial Arts and Vocational Education,* Vol. 45 (September, 1956), No. 7.

Leighbody, Gerald B., "Elementary All Purpose Rooms," *School Shop,* Vol. 16 (March, 1957), No. 7.

Modern School Shop Planning (Ann Arbor: Prakken Publications, 1965).

Moore, Frank C., Carl H. Hamburger, and Anna-Laura Kingzett, *Handcrafts for Elementary Schools* (Boston: D. C. Heath, 1953), Chapter 3.

Newkirk, Louis V., *Integrated Handwork for Elementary Schools* (Morristown, N.J.: Silver Burdett, 1940), Chapters 3 and 4.

Newkirk, Louis V. and William H. Johnson, *The Industrial Arts Program* (New York: Macmillan Co., 1948), Chapters 2 and 3.

Nihart, Claude E., "Industrial Arts in the Elementary School," *Industrial Arts and Vocational Education,* Vol. 40 (October, 1951), No. 8.

Rowand, LeRoy, "Mobile Tool Unit Brings Industrial Arts to Elementary School," *Industrial Arts and Vocational Education,* Vol. 42 (October, 1953), No. 8.

School Shops for Today and Tomorrow (Pittsburgh: Delta Power Tool Division, Rockwell Manufacturing Company, 1960).

"Schoolhouse Planning—the Self-Contained Classroom," *The Nation's Schools,* Vol. 49 (January, 1952), No. 1.

Stanley Tool Guide (New Britain, Conn.: Stanley Tools, 1952).

U.S. Office of Education, *Industrial Arts—Its Interpretation in American Schools* (Washington, D.C.: U.S. Government Printing Office, 1938), Chapter 2.

Wilber, G. O. and N. C. Pendered, *Industrial Arts in General Education* (Scranton, Pa.: International Textbook Company, 1967), Chapters 19–22.

chapter 4 / BASIC SKILLS

The processes and operations described in this chapter are fundamental to a program of elementary industrial arts. Listed at the end of the chapter are a number of references, some for teachers and some for children, which describe additional processes.

WHERE TO GET HELP

The old saying about experience being the best teacher certainly applies to the use of tools. Teachers are encouraged to read the descriptions of operations in the following pages, and then to try them out whenever the opportunity presents itself.

When encountering problems more involved and difficult than those described here, teachers will find it profitable to seek the help of industrial arts, home economics, and fine arts personnel in the school system. These specialists are always happy to demonstrate procedures and recommend materials and equipment within their fields. They often have the equipment needed to do some of the jobs which are beyond the limitations of the tools available in the classroom. Consultants and teachers of allied subjects are expected to furnish such assistance. If they are not available. in a given school, there are probably specialists in nearby junior and senior high schools who can be of help.

Practically every elementary school staff includes someone who is familiar with basic tool operations; he may be another teacher, the principal, or the school custodian. To the extent that they are able to help, these people usually are glad to donate their time and skills.

The teacher should not overlook talents within the class. With the popularity of "do-it-yourself" and the home workshop, many pupils, even the younger ones, are developing surprisingly good skill with tools. This resource should be tapped; the educational advantages are obvious.

Parents of school children often make significant contributions in this area. Many teachers have found parents delighted to participate in building projects. There are many opportunities to strengthen school-home-community relations through such activities.

The classroom teacher has every reason to be confident as the industrial arts work gets under way. Books and other resources are available, and people are eager to help.

PLANNING PROCESSES

Planning, as a necessary part of good education, is a process with which every teacher is well acquainted. Planning occurs at many stages of the school's program as well as in the day-by-day and hour-by-hour work of any classroom. The industrial arts phases of classroom work must be planned carefully to be effective. Where planning is inconclusive, or not done at all, the program rapidly deteriorates to busywork of little or no educational value.

One of the sections in the next chapter describes how choices are made among the many industrial arts activities that might grow out of a particular unit of study. But, there is another vital stage in the planning process. After the decision has been made to construct something, that "something" must be planned if it is to turn out satisfactorily and contribute effectively to the child's learning.

In modern industry, product planning is highly coordinated. Inventors, engineers, architects, and artists work together closely, devoting many hours to conceiving and developing ideas. They must then put those ideas into a language that can be communicated efficiently and accurately to others. Usually, the most effective method uses sketches or drawings, which draftsmen then transform into accurate working drawings, showing all details of the desired product. These working drawings or plans are used to convey the designer's precise meaning to the people who will produce the product.

Although industrial planning is far beyond the scope of elementary school work, the children can be made aware of the basic principles involved. Children can conceive an idea, refine its details, and put it on paper to convey the idea to others or simply to help them remember it. Such planning makes the actual work easier and more efficient. It guides the workers by telling them: (a) What they want to do; (b) How they will proceed; and (c) What materials and supplies they will need.

Planning is done at all levels, beginning in the primary grades, though the nature of the planning varies with the maturity of the children. Planning requires cooperation between teacher and pupil at all levels. The teacher should withdraw gradually as pupils' ability develops and progresses. From the very beginning, it cannot be impressed too strongly on the pupil that *a good worker begins by planning his work.* This is the initial stage of critical thinking and scientific problem-solving.

Following are three descriptions of project planning as it might be carried out in a typical situation:

A. A first grade group has decided to make a mouse cage for use in the classroom. The teacher initiates the planning discussion by asking what the cage should be like, drawing from the pupils ideas of basic design, such as these:

    a. We want to be able to see the mouse.
    b. The mouse should be able to breathe.
    c. The mouse should be able to move about.
    d. We want to be able to get the mouse in and out.
    e. We want to be able to get food to the mouse.
    f. We want to be able to clean the cage.

As these ideas are developed, the teacher illustrates them on the chalkboard, modifying the sketch as the discussion proceeds. If screen wire is used for the sides of the cage, perhaps the sketch will look like Figure 87.

Our Mouse Cage

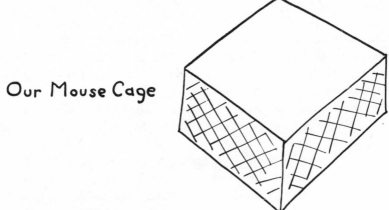

Figure 87. First sketch of mouse cage.

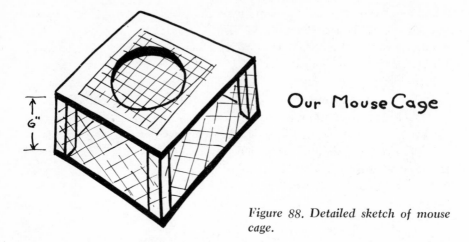

Our Mouse Cage

Figure 88. Detailed sketch of mouse cage.

Now the teacher brings up the matter of size. He might ask, "How long is the mouse?" Then, "Should the cage be the same size?" The idea develops that the mouse needs some room to move, so the cage must be bigger than the mouse. The children develop the concept—then he might say, "Let's see, what do we have to work with?" The teacher holds up two or three pieces of available wood: which is best? A size is chosen for the bottom of the cage, perhaps the end of a fruit crate. Now, of course, the top should be the same size as the bottom. How would it be to cut a hole in the top to get the mouse in and out, and to clean the cage? To keep the mouse from jumping out, a piece of screen can be placed over the hole.

We need some pieces of wood for the corners of the cage. How long must these pieces be? While holding a yardstick in a vertical position on top of a table, the teacher points to 30″. Too tall. She then brings her finger slowly down to 12″. Still too tall. She then points to 6″. Fine. The teacher modifies the sketch, and it now looks like Figure 88.

Even though the dimensions mean little to the children, they are placed on the sketch to show the application of the planning, and to remind the teacher of what is needed. And so the construction work progresses, with the plan nearby for reference. The concept of the importance of planning is taking form. As the children mature and acquire art, number, and language skills, plans can be more accurate, and pupils can play a greater part in the development of plans.

B. In the second example, a fourth grade group has decided to make a store. If the thought does not occur to the pupils, the teacher may suggest using packing crates for the counter. Then a committee of youngsters plan from there, taking into account the construction materials available and the particular space in the classroom where the store is to go. The pupil committee's sketch is presented in a form, such as suggested in Figure 89.

With questions, discussion, and a few pencil or chalk strokes, the teacher reminds the planning group that: (a) Depth should be shown in a plan; (b) Important sizes should be shown; (c) The counter top has thickness, which is shown with two lines; (d) The front of the boxes can be dressed up with advertisements; and (e) A piece of wood across the bottom of the store would make it less wobbly. To determine some of the sizes, a pupil suggests that some boys and girls can be measured. Now, perhaps the plan looks like Figure 90.

While an expert can see a number of details still to be determined, the plan has gone far enough to permit the work to begin. The details are worked out as their need becomes apparent.

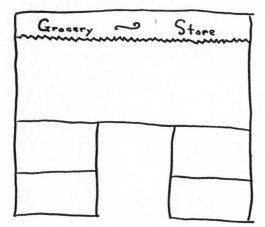

Figure 89. Children's sketch of grocery store.

Figure 90. Detailed version of grocery store sketch.

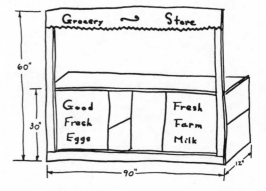

C. In the final example, a sixth grade group is working on personal hobby interests. One girl has planned a scrapbook to hold her photographs. She has decided to use art paper for the pages, poster board for the covers, and loose-leaf rings for the binding. Her plan looks like Figure 91.

She explains that she has a list of the materials she needs: fifty sheets of 9″ x 12″ light blue art paper, two sheets of 9″ x 12″ pink, medium-weight poster board, and two 1½″ loose-leaf rings, all of which are available in the local variety store. She further explains that the holes for the rings will be 2½ inches from the edges and ½ inch in from the ends of the sheets. The holes will be punched with a paper punch. The cover design will be done in blue ink applied with an artist's brush after the design has been sketched lightly in pencil. The work proceeds smoothly.

The differences in level of sophistication among these three examples are apparent, but planning *at the appropriate level* was done in each case.

Complete plans produced by adults often include, in addition to a sketch or drawing, a list of the materials needed, with exact sizes, and sometimes, a list of the steps or procedure to be followed. Most young children are incapable of foreseeing their needs in detail, but teachers can help children to anticipate their needs and to anticipate the operations necessary as work progresses on a project. This is a vital part of the planning process, and, when conditions permit, these more detailed aspects of planning should be encouraged.

Here, one pitfall to be avoided is expecting overly intricate planning by children. Their background of experience is limited, and they need help as they proceed. Devoting too much time to preliminary planning often can dampen the enthusiasm with which children undertake an activity. On the other hand, haphazard activity without any planning results in chaos, frustration, unsatisfactory results, disappointment, and a diminishment of self-

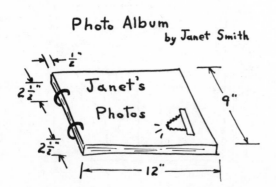

Figure 91. Well-done sketch.

confidence. Only the classroom teacher, who knows each child intimately, can guide the whole process toward optimum educational effectiveness.

Finally, the contributions of industrial arts consultants to the planning process must be mentioned. These people have had broad experience with tools, materials, equipment, and construction processes, and often they can make suggestions for improving plans, avoiding pitfalls, and, in general, making the whole process more efficient. With their experience and power equipment at their disposal, consultants can help classroom teachers and pupils over the rough spots that might develop in constructing some particular project. Where consultant services are available, they should be used.

CUTTING AND SAWING

Following the preliminary planning, the first step in actual construction is selecting the material to be used, and cutting it to the appropriate size.

Sawing Boards

When given a long board from which a piece is to be cut, begin by checking to see whether the board is usable all the way to the end. If not, the board must be squared-off. This is done by placing a try square on the board, as shown, with the handle tight against an edge, and drawing a line on the board along the blade of the try square (Figure 92). This will be a guideline for cutting.

The best tool for the cutting job is the panel saw. Children frequently select the backsaw because it is smaller and appears to be easier to handle. Actually, the backsaw is more difficult to manipulate correctly. With a little instruction and encouragement, even kindergarten children can use the panel saw and achieve satisfying results.

The board to be cut may be placed on low benches or sawhorses (Figure 93). For young children, C-clamps can be used to clamp a short block of wood along the cutting line as a guide for the saw. The saw is then held at an angle of 45° to the board, and pulled backward two or three times to start the cut (Figure 94). Then short back and forth strokes are taken until the cut is well started. These are followed by long, slow, rhythmic strokes until the cut is almost complete. At the very end, short strokes are used again to obtain a clean cut.

The board can either be clamped to the bench with C-clamps, or it can be held steady by one or more helpers. After a degree of skill has been developed, the block used to guide the saw can be dispensed with.

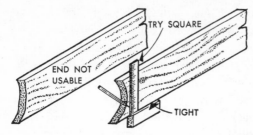

Figure 92. Preparing to square off a board.

Figure 93. Sawing on a low bench.

Sometimes young children like to start by using the half-round cabinet wood file to make a notch for the saw at the beginning of a cut (Figure 95).

Another method is to clamp the board in a bench vise. If this procedure is used, the children will find it easier to cut to the line when the board is placed flat rather than on edge in the vise (Figure 96). Both hands should be on the handle of the saw as pictured. This will keep the hands out of the path of the saw, and also will help the pupil to steer the saw along the cutting line as the sawing proceeds.

When one end of the board has been squared-off, the rule is placed on the board near an edge, and the desired length is marked with a short pencil mark. A penciled, short dash should be used rather than a dot.

Once again the try square is used to draw a line across the board, and the cutting is done as before. The handle of the square must be held tightly against the edge of the board when drawing the line. This time someone should hold the piece being cut to keep it from falling and tearing the last few fibers of the wood.

The compass saw is really designed for sawing gradual curves in thick material or on very large pieces, and for sawing in hard-to-get-at places, rather than for ordinary straight cutting. Because of its lightness and small size, however, children in the lower grades sometimes can do better work with a compass saw than they can do with the panel or backsaw.

The panel saw and the backsaw (Figure 97) are used for cutting dowels, broomsticks, and similar materials. However, for cutting very small sticks,

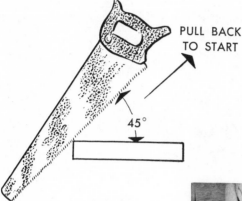

PULL BACK
TO START

45°

Figure 94. Holding a panel saw at the correct angle.

Figure 95. Filling a notch for the saw

Figure 96. Sawing in a vise.

Figure 97. Cutting with a back saw.

up to about the size of kite sticks, the teeth of the panel saw or the back-saw are too coarse. For such purposes the vibrating jig saw, the coping saw, or a hack saw should be chosen.

Cutting to Lines

Accuracy and precision in the work of elementary school children is a recurrent question, so a word here may be appropriate. Precision is a relative thing. The degree of accuracy needed to cut wood for a fence post would be much different from that needed for the leg of a coffee table. Even that degree of accuracy would be totally unacceptable in making a part for a fine watch. But the important element to be considered here, of course, is the child and his limitations. Certainly, accuracy and precision should be encouraged within reason, but they should not be carried to extremes. As children gain in dexterity and experience, they will be able to perform more and more like craftsmen.

In working with wood, the craftsman sometimes cuts to very sharp lines. These lines may be made with a knife, if a pencil line would be too broad. Further, the expert usually leaves the line, cutting just beside it. In some cases, his saw may even split the line. Such exactness, while necessary for the craftsman, obviously does not have a place where young children are concerned. The matter is included here only to point out that precision must be tempered with reason, and to suggest that this precision should be a goal when circumstances permit.

Sawing Panels

Some projects will call for sheets of plywood and various types of panel material. When such material is used, the large sheet to be cut should be placed low enough to be worked on comfortably, and the sizes of pieces needed should be laid out with a rule. A framing square also would be useful here. When the lines have been drawn, one proceeds as before, cutting with a panel saw. Care should be taken that the saw does not travel beyond the corner of a piece to be cut out, or the stock may be spoiled for the next piece to be cut from the length. If a number of pieces of the same width are to be cut, it is a good procedure to cut off a long strip first, and then cut the strip into the desired lengths.

Cutting to Irregular Lines

It is frequently necessary to cut to lines which are not straight, as, for example, in making a lawn ornament or a doll silhouette (Figure 98). For this purpose, either the vibrating jig saw or a coping saw will be needed. Of the two, the jig saw (Figure 55) is much easier to use. Jig saws of the vibrating type have been used safely in grades as low as kindergarten, but local school policies, individual teacher preferences, and the progress of the children will have to be considered.

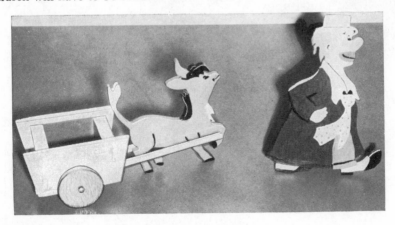

Figure 98. Examples of attractive jig saw work.

The instruction pamphlet accompanying a vibrating jig saw should be consulted first to be sure the machine is in operating order. Most of the newer machines are ready to operate as they come from the packing carton. Generally, they require no lubrication for the life of the machine.

It will be necessary to put new blades in the machine. Models differ somewhat, but most of the new, small, vibrating type jig saws use "pin-end" blades. There is a small slot on the machine that holds the blade at the bottom and another at the top. The blade is placed in the bottom slot first; then the long metal arm is pressed down until the top pin on the blade can be engaged. The metal arm is released slowly, and the machine is ready for operation.

Three precautions are appropriate here:

1. Be sure that the machine is unplugged before inserting or removing blades.
2. Insert the new blade with the teeth toward the operator and pointing downward (Figure 100).
3. Adjust the blade guard (the piece of metal right behind the blade) so that it is about ⅛ inch above the surface of the material to be cut.

Now the machine can be turned on, and the wood, with the cutting lines drawn on it, can be fed into the blade. Very little pressure should be exerted against the wood so that the blade will not bend or break. The saw should be permitted to cut at its own speed. A little experience will indicate how fast the material can be fed into the saw. The material being cut should be held firmly against the table of the saw to prevent chattering.

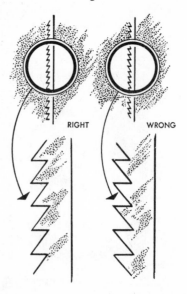

RIGHT   WRONG

Figure 99. Replacing a jig saw blade.

Figure 100. Jig saw blade replacement

When it is necessary to change the direction of cutting, as in cutting a corner, the work should be turned slowly, and as gradually as possible, to prevent twisting and breaking the blade. The blade should be permitted to cut a path for itself. Pulling the material back a fraction of an inch and then pushing it forward again, and repeating the process a few times, will help the saw to cut itself a path around a sharp corner. Technically, this path the saw makes is called a "kerf."

No attempt should be made to cut wood thicker than three quarters of an inch on this jig saw, and it may be difficult to cut stock of that thickness if the wood is hard. Thin plywoods and other wallboards or cardboard will cut easily and produce a smooth edge.

The vibrating jig saw also can be used to cut thin, soft metals like soft aluminum and soft copper, but not steel or iron (ferrous metals) or metal from "tin" cans. Some manufacturers recommend special blades for cutting metal. Whether the machine is used for wood or metal, the procedure is about the same, except that more time must be taken to permit the saw to cut metal. It is difficult to see pencil lines made on metal, so it is recommended that the design be drawn on paper, the paper then can be attached to the metal with rubber cement, and the sawing operation performed, cutting through both the paper and the metal.

To cut a hole in a piece of material, for example, when making a wooden letter "O," another step is required. A hole is first drilled or bored in the material (Figure 101). Next, the top of the jig saw blade is released from its holder, and the blade inserted through the hole in the material to be cut. The blade is then re-attached to the machine and the cutting proceeds.

When it is necessary to cut holes in pieces too large for the capacity of the vibrating jig saw or the coping saw, the compass saw may be used.

The hand tool designed to do approximately the same work as the jig saw is the coping saw. Various blade styles are available; the best for general purposes is the pin-end blade (Figure 102). Obviously, the frame and blade style must correspond.

The method of removing or replacing a blade depends on the style of the coping saw frame. One style requires that the frame be "sprung" to insert the blade. Children are very rarely able to do this. The style recommended has a screw-type handle. Turning the handle in one direction loosens the blade, and turning it in the other direction tightens the blade. Blade replacement is very simple with this style of frame, and children usually can do it easily. In replacing blades, the end of the blade farthest from the handle should be placed in its slot first. Then, the other end of the blade should be

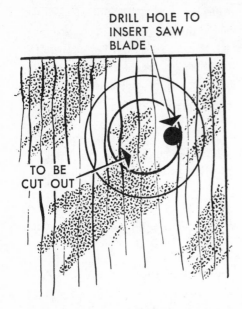

DRILL HOLE TO
INSERT SAW
BLADE

TO BE
CUT OUT

Figure 101. Internal cutting.

Figure 102. Pin-end blade.

inserted in its slot and the handle turned as far as it will go to secure the end of the blade. Only hand pressure is used to tighten the handle, never a tool. When tightening the handle, the metal pin near the handle should be held stationary to prevent the blade from being twisted.

Here again, the direction in which the teeth of the blade point is important. If the wood to be cut is to be clamped upright in a vise, the teeth should point away from the handle (Figure 103). If the procedure illustrated in Figure 104 is to be used, the teeth should point toward the handle of the saw.

If a vise is used, the operator stands before the bench and moves the saw back and forth. If the material to be cut is clamped to a bench, the operator kneels or sits, and moves the saw up and down. When thin material is to be cut, it is desirable to clamp a piece of thicker wood to the piece being cut to prevent the piece from bending and vibrating. Obviously, the thicker wood must be placed so that it does not cover the cutting lines and interfere with cutting.

Youngsters often find it convenient to place both hands on the handle of the saw, but in any case, they must take care to hold the saw at right angles to the work to produce cuts as square and true as possible.

In the previous chapter, it was suggested that coping saws of the adjust-

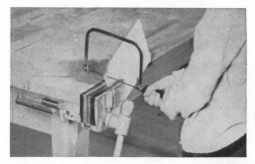

Figure 103. Using a coping saw with the work in an upright position.

Figure 104. Using a coping saw with the work held flat.

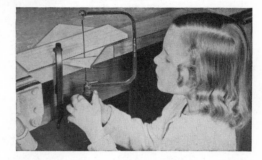

able type be procured so that the blade may be turned when necessary. When the position of the saw makes it desirable to turn the blade, the handle is loosened slightly, and the front and rear turning pins turned the same amount to keep the blade from twisting.

Finally, the precautions regarding the forcing or bending of jig saw blades apply also to the use of the coping saw. Coping saw blades are somewhat fragile, but when correctly and carefully used, they will last a long time. They should be discarded when dull or broken.

Cutting Metal

Reference was made to the use of the jig saw for cutting to irregular lines in soft, thin, nonferrous metals. When cutting the tin plate of which "tin" cans are made, and other sheet steel such as galvanized iron, the jig saw should not be used because the metal is too hard. The appropriate tool for cutting such material is tin snips.

Since pencil lines are not satisfactory on metal, the scratch awl instead of a pencil should be used for marking. For irregular shapes, a paper pattern can be attached to the metal with rubber cement.

After the lines are made or the pattern is attached, the tin snips are used much like a pair of scissors (Figure 105). Care must be taken so that the children's hands are not cut on the sharp edges of the metal. Resting the tin snips on the bench, as shown, provides good leverage and facilitates cutting.

Metal from discarded cans may be used where small pieces of metal are needed, as in reinforcing the corners of small wooden frames. Both ends of the can should be removed with a wall-style can opener. Then, the cylinder is cut apart and the metal flattened out by hammering with a wood or rubber mallet.

Tin snips, of course, can be used on softer metals such as aluminum, copper, and brass, and they serve very well for cutting screening and poultry netting.

For cutting wire and for cutting the heads off nails to make "drill bits," the side-cutting pliers are used.

Figure 105. Cutting metal with tin snips.

Figure 106. Cutting with a hack saw; the metal is held in the machinist's vise.

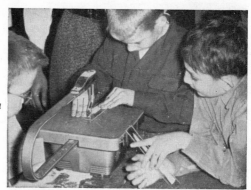

Figure 107. Cutting plastics on the jig saw; the metal is held in the machinist's vise.

Occasionally it may be necessary to cut heavier metals such as small steel rods, angle iron, or bolts. For such jobs, the hack saw is used. This tool was not recommended in the minimum list of tools for classrooms, because it is used rarely. If one is procured, it should have an adjustable frame and use 10″ blades with 24 teeth per inch.

The metal to be cut is held securely in a machinist's vise. The hack saw is grasped with two hands, one on the handle and one at the top front end of the frame (Figure 106). The sawing is done with slow, rhythmic strokes, using as much of the length of the blade as possible.

When cutting a bolt that is too long, the bolt is held in the vise at the waste end to avoid damaging the threads. Also, the nut should be placed on the bolt before cutting; otherwise it will be difficult to start the nut on the bolt after cutting, since sawing off the bolt may damage one or two of the beginning threads. When the nut is removed after cutting, the nut tends to repair the threads at the newly cut end.

As stated previously, the hack saw may be used to cut materials softer than metal. It is good for sawing small wooden sticks. Although it cuts more slowly than regular woodworking saws, it produces a smooth cut.

Cutting Other Materials

In addition to wood and metal, many other materials can be cut by one or more of the processes previously described. Notable exceptions are very hard materials, such as glass, stone, concrete, and brick, which are beyond the scope of this discussion. However, materials such as rubber, cloth, thin leathers, paper, thin cardboard, and metal foils, can be cut with scissors or short-blade knives.

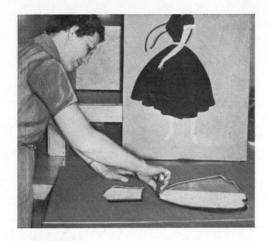

Figure 108. Cutting heavy poster board for a clothing-fabric display.

Most plastics can be cut by the same processes used to cut wood (Figure 107). Linoleum and materials such as heavy leathers and heavy poster board, are cut by running a sharp knife or razor blade (in a razor blade holder) along a straight edge like the framing square, with scrap material underneath to prevent damage to the bench or table (Figure 108).

MAKING HOLES

Making holes in materials is one of the simplest and yet one of the most vital of industrial processes. Various types and shapes of holes affect a product's appearance and function, and many of the primary means of fastening things together require holes through which fastening devices must pass.

Round Holes in Wood

First, the location of holes to be drilled or bored should be indicated with a mark similar to a plus sign (+). The place where the lines cross will be the center of the hole. This mark will result in a more accurate hole location than a small pencil dot or some other method of marking.

Next, depending on the size of the hole required, either a hand drill or a brace should be selected. For holes up to $\frac{3}{16}$ inch in diameter, the hand drill should be used; for larger holes, children will get more satisfactory results with the brace. Hole sizes and the tools cutting the holes always are designated by the diameter, or the distance across at the widest part.

To drill a small hole, a twist drill bit of the correct size is selected and fastened securely in the chuck of the hand drill. When inserting the bit

Figure 109. Turning the chuck on the hand drill.

Figure 110. Drilling a hole.

in the hand drill, the tool is held in one hand, with the first two fingers on the crank handle, as shown. It will now be possible to turn the chuck with the other hand (Figure 109). As the chuck is turned, three metal lugs in the end of the chuck will open or close, depending on the direction in which the chuck is turned. The twist drill bit should be inserted between the lugs, and the chuck should be tightened, using only the hands. To remove the bit, the hand drill is held in the same manner, and the chuck is turned in the opposite direction.

With the bit in the chuck, the hand drill is ready for use. The end of the twist drill bit is placed wherever a hole is required (Figure 110). Slight pressure is exerted toward the wood, and the crank handle is turned in a clockwise direction until the bit makes the desired hole. To remove the tool, the operator continues to turn the hand drill *in the same direction*, while it is being withdrawn, to remove the cutting chips from the hole.

For drilling small holes (less than $\frac{1}{8}''$) in soft wood, a nail may be used as a drill bit. The head of the nail is nipped off with side-cutting pliers, and the nail then inserted into the chuck of the hand drill as if it were a twist drill bit. The advantage is that twist drill bits are hard and brittle, and small ones will break if the children do not hold the hand drill steady; nails are soft and comparatively flexible, and they are inexpensive. For holes from $\frac{1}{8}''$ to $\frac{3}{16}''$ in diameter, standard twist drill bits should be used.

For holes larger than $\frac{3}{16}''$ a different kind of bit is used in conjunction with the brace. Instead of being cylindrical to the end, like twist drill bits, the bits designed for use in the brace have a squared end called a tang (Figure 111). There are various types of bits designed for use with the brace, but the auger bit is the most common. Auger bits are available in various sizes. Stamped somewhere on the shank or squared end of an auger bit is a numeral indicating the diameter in sixteenths of an inch. For example, a No. 4 bit will bore a hole $\frac{4}{16}$ of an inch (or $\frac{1}{4}$ inch) in diameter; a No. 16 bit will bore a hole $1\frac{6}{16}$ of an inch (or 1 inch) in diameter.

To place a bit in the brace, the chuck of the brace is grasped with the left hand and held firmly (Figure 112). Then, the right hand grasps the handle of the brace and turns. Turning the handle in one direction will open the lugs in the end of the chuck, and turning it in the opposite direction will close them. Before tightening, the chuck should be opened wide enough to allow the squared end of the bit to go as far as possible into the chuck. The squared end of the bit will not be visible if the bit is properly fastened in the chuck.

In boring a hole, the screw tip on the end of the auger bit is placed wherever the center of the hole is to be (Figure 113). Then, the brace is

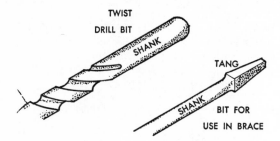

Figure 111. Bits.

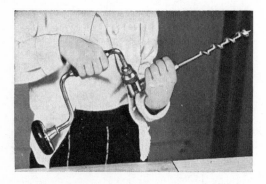

Figure 112. Placing a bit in a brace.

held as shown, with one hand on the handle and one on the knob. The knob should be held as steadily as possible, with slight pressure exerted toward the hole. The handle is turned in a clockwise direction and the boring proceeds. Someone should watch the screw tip of the brace emerge from the other side (Figure 114) of the wood. As soon as it appears, the brace should be turned counter-clockwise and withdrawn from the wood. Then, the wood should be turned around and the hole completed by boring from the other side. If the bit were simply forced through the wood from the original side, the wood would split, leaving a jagged hole.

When holes are made with the hand drill and twist drill bits, the process is called "drilling"; when brace and auger bits are used, the process is called "boring."

Figure 113. Boring a hole.

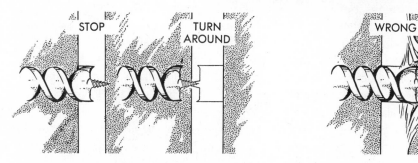

Figure 114. Left: correct way; right: wrong way to bore a hole.

Figure 115. Holes, ⅝" (No. 10 auger bit), drilled in squares of ½" plywood; the birch dowel is ½" in diameter.

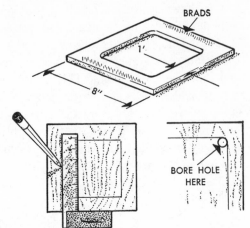

Figure 116. Cutting a square hole.

Irregularly Shaped Holes in Wood

The process of making holes of irregular shape in wood can be illustrated with the small waffle-weaving loom in Figure 116. One very simple way to make this frame is to cut a 6-inch square hole in the middle of an 8-inch square piece of ¾-inch fir plywood. The first step is to cut an 8-inch square out of ¾-inch plywood. Next, with pencil, rule, and try square, lines are drawn for the square hole. Then holes of about ½-inch diameter (No. 8 auger bit) are bored in the corners as shown. Now the center section is cut out either with a jig saw or a coping saw, as described in the preceding section on cutting and sawing, or the compass saw may be used, with the four bored holes as starting points for the saw. Finally, a file and sandpaper are used to smooth the sides of the hole before finishing the loom and placing the nails or pegs.

This process, with variations, can be used for cutting almost any irregularly shaped hole in wood, the basic operation being one of drilling or boring round holes first, and using saws from then on.

Holes in Metal

Holes can be made in metal, too. Hole locations should be marked with a plus sign as on wood, using a scratch awl rather than a pencil.

In thin material, like the metal of which tin cans are made, small holes can be punched with the scratch awl simply by hitting the wooden handle of the scratch awl with the flat of the hand (Figure 117). Or, a common nail and a hammer can be used to accomplish the same purpose. In either case, when punching holes in flat metal, scrap wood should be placed under the metal to avoid damage to the bench or table.

Figure 117. Punching a hole in the bottom of a can.

Figure 118. Bean-bag game; holes are punched in the can for fastening to the base.

Figure 119. Center punch.

The underside of these punched holes will be ragged and sharp. These ragged edges, or burrs, should be filed, or hammered down to prevent cuts.

For metal too thick to be punched, the hand drill and twist drill bits may be used. The improvised "nail bits" described earlier will not work on metal. *Auger bits should never be used on metal.*

When drilling holes in metal, a punch mark must be made to guide the twist drill bit, otherwise the bit will wander when the drilling process is started. For this purpose a center punch is used (Figure 119). The point of the center punch is placed exactly where the center of the hole should be and the punch is struck with a hammer. The center punch is struck only once, as if it were being driven into the metal. The depression thus made will serve well as a starting point for the bit.

Drilling holes in metal is basically the same as drilling holes in wood,

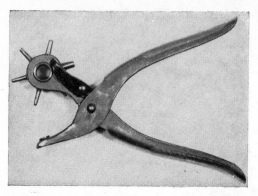

Figure 120. Leather punch.

except that it is slower and requires more exertion. And again, the burrs on the underside of the hole should be filed off or hammered down. The use of power drills should not be attempted without a demonstration by a skilled person, but after a demonstration, children can operate power drills safely.

Holes in Other Materials

The hand drill and twist drill bits can be used on heavy cardboard, wallboard, pressed wood, linoleum, plastics, angle iron, sheet metal, and practically anything else, except very hard materials such as stone, glass, and concrete. When drilling holes in plastic the drill will need a start, as in drilling metal, but one must take care to tap the nail or scratch awl gently to avoid damaging the material.

An ordinary paper punch can be used to make holes in many thin materials, and for those which are a little tougher, a leather punch usually will do very nicely (Figure 120).

Auger bits should be used only on wood. They are delicate tools, and when their cutting ends are damaged, they are practically worthless. Auger bits should be stored in such a way that the cutting ends do not come into contact with anything harder than wood. When properly and reasonably cared for, auger bits will last and work well for a long time. They can be sharpened, as can twist drill bits, but only a skilled craftsman can do a satisfactory job. Sharpening is required when these tools cease to work well.

MAKING THINGS SMOOTH

Usually before parts are assembled and painted or otherwise finished there are rough surfaces requiring smoothing. Practically all such surface preparation in elementary grades can be done with one or more of these:

(a) sandpaper, (b) file, and (c) block plane. For most projects, files and sandpaper are sufficient, and in some instances, sandpaper alone will do. Block planes are used less frequently.

Sandpaper

Technically, sandpaper is referred to as a "coated abrasive." The supply list in Chapter 3 recommended the medium grit (degree of coarseness) of flint sandpaper. A more complete list of supplies also might include fine and coarse sandpaper, but many teachers get along very well with only the medium grit. The differences in the grits are that coarser sandpapers cut away the wood faster and finer sandpapers produce a somewhat smoother surface. As a compromise, medium sandpaper produces both results reasonably well. Also, after medium sandpaper has been used for some time, it becomes worn and acts about the same as fine sandpaper.

For economical and efficient use, the large sheets (9″ x 10″) of sandpaper are torn into six parts, first by tearing in half the long way, and then by tearing each half into thirds. The tearing operation is performed by folding the sandpaper with the grit side inward. Next, the fold is run over the edge of a bench to make the crease sharp (Figure 121). The paper is then placed on a fairly sharp edge of a bench, with the grit side down, and torn carefully (Figure 122).

If the sandpaper is torn into pieces as explained above, it can be used with the sanding blocks shown in Figure 123. Three or four of these blocks should be made and painted in distinctive colors. A screw eye in the end of each one will allow it to be hung in a definite place on the tool panel.

Figure 121. Creasing sandpaper.

Figure 122. Tearing sandpaper.

The practice of using scrap wood, picked up at random for sanding blocks, should be discouraged, since inappropriate sizes may be difficult for children to handle. Also, the sandpaper will slip off such blocks, tear, and be wasted.

In preparing to sand, one of the small pieces of sandpaper (one sixth of the large sheet) is fitted to the sanding block, and the paper folded snugly over the two edges. When this is done properly, the paper will fit the block almost exactly. It is not necessary to fasten the paper to the block, since the fingers hold the block and the paper at the same time. Sometimes, in the lower grades, teachers use thumbtacks on each edge of the block to secure the paper, and there is no objection to this practice.

When sanding the end of a board which has been sawed, the board should be positioned upright and fastened in the vise as shown in Figure 124. Then, the block with the sandpaper is held flat on the end of the board with both hands and pushed back and forth, all the way across the board. The block should be held as steady as possible, and not rocked, which would produce an uneven surface. If the board is too long to place upright in a vise, it can

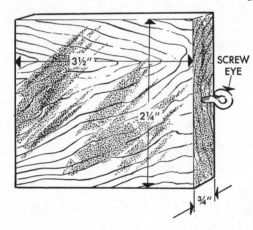

Figure 123. Well-proportioned sanding block.

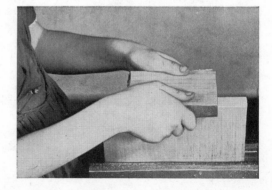

Figure 124. Sanding the end of a board.

be laid flat on the bench, clamped in place with a C-clamp, and the sandpaper block held in the same relative position to the board as described.

Later the sandpaper and block can be run over the sharp corners of the wood once or twice to remove any "whiskers" and sharp corners.

When it is necessary to smooth the faces and edges of boards, sanding should be done in the same direction as the grain of the wood, otherwise the sandpaper will produce scratches in the wood.

The sanding block also can be used for sanding convex shapes, like the edges of wooden wheels. When sanding concave shapes, the sandpaper should be wrapped around something round, like a short dowel or piece of broomstick. For sanding large concave curves, a piece of cork bulletin board material makes a very good backing for the sandpaper in place of the sanding block. And lastly, when sanding around very small curves and corners, it may be necessary to use the sandpaper without a block. A small piece of sandpaper can be used and merely folded to provide some rigidity. *Whenever possible, some type of block should be used with sandpaper.* One exception is sanding between coats of paint or other finishing substances. For this purpose no sanding block is used because a lighter, even pressure is required.

The sandpaper and block should be tapped on the workbench occasionally to dislodge sawdust and small particles of wood. When sandpaper becomes clogged, it will not cut properly. The wasteful use of sandpaper should be discouraged, but when it wears out it must be discarded.

If greater smoothness is desired than that produced by the first sanding, the process can be repeated with a paper of finer grit.

Materials other than wood can be smoothed with sandpaper. These include the edges of cardboard, linoleum, fiber wallboard, and pressed wood. Plaster and unglazed clays also can be smoothed with sandpaper. Flint sandpaper cannot be used on metal, glass, and other very hard materials, except when rubbing down paints and finishes, as described in a later section.

Files

Sandpaper is suitable for most of the smoothing work children have to do. The two principal jobs for which files will be needed are removing burrs and sharp edges from metals, and removing more wood than can be removed with coarse grit sandpaper (Figure 125). An example of the latter would be the use of a file on a wooden silhouette cut with a coping saw or jig saw, where the cut wavered from the desired outline. If the deviation from the layout line is considerable, recut the outline using the saw again.

Figure 125. Filing an irregular edge.

When using files, the following points should be kept in mind:

a. Files without handles *should not be used* by children.
b. Files should be kept clean by brushing them frequently with a file card to remove sawdust and chips.
c. Files cut only on the forward stroke.
d. Files almost always should be held with one hand on the handle and the other hand near the tip.
e. Files are designed to remove only relatively small amounts of material.

For filing flat or convex edges of a piece of wood, the flat surface of the half-round cabinet file is used. For filing concave shapes, the rounded part of the file is used. The wood is placed in the vise (Figure 126) and the file is applied as shown. The file is pushed away from the operator while slight downward pressure is exerted. The file is then lifted completely off the wood for the return stroke, and another forward stroke taken. Long, rather slow and rhythmic strokes are used, employing the greater part of the file's length. Children should be encouraged to try to remove any unwanted bumps left over from sawing.

If filing wood produces a squealing or squeaking sound, the edge being filed should be moved closer to the jaws of the vise.

The file should be brushed frequently with the file card (Figure 127). This will dislodge sawdust and bits of wood that can prevent efficient cutting.

Wood files are used frequently for shaping small pieces of wood for such things as the fuselage (body) of a model airplane. In general, the file is used as described above. If large amounts of wood must be removed, a rasp may be used (Figure 128). The file has grooves on its cutting surface, and the rasp has sharp points or teeth. It is used in the same way a file is used. For work on balsa wood, the rasp is almost a necessity, because the fibers of this very soft wood resist the cabinet file. The rasp is coarse, and it produces a fairly rough surface. The cabinet file can be used after the rasp to produce a finish of greater smoothness. The final smoothing can be done with sandpaper.

For filing off burrs on metal, the mill file should be used. The half-round cabinet wood file should not be used on hard metals, or the tool will be permanently damaged.

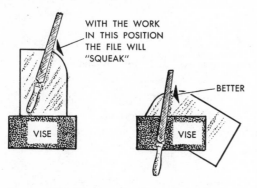

WITH THE WORK
IN THIS POSITION
THE FILE WILL
"SQUEAK"

BETTER

VISE

VISE

Figure 126. Placing work in a vise for filing.

Figure 127. Using a file card to clean out chips from file grooves.

Figure 128. Rasp.

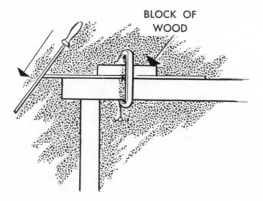

BLOCK OF
WOOD

Figure 129. Removing sharp burrs from metal.

The metal should be clamped on the bench, and the mill file used as shown in Figure 129, the file being lifted off the material on the return stroke. *Extreme care must be taken to prevent injury from sharp metal edges.* The purpose of removing metal burrs, of course, is to make the metal safe to handle. The filed edges, therefore, should be carefully checked to make sure that they have been made completely harmless. Mill files should be cleaned with the file card.

The Block Plane

The block plane was in a separate category in the list of classroom tools. The principal reason for considering this tool separately is that unless someone is available who can sharpen the cutter frequently, its cutting action is quickly impaired. In fact, the block plane should be left off the list of tools unless it can be sharpened regularly by an industrial arts consultant, shop instructor, or other qualified person. *A block plane with a dull cutter is worse than none at all.*

The primary purpose of the block plane is to smooth the straight edges and ends of boards. The roughness from a saw, for example, can be removed with this tool. The block plane cannot be used on curves or pieces of wood with an irregular shape.

Ordinarily, the block plane is not used by children in Kindergarten and Grade 1. In Grades 2 through 4, most children can manipulate the tool if the teacher makes the necessary adjustments, and in Grades 5 and 6 most children can adjust and manipulate the block plane rather successfully.

The block plane requires adjustment before use. Although various makes of the block plane differ somewhat, the description included here applies to all block planes with minor exceptions.

In order to understand the adjustment of this tool, it should be taken apart. The tool is held in the left hand with the bottom of the plane in the palm of the hand (Figure 130). *One should be careful that the sharp cutter does not come in contact with the hand.* The plane is held with the bottom down and the adjusting nut toward the operator. Now the cap screw is loosened. This makes it possible to pull the cap toward the operator and lift it completely off the plane. The cap is laid down and the cutter is lifted off the plane and examined. The cutting edge should be free from nicks, and it should appear to be sharp. If the cutting edge appears shiny it is probably dull . If the cutting edge appears dull or nicked the cutter probably needs sharpening. If one is in doubt about the condition of the blade, he should consult someone well versed in tools.

To put the tool back together, the plane is held as before and the cutter replaced with the bevel up. When the plane is ready to use, the cutting edge should barely protrude through the opening in the bottom of the plane.

Next, the cap is replaced and the cap screw tightened by hand until it is snug. Now the plane is turned over and the cutting edge examined. If one corner of the cutter protrudes more than the other, the cap screw is loosened slightly and the cutter straightened. After the cutter is straightened, the cap screw is tightened again. Turning the adjusting nut should cause the cutter to protrude more or less, depending on the way in which the nut is turned.

The only way to gain proficiency in the use of the block plane is to practice. Do not be discouraged if early attempts are unsatisfactory; use scrap wood for practice, and keep trying.

Perhaps the best way to begin is by planing the edge of a board. After the piece to be planed is fastened securely in a vise, the operator stands in position as illustrated in Figure 131. The plane is held flat on the edge of the wood and pushed along. The plane should be held as flat and as steady as possible, making sure that it cuts from the very beginning to the very end of the stroke. Young children will have to use two hands, one hand on the finger rest and one hand grasping the body of the plane.

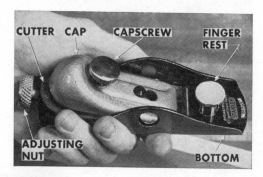

Figure 130. Block plane.

Figure 131. Planing the edge of a board.

If the plane is operating properly, only a moderate amount of force (downward and forward) should be needed to push the plane and cut the wood. If no shavings appear at all, or if too little wood is being removed, the adjusting nut on the plane can be turned to make the cutter protrude more. If too much wood is being removed, or if too much force is required to push the plane, the adjusting nut can be turned in the opposite direction to make the cutter retract and protrude less. *Shavings stuck in the cutter slot in the bottom of the plane should be removed with great care.*

If planing in one direction on the edge of a board produces a rough surface, or if the plane appears to stick part way along, one should try planing in the opposite direction (Figure 132). Planing should be done in the direction that produces the best results.

When planing the end (end grain) of a board, an additional step is required. Because of the structure of wood, if you were to plane all the way across the end of a board the grain would split and break at the end of the stroke. There are a number of ways to prevent this. The method found to be most satisfactory for youngsters is to make a small chamfer on the corner of the board with the cabinet wood file as shown in Figure 133. The length of this chamfer should be ⅛ to ¼ of an inch. Now the block plane can be used as before, across the entire width of the board. When the chamfer is almost removed by planing, file to renew it.

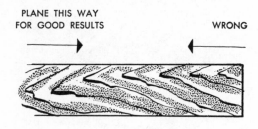

Figure 132. Note the grain of the wood.

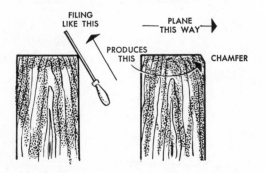

Figure 133. Filing a chamfer before planing end grain.

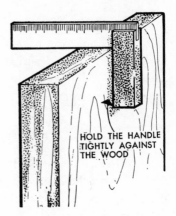

Figure 134. Testing for squareness.

Planing end grain has a "feel" which is somewhat different from planing edge grain. More force is needed, and sawdust rather than shavings is produced. Practice will soon bring satisfactory performance. Normally, a lighter cut is taken on end grain than on an edge.

When ends and edges are to be planed on the same piece, the ends should be planed first, so that the edge planing removes the chamfers, leaving square corners. For some work, a small chamfer left on the corner of a board would not be objectionable.

As previously stated, a high degree of accuracy is not to be expected from children. In the upper elementary grades, however, many children will be able to produce reasonably square edges and ends in planing. Accurate work, certainly, should be encouraged when circumstances permit. The try square can be used to check for squareness (Figure 134). The tool and board are held up to the light to see whether the plane should be tilted slightly one way or the other, to produce a cut that is as square as possible.

The plane should be used on wood (including plywood) only. The cutting edge should be checked for sharpness at frequent intervals or as soon as the plane ceases to work well. A dull cutter is useless, producing unsatisfactory results and discouragement.

FASTENING PIECES TOGETHER

The fastening processes used in elementary industrial arts fall into four general classifications. They include fastening with:

a. Glue, paste, and rubber cement.
b. Nails, tacks, brads, and corrugated fasteners.
c. Wood screws.
d. Stove bolts and carriage bolts.

Other important methods of joining parts together, such as soldering, brazing, welding, and riveting, are rarely used on the elementary level unless a consultant and a shop are included in the industrial arts program. In such programs, soldering and simple riveting are sometimes done in the upper elementary grades.

Glue, Paste, Rubber Cement

Since the properties and uses of paste and rubber cement are so commonly known, little need be said about them here. Rubber cement is very useful for fastening patterns temporarily to heavier materials like wood, metal, or plastic, in preparation for sawing or cutting.

Glue has the advantage of being easy to use and is an excellent means of fastening parts of quite a variety of materials, including wood. Often pieces are too small or thin for fastening with nails or screws, and glue of the proper type will provide an adequate bond for the purposes.

The glues most frequently used in industrial arts work are polyvinyl resin glues for general-purpose work (Figure 135), and rapid-drying cellulose (airplane) glues for work on small models and other projects where fast drying is essential. Cellulose glues should be purchased in small tubes rather than jars to reduce waste from drying, and to eliminate the danger of broken jars. For similar reasons, polyvinyl glues should be procured in plastic squeeze bottles. Some manufacturers provide glue in glass jars or cans, and furnish one or more dispensers which can be refilled as required.

Figure 135. Polyvinyl resin glue in plastic squeeze bottle

When glue is used, two points must be kept in mind: the surfaces to be joined must fit together well, and the pieces fastened should be held together securely while the glue dries. Drying time is ordinarily indicated on glue containers. For holding pieces together while the glue dries, either C-clamps can be used, or some other devices, such as nails or screws, can be used along with the glue. Sometimes a weight may serve to hold the pieces together.

When the surfaces to be joined fit well and are clean, the glue is spread on both surfaces either with a small stick or a small brush (which is cleaned immediately after use). Then, the pieces are placed together and clamped, nailed, or otherwise held firmly in place until dry. Any excess glue should be removed with a damp cloth before it has a chance to dry and harden. For glues not soluble in water, consult manufacturer's directions.

Nails, Tacks, Brads, Corrugated Fasteners

These four fastening devices are similar in that all of them are driven into place with a hammer. This type of fastening is very fast and simple, and for many jobs it provides adequate strength. However, for anything subject to vibration or movement, such as a hinged joint, some other method of fastening should be used. Nails in moving parts sooner or later work themselves loose and the pieces come apart. Also, where unusual strength is needed, as in holding together the parts of a workbench, nails would be a poor choice.

One very important principle that applies in this section as well as in the section on wood screws is that thin pieces should be fastened to thick ones, rather than vice versa, as shown in Figure 136. In other words, a nail first should be driven through the thinner of two pieces, thus giving the nail greater holding power.

In selecting a size and type of nail, tack, etc., for a particular job, one should be guided by the nature of the pieces being fastened, and the strength desired. The following are some typical construction problems together with recommendations for means of fastening:

Example 1. In fastening muslin to ¾" wooden frames to make a puppet stage, one would need a fastener about ½" long with a relatively large head so that the muslin would be held securely and not tear. The choice then should be upholsterer's tacks of the length indicated by the thickness of the wood.

Example 2. For fastening ¼" plywood to 1" x 2" pine for small plant flats, longer nails are used (Figure 147). They should go through the plywood first

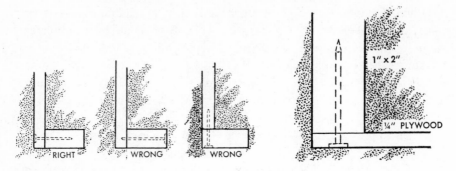

Figure 136. Nailing.   Figure 137. Nailing plywood.

and extend about an inch into the side pieces. Nails, about 1¼" long, would be satisfactory. The nails should be fairly thin so as not to split the side pieces. Accordingly, box nails, rather than common nails, should be used. The heads of finishing nails are too small for this job, because of the weight of the soil in the plant flats. The classroom supply list included 4d box nails, which are 1½" long, certainly close enough for this purpose.

Example 3. For fastening screening or poultry netting to wooden frames to make an enclosure for a small pet, a good choice would be double-pointed tacks. The screen wire could not slip off, as it might slip off the heads of ordinary tacks.

Example 4. If ¼" plywood were to be fastened to ½" pine for a small treasure chest, an appropriate choice for fastening would be glue and 1", No. 20 brads. Very little strength is needed, the wood is thin, and the heads of the nails should be small so that they will not spoil the appearance of the finished project.

Corrugated fasteners are used for fastening pieces edge to edge or end to edge, as in making stage scenery flats. Children sometimes have difficulty using these fasteners, however, and many teachers prefer to use ¼" plywood or hard wallboard triangles (Figure 138) nailed or tacked over the joint as shown. These triangles add considerable strength, and are sometimes used in conjunction with corrugated fasteners.

For smaller frames, such as picture frames, where the thickness of these plywood triangles might be objectionable, triangular pieces can be cut from thin metal like the metal from food containers. Here again tacks would be appropriate as fastening devices.

If corrugated fasteners are used, the pieces to be joined are placed in their respective positions and the corrugated fasteners are driven with a hammer.

The fasteners should be located far enough from the edge of small pieces of wood so that the wood does not split. Experimentation with a few of these fasteners and some pieces of scrap wood will show the teacher how they can best be used and what their limitations are.

The supplies chart in Chapter 3 should be consulted when selecting fastening devices (pages 110 through 117).

For the operation of hammering, the pieces being fastened should be placed solidly on some stable working surface. When pieces being nailed bounce around, it is difficult, if not impossible, to do well. The hammer is grasped comfortably, well away from its head, with one hand. The nail or other fastening device is held in the fingers of the other hand and tapped lightly two or three times to start it (Figure 139). Then the fingers are moved *well away from the nail* and the hammer is used to finish the nailing process. The children should be encouraged to hold the hammer in just one hand, as it is practically impossible to hit the nail squarely if two hands are used.

Obviously, it is important for the nail to be started straight; otherwise it may come out the side of one of the pieces being joined. If a nail has started to go in crookedly, it should be pulled out and started in a different place; otherwise it will follow the crooked hole. It is important for the nail to be hit squarely. If the face of the hammer meets the nail at an angle, the nail is likely to bend. One of the common causes of trouble here is grasping the hammer too close to its head. Aside from this, it is just a matter of time and practice until skill is developed.

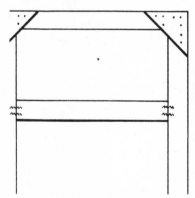

Figure 139. Starting a nail.

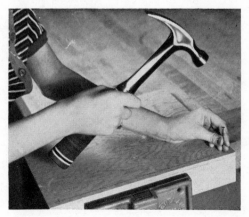

Figure 138. Corrugated fasteners and plywood triangles.

When a nail starts to bend, it should be straightened immediately. This can be done either by tapping the side of the nail with the hammer to straighten it, or by grasping the nail in the claw of the hammer and bending it straight again. If this does not help, the nail should be withdrawn, and a new nail used.

After the nail has been driven almost all the way into the wood, continued hammering might produce hammer marks on the surface of the wood around the nail. For most work, a few hammer marks may not be objectionable, and inexperienced hands can be expected to miss the nail occasionally, but there is a way to prevent them. When the nail has only a very little way to go, a nail set can be placed on the head of the nail. The nail set is held steady with one hand and struck with a hammer held in the other hand. In this manner the nail can be driven all the way into place.

It is sometimes desirable to drive the head of a nail below the surface of the material being fastened. This operation is called "setting the nail" (Figure 140), and is required where a nicely finished surface is necessary. Nails with small heads, like finishing nails or brads, should be used because they can be driven down into the wood. The nail set also is used for this purpose, as previously described. The nails should be driven only slightly below the surface, about $\frac{1}{16}$ of an inch. Later the small holes can be filled with putty or a similar substance to provide a flat surface before the finish or a coat of paint is applied.

Sometimes a nail driven too close to the edge or the end of a piece causes the wood to split. This can be prevented by drilling a hole in the piece through which the nail passes (Figure 141). The hole can be drilled either with a carbon-steel twist drill bit or with a nail of the size that will be used for nailing, as explained in the section on making holes. Ordinarily, no drill-

Figure 140. Setting a nail.

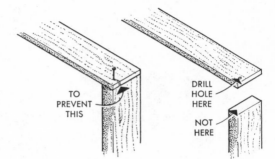

Figure 141. Drilling prevents splitting.

TO
PREVENT
THIS

DRILL
HOLE
HERE

NOT
HERE

Figure 142. Drawing a nail.

Figure 143. Drawing a nail using a block to protect wood surface.

ing should be done in the piece that the nail is expected to hold; otherwise the holding power of the nail will be greatly reduced.

When it is necessary to withdraw a nail, the claw of the hammer is used as shown in Figure 142. To avoid denting the wood with the hammer, a piece of scrap wood can be placed between the head of the hammer and the surface to be protected (Figure 143). A piece of scrap wood placed in this way is also useful in pulling a long nail, because it provides added leverage and makes it easier to pull the nail.

It will sometimes be necessary to take apart pieces which have been nailed together. The basic procedure can perhaps be best illustrated by describing the process of taking apart a box or crate. The pieces from such boxes and crates often can be used if they have been carefully taken apart.

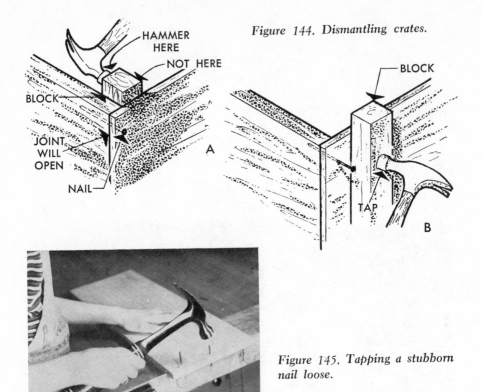

Figure 144. Dismantling crates.

Figure 145. Tapping a stubborn nail loose.

The simplest procedure for children involves the use of a fairly sturdy block of scrap wood. A piece of wood 2 inches by 2 inches and 12 inches long is ideal for taking apart an orange crate (Figure 144). The block is placed along a corner where the box is joined together. The block is hammered in order to remove the nails holding the box together as shown at A. After the joint has been opened about half an inch or so, the side of the box is tapped back into place as shown at B, and the nails will stick out far enough to be pulled with the claw of the hammer.

If an attempt is made to take apart a box or crate by hammering directly on the sides of the box or crate without the use of a block, the thin side pieces of the crate will very likely be cracked or broken by the hammer.

While the hammering is being done, the box can be held steady by standing in it or by having a helper hold it.

Occasionally, nails remain fast and the heads may even make a hole in the thin side pieces, but this should not happen often if the procedure described here is followed. When a nail sticks in the thin side piece, it can be removed by tapping lightly on the point to loosen it (Figure 145), and then pulling it in the usual way.

Wood Screws

Although it takes a little longer to fasten parts with wood screws than it does with nails, there are two advantages to using screws. Other things being equal, screws have greater holding power, especially if the parts are subject to movement or vibration. Secondly, things fastened with screws can be taken apart and reassembled more successfully than if they were fastened with nails.

Here again the principle applies that thinner pieces should be fastened to thicker ones. The screw should go through the thinner of the two pieces first, as with nails.

The wood-screw styles mentioned in the discussion of supplies will meet practically any need that is likely to arise. Flat-head (F.H.) screws are used where the screw heads are to be set below the surface. Whether round-head (R.H.) and oval-head (O.H.) screws should be used for a particular job depends primarily on the appearance desired. However, when a washer is used to keep the screw head from biting into the material being fastened, a round-head screw should be chosen. The size of screw to be used depends, of course, on the materials being fastened.

The process of fastening with screws is illustrated by Figure 146. To make a flannelboard the $\frac{3}{4}$" x 2" x 32" tray is fastened to a sheet of $\frac{1}{4}$" plywood. When the pieces are ready to assemble, they are placed on the bench as shown. Then a light pencil line is drawn along the plywood, $\frac{3}{8}$ inch from the edge. This is where the screws will be placed; they will be located exactly along the middle of the $\frac{3}{4}$" piece. Next, short pencil marks are made where the screws are to be located, perhaps every six inches or so. F.H. screws should be used so the heads will not protrude and scratch fingers or table tops. The screw size should be about $1\frac{1}{4}$", No. 8, or as close to that as found in the available supply of screws.

Now a drill bit is selected. This is done by holding a screw and a drill bit side by side to compare the sizes. The holes to be drilled first should be about the size of the *unthreaded* part of the screw. This is known as the shank of the screw, and the holes to be drilled are called shank holes (Figure 147). The plywood is taken off the tray, and all of the shank holes are drilled in the plywood. This size hole is *not* drilled into the tray piece.

Next, the shank holes are countersunk (Figure 148). The brace countersink is inserted in the brace and the brace is used as described in a previous section. The purpose of this step is to produce a recess in the wood for the head of the screw. To determine how deep to countersink the holes, the operator can place a screw in a countersunk hole to see how the screw head fits.

The plywood, with all of the shank holes drilled and countersunk, is now placed on the tray as it was before, and a drill bit (or a nail) is selected for drilling the anchor holes. These are the holes to be drilled into the tray. They must be somewhat smaller than the screws. These holes should be approximately the same diameter as the lower part of a screw, not counting the threads (Figure 150).

The plywood and tray are now either held carefully by a helper or clamped together in position with C-clamps and the anchor holes drilled into the ¾" tray piece. These holes should be about as deep as the screws are long. As a rule, the depth of these holes can be gauged closely enough by eye. If desired, a small rubber band can be placed on the drill bit to show when drilling should be stopped.

All of the anchor holes can be drilled first, or one hole can be drilled near each end, and the screws put in place. Then the clamps are removed and the rest of the holes are drilled, and the screws are driven into the wood.

The screws should be driven with a screw driver of the correct size. From the screw drivers available, the one that fits the screw slots best should be chosen. If a screw driver is too big or too small, the job will be more difficult than it needs to be, and damage to the work or injury to the operator may result.

The tip of a screw driver should be flat (Figure 151). If it is nicked or rounded by wear it should be put aside and not used until it can be reground by a competent craftsman.

The screws are inserted in the holes and turned with the screw driver until they are snugly in place, the heads just slightly below the surface of the wood.

Children sometimes have difficulty keeping a screw driver in the slot of the screw. They should be encouraged to hold the tool in line with the screw and to exert pressure on the screw driver toward the screw (Figure 152). If the screw driver wiggles or leans, it will slip out of the slot. If the screw driver slips too often, the head of the screw may be chipped, in which case a new one should be used. Again, practice is needed to achieve skill.

The holes for oval-head screws are countersunk less deeply, and in soft

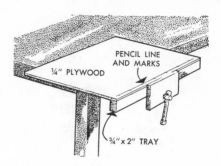

Figure 146. A vise can help in layout and fastening.

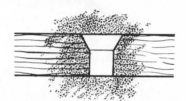

Figure 148. Countersunk hole.

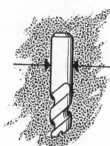

Figure 147. Shank hole size.

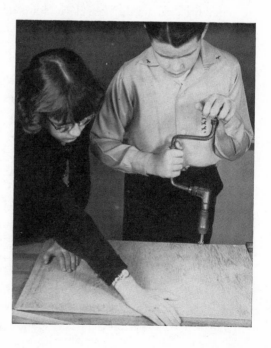

Figure 149. Countersinking.

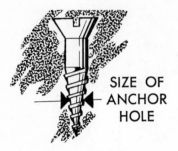

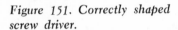

SIZE OF
ANCHOR
HOLE

Figure 150. Anchor hole size.

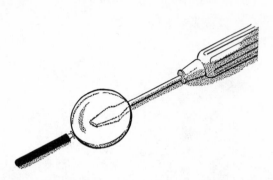

Figure 151. Correctly shaped
screw driver.

woods it may not be necessary to countersink at all, since the screw will pull itself into the surface of the wood when turned. When using round-head screws no countersinking is done.

The process of inserting similar threaded devices such as screw eyes (Figure 153) and cup hooks (Figure 154) is very much like that described above, except that no shank holes are needed. With cup hooks and the like, no screw driver is used; these devices are turned into the wood with combination pliers, or, instead of using pliers, a nail can be inserted into the eye of a screw eye to turn it.

In designing and planning objects to be made, one should bear in mind that wood screws do not hold well in end grain. It is not always possible to avoid using screws in end grain, but when some alternative is possible it should be considered.

When driving screws that must permit movement of the parts fastened, as at the top of the upright pieces in the easel shown on page 222, only minor changes are needed in the procedure described above. First, the shank hole, which is the hole in piece (A) in Figure 155, must be large enough to permit the shank of the screw to turn freely, but not so large as to be excessively loose. Next, it is well to place a plain washer under the head of the screw to prevent it from biting into the wood. Another washer between pieces (A) and (B) will help the hinged joint to work more freely. Then, a little soap or candle wax is rubbed on the shank of the screw and on the washers before putting them in place to provide lubrication for the joint. Finally, the screw is not tightened completely, but rather left a little loose to permit the pieces to move.

Figure 152. Using the screw driver.

Figure 153. Placing a screw eye.

Figure 154. Placing a cup hook.

When metal is fastened to wood with wood screws, the process is essentially the same as when fastening wood to wood. Ordinarily round-head screws are used to eliminate the necessity of countersinking holes in the metal. If it is desirable to countersink the holes in the metal, an ordinary twist-drill bit large enough to accommodate the head of the screw should be used. *The brace wood countersink is never used on metal.*

Most commercially produced metal devices, such as hinges and corner braces, have holes already countersunk to take F.H. or O.H. screws. One merely has to select screws of a size that will fit the holes.

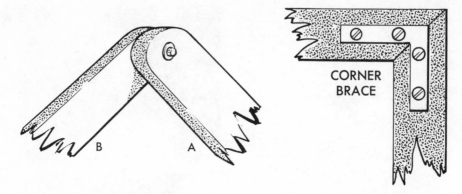

Figure 155. Hinged joint.   Figure 156. Corner brace.

In using corner braces (Figure 156), the pieces to be fastened are placed in position, the corner brace is located, and a pencil is used to draw the outline of one of the holes. Then, the corner brace is removed and the anchor hole for one screw is drilled in the center of the penciled circle. The shank hole is already in the metal. The corner brace is again put in place and the first screw is driven. Now the other holes are drilled with the corner brace in place. One hole is drilled at a time and a screw inserted before the next hole is drilled. If children try to drill all the holes at one time, the holes in the corner brace may not correspond with the holes they have made. Proceeding with one hole at a time prevents this result.

The process of attaching hinges and similar devices is essentially the same as that used to attach corner braces. When mounting hinges, it is helpful to place a couple of pieces of thin cardboard between the pieces to be hinged before drilling the anchor holes and inserting the screws. The cardboard keeps the hinged parts from binding. Also, paint and other finishes should be applied before attaching hinges, because the thickness of the paint film might cause binding of the hinged joint.

A final suggestion concerns large wood screws that might be difficult to turn into the wood. Even if shank and anchor holes of appropriate size have been drilled (or bored), the screws will turn easier if the threads are rubbed on a piece of soap or wax before the screws are inserted in the holes.

Stove Bolts, Carriage Bolts

Other things being equal, bolts provide more holding power than the other fasteners described in this section. Another advantage is that wing nuts can be used with bolts to permit tightening or loosening with only the fingers (see easel on page 222).

Stove bolts are available with either flat heads or round heads, both head types having slots like those of wood screws. Carriage bolts have a rounded head without a slot and a squared section on the shank just below the head.

In bolting parts together, the first task is to select the proper style and size of bolt. Bolts are designated by their style, shank diameter, and length as: F.H. stove bolt, $\frac{1}{4}$" x $1\frac{1}{2}$"; or carriage bolt, $\frac{5}{16}$" x $2\frac{1}{2}$"; etc. One should measure carefully the combined thicknesses of the pieces to be fastened and add $\frac{1}{4}$ inch to allow for the washer and the nut on the threaded end of the bolt. Thus, if one were fastening two pieces, each of which measured $1\frac{5}{8}$ inches think, he would put the pieces together and measure them. In this case, the combined measurement would approximate $3\frac{1}{4}$ inches, to which should be added $\frac{1}{4}$ inch, which means that $3\frac{1}{2}$" bolts would be needed for the job. The choice of diameter for the $3\frac{1}{2}$" bolt depends on the amount of strength needed. For general purposes, bolts up to 1 inch in length should be $\frac{1}{8}$ inch in diameter; bolts from 1 inch to 2 inches in length should be $\frac{3}{16}$ inch in diameter; bolts from 2 inches to 3 inches in length should be $\frac{1}{4}$ inch in diameter; and bolts from 3 inches to 4 inches in length should be $\frac{5}{16}$ inch in diameter.

In general, stove bolts should be used for any job where the bolt length is to be $1\frac{1}{2}$ inches or less. If the bolt length is to be greater than $1\frac{1}{2}$ inches, carriage bolts should be chosen. These are, of course, only general rules; where the specifications for a job call for a certain style and size of bolt, such bolts should be used.

It should be pointed out that the squared shank on a carriage bolt, near the head, restricts the use of carriage bolts to wood, since this squared shank bites into the wood and wedges itself in place. Carriage bolts cannot be drawn into metal in this manner. Stove bolts, on the other hand, can be used to fasten almost anything through which holes can be drilled or bored.

The plain washer is the type most commonly used in elementary industrial arts. It looks like a little metal doughnut. The primary function of these washers is to keep fasteners from biting into the surface of the material being fastened (Figure 157). Ordinarily, no washer is needed under the head of a carriage bolt, because the head is large enough to serve as its own washer. Washers cannot be used under the heads of F.H. bolts.

When a job involves fastening metal to metal, as in assembling or repairing an all-metal toy, for example, lock washers will be needed. These washers are split and sprung. Their function is different from plain washers.

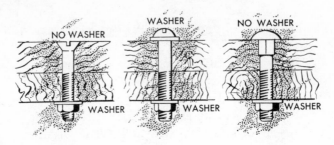

Figure 157. When to use plain washers.

When wood is fastened with a bolt, the wood is squeezed by the bolt. Then the natural resiliency of wood exerts a constant force on the head of the bolt and on the nut, causing enough friction to keep the nut from working loose once it has been properly tightened. Since metal does not have enough resiliency to do this, a lock washer, with its built-in spring tension, is used to obtain the same result. Without the lock washer, vibration will cause a nut, eventually, to work itself loose from the bolt, and pieces then come apart.

The actual process of fastening with bolts is relatively simple. Holes are drilled or bored wherever the bolts are to be placed. The holes must be large enough to permit the bolt to pass through freely, but not so large that the bolts fit too loosely. If flat-head stove bolts are used, countersinking is necessary; most of the other bolts do not require it.

After a hole is made, the bolt is inserted, with washers where needed, and the nut is turned on the bolt with the fingers. The heads of carriage bolts should be tapped into place with a hammer to wedge the squared shank into the wood. This is not done with stove bolts. Finally, the adjustable wrench is used to tighten the nut.

The adjustable wrench is adjusted to fit the nut snugly, and applied to the nut so that force is exerted on the immovable jaw of the wrench (Figure 158). If the wrench is applied backward, it may slip off the nut and cause

Figure 158. Using the adjustable wrench.

bumped or scratched knuckles. Of course, when loosening nuts, the position of the tool is the reverse of that shown in the illustration, since the force will be in the opposite direction.

When using the wrench on the nut of a stove bolt, the bolt itself may also turn. This can be prevented by holding a screw driver in the slot in the head of the bolt. A carriage bolt is not likely to turn, because the squared shank holds it in place as force is exerted on the nut.

PAINTING AND FINISHING PROCESSES

As used here the term, "finishing processes," refers to and includes:

a. Preparing surfaces for the application of finishing materials such as paints, shellacs, varnishes, and enamels.
b. Selecting and preparing these materials for application.
c. Applying them.
d. Cleaning up after the work is completed.

Preparing Surfaces

A question that is commonly asked is whether parts should be assembled before or after painting. The answer depends on the nature of the project. Ordinarily, nonmoving parts, which are to be permanently fastened, should be assembled first and then painted. However, it is practical to finish and then assemble moving parts, such as wheels on toys, and parts that would be difficult to reach with a paint brush after assembly. Sometimes parts can be assembled, then taken apart for painting, then reassembled. In this way holes are already drilled and screws go back in place easily.

Just what is involved in the preparation of surfaces depends on the results expected. For some articles, surface preparation consists in a thorough wiping with a dust rag. In other instances, it might be necessary first to do some sanding to remove wood whiskers or rough spots that escaped the smoothing processes described earlier. If a transparent finish such as shellac is to be applied, pencil marks and smudges should be erased and sanded away; otherwise they will be preserved by the transparent finish and will mar the appearance of the completed article.

If nail holes and small depressions in wood surfaces are to be filled, another step is needed. For this purpose, a commercial hole filler or a homemade mixture of fine sawdust and glue can be used. The material is simply pressed into the holes with the fingers, a small stick, or a putty knife. All excess

Figure 159. Painters at work.

material should be removed so that it does not harden on the surface. After the substance used to fill the holes has hardened, sandpaper on a sanding block can be used to smooth over the spots. Most commercial hole fillers dry and harden very quickly when exposed to air. The cans or other containers, therefore, should be kept tightly covered when not in use. Children have a tendency to use a great deal more of this type of material than is needed for any given job. Therefore, they should be supervised closely when using hole fillers. Most teachers prefer not to have their pupils use them, since they are not expected to produce perfectly finished surfaces.

If a job involves painting over a surface that already has paint or some other finish on it, the surface should be sanded first with fine sandpaper or worn medium sandpaper. This step will remove bumps and rough spots and provide a better bond for the new coat of paint.

Finally, all surfaces should be free from dust and dirt before the new finish is applied.

Selecting and Preparing Finishing Materials

It was explained in Chapter 3 that many teachers get along very well with only water-soluble, latex-base paints. These are easy to use and they produce very fine results for our purposes. Latex-base paints are opaque, and are available in white and a great variety of colors. Various colors *of the same brand* can be mixed to produce almost any shade desired.

If a natural finish is desired, that is, if the grain of the wood is to be visible, a transparent finish will be needed. For this type of finish, shellac, varnish, or clear lacquer can be used. Because varnish is somewhat difficult for children to apply properly, it is seldom used in the elementary grades. Also, very little use is made of clear lacquer, because it is difficult to apply and expensive. Where consultants and shops are part of the industrial arts program, these two finishes may be used satisfactorily in the upper grades.

The best choice among transparent finishes seems to be white shellac. Shellac should not be used for objects that are to be used outdoors, unless it is to serve as a sealer coat which will be covered with oil paint. It is very satisfactory, however, for indoor use, and it is relatively easy to apply. Paste wax applied over the last coat of shellac will give a pleasing effect.

The advantage of using shellac under oil paint is that it seals the wood, minimizing the absorption of moisture and preventing the paint from soaking in and producing dull spots. Shellac should not be used under latex-base paints, however, because it sometimes causes them to peel.

If an opaque finish will be exposed to weather for long periods, "outside" oil paints can be used. These finishes are more glossy than the water-soluble paints, although they do not have the gloss of enamels or lacquers. "Inside" oil paints can be used for things that will not be exposed to weather, but rather than be troubled with too many kinds of finishes, most teachers use only outside paint, if they use oil paints at all. The chief difference between inside and outside paints, as far as we are concerned, is that the latter may take a longer time to dry.

Enamels and colored lacquers are more expensive and more difficult to apply than outside oil paints. They are not recommended unless a consultant is available to give advice regarding their use.

In the past, some teachers used ordinary water colors and tempera paints for industrial arts work. These paints, of course, rub off and are certainly not waterproof, which makes them rather unsatisfactory for many purposes. Furthermore, the water-soluble, latex-base paints are so easy to work with and produce results which are so much more satisfactory, that they are now much more popular than water colors in industrial arts work. Water colors are, of course, useful for making stage scenery and the like where the finished product is not expected to last very long. There are processes for preserving water colors almost indefinitely, but these demand more skill than can be expected of pupils in lower grades.

It must be remembered that for every finishing substance, there is a proper brush cleaner, thinner, and solvent. If shellac is used, alcohol must also

Figure 160. Consultant helps second graders. The right finish makes a model house realistic.

be procured. For varnish, inside and outside oil paints, and enamels, turpentine is needed. For lacquers, lacquer thinner is needed. For the water-soluble latex-base paints, the only requirement is plain water.

The object to be finished should be placed either on a bench or table, or on the floor, and the area should be protected either with newspapers distributed liberally, or, even better, with a large piece of canvas from an old awning, or with a commercial drop cloth. These drop cloths can be purchased from paint and hardware stores and from firms dealing in school supplies.

The painter should wear a protective garment, such as a smock. Aprons are not satisfactory because they leave too much clothing exposed. Men's shirts make excellent smocks. Jeans and old shoes provide an added measure of protection for clothing.

The containers of all finishing substances must be kept tightly covered when not in use, or the paints, shellac, and other finishing materials will deteriorate and be wasted. Cans are opened with a screw driver or special paint-can opener, never with a sharp object such as a chisel or ordinary can opener. A paint-can cover should be pried up a little at a time, working all the way around the can until the cover comes off (Figure 163). The can is grasped securely while the cover is being removed, and the hand holding the can is placed so that it will not be injured if the screw driver or paint-can opener should slip. It is advisable to place a paper plate and some fully opened newspaper sheets under the can in any case to minimize damage in the event of spilling. After the cover has been removed, it should be placed paint-side-up on additional pieces of newspaper, in a place where it will not be stepped on accidentally. Teachers, familiar as they are with children's activities, will appreciate the necessity of including these precautions.

When the can has been opened a clean stick is used to stir the finishing substance. With experience one can tell by the way the substance stirs whether it is of the proper consistency. Sometimes paint and shellac become thick from standing, and the ingredients separate. After a little stirring, or after the separated ingredients are well blended, the stirring stick can be lifted to permit the finishing substance to drip off the stick into the can. The drips provide a clue to the condition of the finishing substance. If the drips seem to "pile up," the material is too thick and must be thinned. *The correct thinner must be used.* A very small amount of thinner, about a teaspoonful or so, is added at a time. Then the substance is stirred and tested again. This stirring should be done about every fifteen minutes while the finish is being applied to maintain the proper consistency and mixture of ingredients.

Now the excess is brushed off the stirring stick and wiped off the brush into the can (Figure 161). The wet end of the stirring stick is placed on the upturned can cover, and the paint can now be applied.

Figure 161. Removing a can cover.

Figure 162. Wiping excess thinner from brush.

It may be wise, at this point, to pour a small amount of the finishing substance into one or more small, clean cans which have been collected for this purpose. This also reduces the damage and loss in case of spilling. When there are two or more painters, each painter should have his own container. The original container should then be covered, if it is not being used.

When mixing paints, enamels, and lacquers to produce desired shades of color, one must be careful to mix together only the same type of finishing materials. Oil paints, for example, cannot be mixed with latex-base paints or the entire mixture will be ruined. To be safe, one should restrict mixing to the same brands, since various brands of even similar finishes sometimes vary enough chemically to prevent their mixing properly. Certainly, one should mix only as much of any given finish as is needed for the job at hand.

Applying the Finishing Substance

One should first decide where he will begin; then, arrange the container of paint or other finishing substance and the object to be finished for greatest working convenience. Ordinarily, hard-to-get-at parts of an object should be done first; the most accessible parts last. This prevents undue reaching over wet surfaces and possibly touching them accidentally. Ends and edges usually should be done before faces of pieces, insides and bottoms before outsides and tops. The container should be placed where it can be reached easily and placed on a newspaper, drop cloth, or paper plate for protective purposes.

The brush is dipped in the finishing substance so that not more than one third of the length of the bristles is immersed. Then, the brush is wiped lightly against the edge of the can to remove excess liquid. This is done to both sides of the brush, but not with undue pressure for that will remove too much liquid.

In applying the finish, a slight pressure is exerted on the brush, causing the bristles to bend a little. Fairly long strokes should be used, rather than a dabbing motion. The finishing substance is applied as evenly and as smoothly as possible, to obtain an even finish. Best results are usually achieved by brushing with the grain of the wood rather than across the grain.

When shellac, fast-drying enamel, or lacquer are used, one should work rather quickly, completing a small section at a time, but not going over it once an area has been done. Rebrushing with these rapid-drying substances may cause troublesome brush marks and piling up, which produce an unattractive surface. With water-soluble paints and outside oil paints, this is not a serious matter because of their drying characteristics. Even with these paints, however, one should develop a painting technique that gets the job done quickly, and then leaves well enough alone until the finish is dry.

One difficulty that seems to occur frequently is dripping on corners and edges of pieces being finished. This is caused by brushing in the incorrect direction. One should brush off the surface at edges rather than toward the surface, as illustrated in Figure 163. The job should be inspected while in progress and when the work has been completed, for missed spots or drips. As soon as they are noticed, missed spots can be touched up and drips can be brushed over to smooth them out. After the finish begins to dry and get tacky, it is best to let it dry completely. The next coat of finish can be used to repair any defects.

One coat of finish is frequently sufficient, but if the first coat soaks in leaving dull spots, or if there are missed spots and drips, a second coat may be needed. After the first coat is thoroughly dry, it is sanded lightly with fine sandpaper or worn medium sandpaper. Large sheets of sandpaper should be torn in sixths, as explained earlier, and the small pieces folded once or twice. The paper is folded and used without a sanding block. The principal purposes of sanding here are to remove any gloss and surface dirt, thus providing a good bond for the next coat, and to smooth out any imperfections in the preceding coat. Large drips may have to be scraped away with a knife and then sanded smooth.

The second coat is applied in much the same manner as the first, with perhaps a little more care if this is to be the last application. In unusual

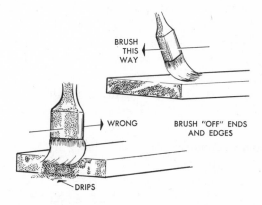

Figure 163. Brush off ends and edges.

cases, third and fourth coats may be applied. Sanding is done between all coats but not usually after the last coat except for wax finishes or other very fine finishes.

Proficiency in finishing is developed primarily through practice. Children ordinarily approach this work with enthusiasm, and with a reasonable amount of instruction, the results they achieve will be most satisfying.

Cleaning Up After Applying Finishes

Unfortunately, many finishing operations bog down at this point. Everyone has had the experience of coming across brushes that were placed in water or solvents to be cleaned "tomorrow" and long since forgotten. Often such brushes are completely ruined, or much the worse for the treatment they have received: bristles out of shape, bristles coming loose, and handles covered with paint.

Cleaning up is an integral part of the finishing process, and it should be performed without fail. *In planning work periods, time should be allowed for cleanup.*

If shellac has been used from a container with a rubber cap, only a cloth dampened with alcohol will be needed to clean off the brush handle and the outside of the shellac container. Then, new shellac is added to bring the level in the container high enough to cover the bristles of the brush, and the brush and rubber cap are replaced on the container. Hands can be cleaned with an alcohol-dampened cloth, but they then should be washed immediately with soap and water. Unused newspapers and clean, folded cloths can be put away for future use. Newspapers and cloths which have absorbed shellac or alcohol, however, should be either taken directly to the school incinerator or placed in a covered metal can, so they cannot cause a fire by spontaneous combustion. *The proper disposition of used cloths and newspapers is very important.* Shellac brushes can be cleaned with alcohol. Shellac brushes which have become stiff and hard because they were not properly cleaned can sometimes be softened again by immersing the bristles in shellac for a day or two. Alcohol has little effect once the bristles become stiff.

For all finishing substances other than shellac in the rubber-cap container, the cleanup begins differently. The brush is used to remove the finishing substance from the outside of the container. Then it is used to pick up any liquid resting in the grooves around the top edge of the can. Finally, the brush is wiped as dry as possible on the inside, top rim of the container.

If one or more small cans of the same substance were used, these are all emptied into the main container, and the small cans cleaned out as well as possible with the brush. All the liquid thus picked up on the brush is also wiped back into the main can. The brush is pressed against the top inside edge of the can and drawn upward to remove as much of the liquid as possible.

The container is covered by placing a wiping cloth over cover and can and then using a hammer to tap the cover tightly in place, hitting it around the entire edge. The cover should not be struck so hard as to bend it out of shape, but it must be hit hard enough to close the can securely. The cover should not be struck anywhere except on the edge. The cloth prevents splashing as the cover is hammered on. Once the cover is securely in place, it is supported by one hand, as the can is tipped upside down for an instant to permit the finishing substance to seal the can, making it air-tight. Then, the outside of the can is cleaned with a cloth or paper towel dampened with the appropriate solvent and the can is put away. To prevent fire from spontaneous combustion, the cloth or paper towel used to clean the outside of the can should be taken directly to the school incinerator or placed in a covered metal can provided for the purpose.

If water-soluble paint has been applied, the brush, stirring stick, paint container, and wiping cloth are taken to the sink and washed out with water which is cool to lukewarm in temperature. The brush is held under the stream of water and the paint washed away. After most of the paint is removed, the bristles of the brush are spread apart with the fingers, still holding the brush under the stream of water. Then, the brush is rubbed on a bar of ordinary soap, and the lather is worked well into the bristles (Figure 164). The lather is rinsed off and the process repeated until there are no further traces of paint. The run-off water squeezed from the bristles should be perfectly clear. Dried paint on bristles or handle can be rubbed off with very little effort by using a water-dampened scouring pad. Once the bristles of the brush have been squeezed as dry as possible, and shaped with the fingers to the original brush shape, the brush is placed on a paper towel or newspaper to dry.

The stirring stick and small cans can be scrubbed clean with the scouring pad if desired, and the wiping cloth can be washed with soap and water. If this paint is allowed to dry thoroughly, it is very difficult to remove from cloth, so any paint that accidentally gets on clothing should be removed immediately. The same applies to spots on floors or furniture. Last, the sink itself is wiped clean and the hands washed.

A different process is required to clean brushes used to apply oil paints, varnish, enamel, shellac, and lacquer. Although all of these materials are removed from brushes in the same way, the brush cleaners used will vary. The cleaner for shellac is alcohol; the cleaner for lacquer is lacquer thinner; and the cleaner for varnish, oil paints, and enamel is turpentine. As stated before, these cleaners may not be used interchangeably. Even the so-called "universal" thinners have their limitations and are not truly universal. Teachers are strongly urged to procure the cleaners recommended above for each type of finishing substance used.

A small amount of cleaner, half an inch or so, is placed in a shallow can like the familiar tuna fish can. Then the brush is worked back and forth and around in the cleaner, forcing the full length of the bristles down into the solution (Figure 165). This is repeated until the cleaner washes most of the finishing substance from the brush. Occasionally, the brush is wiped on the top edge of the can to squeeze out the cleaner. This also helps in working the finishing substance out of the bristles. When this process has been repeated a few times, the used cleaner is dumped into a larger can. Then the small can is wiped clean and dry with a paper towel or cloth. A new supply of cleaner is placed in the small can and the entire process repeated. In fact, this is repeated until no finishing substance can be removed from the brush by the cleaner. The bristles of the brush are

Figure 164. Brushes used in water-soluble paints are cleaned with soap and water.

Figure 165. Cleaning a brush used in oil paint.

spread apart with the fingers to see whether any finishing substance remains. If so, the brush should be cleaned again. If the bristles appear entirely clean, the cleaner is squeezed out and the bristles shaped as before, and the brush laid down on a paper towel or newspaper to dry. Any finishing substance left on the handle or other parts of the brush should be removed with a cloth dampened with the proper cleaner. The same applies to the outside of the finishing-substance container and to any spots left on the floor, furniture, or shoes. The can of dirty or used cleaner is not dumped in the sink, because such material will clog drains. Rather, it is removed to the school incinerator and disposed of by the custodian.

Oil paints, shellac, and similar substances also can be removed from hands or face with a clean cloth slightly dampened with the appropriate cleaner. *The teacher should supervise the pupils very closely since these cleaners must be kept well away from eyes.* Furthermore, it is very important that the skin be washed well with soap and warm water to remove all traces of these cleaners, especially turpentine, which can cause skin burns.

Most of these finishing substances cannot be successfully removed from clothing, except by a professional dry cleaner, and sometimes even he is unable to restore the cloth. Therefore, every effort should be made to protect clothing with smocks or old shirts as already mentioned. Carbon tetrachloride usually is quite effective as a spot remover for these finishes, but since it is harmful if taken internally, *it should not be in an elementary school classroom.*

Of particular concern is the disposal of newspapers, paper towels, and wiping cloths saturated with these finishing substances and cleaners. *They are highly flammable.* They should be taken to the school incinerator and turned over to the school custodian as soon as they have served their purpose. They should not be left lying about. The only acceptable alternative is a tightly covered metal container which is placed well away from all heat sources. Even this container should be emptied at the earliest possible moment.

All of these precautions are necessary where shellac, varnish, oil paints, enamel, and lacquer are used, which is one of the primary reasons why many teachers use water-soluble latex-base paints exclusively. Where consultants and shop facilities are available, the necessary precautions are taken as a routine matter. Classroom teachers understandably prefer to relieve themselves of these troublesome matters, and fortunately they can now do so without curtailing their programs, since the water-soluble paints are available.

Figure 166. Spray paints simplify the clean-up.

If the cleaning up is done as described, finishing experiences can be very enjoyable and completely safe. Besides, there is great satisfaction in reaching for a brush and finding it soft and pliable and ready for the job at hand. Containers kept clean and properly sealed and in their proper places add to one's enthusiasm in undertaking a task. In fact, the whole school program profits from cleanup routines that keep supplies, tools, and equipment in workmanlike condition, always ready for a new adventure.

SELECTED REFERENCES

The references listed here describe processes. Those listed at the end of Chapter 5 describe *things to make and do*. References that do both are listed in both places. The numerals in parentheses following some of the references indicate the grade levels for which those books are appropriate as specified in *The Children's Catalog*, 11th ed., 1966, published by H. W. Wilson Company, New York. These grade-level recommendations are included with the permission of the H. W. Wilson Company.

References for Ceramics Activities
Olson, Delmar W., *Pottery* (Scranton, Pa.: International Textbook, 1953), 113 pp.
Scobey, Mary-Margaret, "Helping Children Work With Clay," *Industrial Arts and Vocational Education*, Vol. 44 (November, 1955), No. 9.

Seeley, Vernon D. and Robert L. Thompson, *Activities in Ceramics* (Bloomington, Ill.: McKnight and McKnight, 1956).
Zarchy, Harry, *Ceramics* (New York: Alfred A. Knopf, Inc., 1954), 171 pp.

References for Paper and Cardboard Activities
Anderson, Mildred, *Papier Mâché and How to Use It* (New York: Sterling Publishers Co., 1965), 96 pp.
Araki, Chiyo, *Origami in the Classroom* (Rutland, Vt.: Chas. E. Tuttle, 1965), 44 pp.
Johnson, Pauline, *Creating With Paper* (Seattle: University of Washington Press, 1958), 207 pp.
Sarasas, Claude, *The ABC's of Origami; Paper Folding for Children* (Rutland, Vt.: Chas. E. Tuttle, 1964), 55 pp.
Schneider, Herman, *Science Fun With Milk Cartons* (New York: McGraw-Hill, Inc., 1953), 159 pp. (5–8).
Weiss, Harvey, *Paper, Ink and Roller; Printmaking for Beginners* (New York: W. R. Scott, 1958), 64 pp.

References for Puppet Activities
Bufano, Remo, *Remo Bufano's Book of Puppetry* (New York: Macmillan Co., 1950), 232 pp. (5–8).
Cummings, Richard, *101 Hand Puppets* (New York: David McKay, 1962), 147 pp.
Jagendorf, Moritz A., *First Book of Puppets* (New York: F. Watts, 1952), 66 pp. (4–6).
Pels, Gertrude J., *Easy Puppets* (New York: T. Y. Crowell, 1951), 104 pp. (3–6).

References for Textiles Activities
Alexander, Marthann, *Weaving Handcraft* (Bloomington, Ill.: McKnight and McKnight, 1954), 91 pp.
Atwater, Mary M., *The Shuttle-Craft Book of American Hand Weaving* (New York: Macmillan Co., rev. 1951), 275 pp.
Chapman, Jane A., *Girl's Book of Sewing* (Greenberg, 1952), 95 pp. (4–9).
Dow, Emily R., *How to Make Doll Clothes* (New York: Coward-McCann, Inc., 1953), 96 pp. (5–8).
Leeming, Joseph, *Fun With Fabric* (Philadelphia: J. B. Lippincott Co., 1950), 96 pp.
Picken, Mary (Brooks), *Singer Sewing Book* (New York: McGraw-Hill, Inc., rev. 1953), 244 pp.
Scobey, Mary-Margaret, "Textiles in the Elementary School Curriculum," *Industrial Arts and Vocational Education*, Vol. 44 (Sept., 1955), No. 7.
Zarchy, Harry, *Weaving* (New York: Alfred A. Knopf, Inc., 1953), 44 pp. (5–9).

References for Wood Activities

Beim, Jerrold, *Tim and the Tool Chest* (New York: Wm. Morrow and Co., Inc., 1951), (1–3).

Cramlet, Ross C., *Woodwork Visualized* (Milwaukee: Bruce Publishing Co., 1950), 158 pp.

Crocker, Constance H., *Creative Carpentry* (Boston: Houghton Mifflin Co., 1951), 39 pp. (4–8).

Feirer, John L., *Industrial Arts Woodworking* (Peoria, Ill.: Chas. A. Bennett, 1950), 290 pp.

Hunt, Ben, *Whittling With Ben Hunt* (Milwaukee: Bruce Publishing Co., 1959), 160 pp.

Zarchy, Harry, *Woodworking* (New York: Alfred A. Knopf, Inc., 1952), 44 pp. (4–6).

References for Other Activities or a Variety of Activities

Baillie, E. Kenneth, *Homespun Crafts* (Milwaukee: Bruce Publishing Co., 1952), 159 pp.

Boy Mechanic, 6th ed. (New York: Popular Mechanics, Inc., 1952), 312 pp. (5–9).

Brown, Mamie E., *Elementary Handcrafts for Elementary Schools* (Exposition Press, 1956), 104 pp. Chapters 2–8.

Carlson, Bernice W., *Make It Yourself* (Nashville: Abingdon Press, 1950), 160 pp. (3–6).

———, *Make It and Use It* (Nashville: Abingdon Press, 1958), 160 pp. (3–6).

Champion, Paul V., *Creative Crate Craft* (Milwaukee: Bruce Publishing Co., 1951), 110 pp.

Cherry, Raymond, *General Leathercraft* (Bloomington, Ill.: McKnight and McKnight, 1955), 144 pp.

Cox, Doris E. and Barbara W. Warren, *Creative Hands* (New York: John Wiley & Son, Inc., 1951).

Dow, Emily R., *Crafts for Fun & Fairs* (Barrows, 1964), 271 pp.

Downer, Marion, *Kites: How to Make and Fly Them* (New York: Lothrop Lee & Shepard Co., Inc., 1959), 64 pp. (4–7).

Griswold, Lester, *Handicraft* (Englewood, N.J.: Prentice-Hall, Inc., rev. 1952).

Groneman, Chris H. and John L. Feirer, *General Shop* (New York: McGraw-Hill, Inc., rev. 1956), 342 pp.

Hallen, Julienne, *How to Make Foreign Dolls and Their Costumes* (Homecrafts, 1950), 93 pp.

Hunt, W. Ben, *The Golden Book of Crafts and Hobbies* (New York: Golden Press, 1957), 111 pp.

Ickis, Marguerite and Reba S. Esh, *Book of Arts and Crafts* (New York: Association Press, 1954), 275 pp.

Jones, E. W., *General Electricity* (Bloomington, Ill.: McKnight and McKnight, 1954), 120 pp.

McCall's Book of Paper, Wood and Paint Crafts (New York: Golden Press, 1965), 48 pp.

Meyer, Jerome S., *The First Book of Mechanical Drawing* (New York: F. Watts, 1963), 66 pp.

Moore, Frank C., Carl H. Hamburger, and Anna-Laura Kingzett, *Handcrafts for Elementary Schools* (Boston: D. C. Heath and Co., 1953), Chapters 5–12.

Musciano, Walter A., *The Model Plane Manual* (McBride, 1952), 160 pp.

Newkirk, Louis V. and LaVada Zutter, *Crafts for Everyone* (Scranton, Pa.: International Textbook, 1950), 210 pp.

Ota, Koshi, *Printing For Fun* (New York: Astor-Honor, 1960), 53 pp.

Robertson, Seonaid, *Creative Crafts in Education* (Cambridge, Mass.: Bentley, 1953), 286 pp.

Ruley, M. J., *Practical Metal Projects* (Bloomington, Ill.: McKnight and McKnight, 1955), 88 pp.

Projects in General Metalwork (Bloomington, Ill.: McKnight and McKnight, 1951), 80 pp.

Schloat, G. Warren, *Playtime for You* (New York: Charles Scribner's Sons, 1950), 63 pp. (K–2).

Snook, Barbara, *Costumes for School Plays* (Newton Center, Mass.: C. T. Bradford, 1965).

Weiss, Harvey, *Clay, Wood and Wire* (New York: W. R. Scott, 1956), 48 pp.

Zarchy, Harry, *Here's Your Hobby* (New York: Alfred A. Knopf, Inc., 1950), 233 pp.

——, *Leathercraft* (New York: Alfred A. Knopf, Inc., 1953), 44 pp. (5–9).

——, *Sculpture; Soap and Other Materials* (New York: Alfred A. Knopf, Inc., 1952), 44 pp. (5–9).

chapter 5 / PROJECTS AND ACTIVITIES

Since industrial arts activities should grow from the curriculum, it is impossible to prescribe specific activities. This is so because the general curriculum framework varies from school to school, and the actual classroom work varies even within a given curriculum framework. This section, therefore, provides only clues to possible industrial arts activities. It offers examples which may (or may not) be appropriate in a given classroom situation.

STARTING WITH THE CURRICULUM

Without exception, good industrial arts activities are inspired by the curriculum and contribute to the quality of learning. Sometimes an industrial arts activity seems to suggest itself as a teacher considers ways of achieving educational goals. Study may be needed to see what activities show promise. When industrial arts activities can make no contribution whatever to a particular unit of classroom work, other avenues to the achievement of educational goals must be sought.

Here are some typical industrial arts activities relating to grade levels and areas of learning. The teacher can make the best use of the suggestions if he studies them in their entirety. He can then consider the most promising possibilities in terms of the grade level with which he is concerned. An activity suggested for a first grade might also be appropriate in the fifth grade with variations in the approach, development, and concentration.

Figure 167. Light bulb mock-up is part of fifth grade science.

For example, plant flats can be constructed in the first grade to enable children simply to observe plant growth; plant flats can also be constructed in the fifth grade for a comparison of the effectiveness of various plant foods.

The suggestions are not intended to limit the work of any grade level. They are presented to illustrate the activities that children and teachers have carried on successfully. Further, the material is intended to stimulate other ideas, since no such list could be all-inclusive.

POSSIBLE INDUSTRIAL ARTS ACTIVITIES

KINDERGARTEN

Health and Safety
Observe traffic lights and signs
Draw and construct traffic signs
Set up "roads" on playground
Make toy cars and trucks from milk cartons

Science
Make pet cages
Arrange pulley systems

Construct boxes for planting
Observe growth of plants
Play with magnets
Make steam
Freeze water
Touch and feel many substances
Care for classroom pets

Music and the Arts
Construct rhythm instruments
Model objects with clay
Make toys
Make gifts for holidays
Make hats and table decorations for parties

Social Studies
Visit school heating plant
Observe outdoor construction work
Build with blocks
Construct playhouses
Make trucks, boats, planes
Construct simple furniture

FIRST GRADE

Health and Safety
Plan safety rules
Construct first aid kit
Discuss and practice correct use of tools
Construct stick puppets for demonstrating safe living

Language Arts
Construct reading chart stand
Make "movie" box
Draw plans of school building and area
Invite mailman to class

Mathematics
Construct counting frames
Make individual counting sticks
Make oversized dominoes
Number nail cans

Construct calendar with movable dates
Collect and construct early time-telling devices
Construct classroom store
Construct flannelgram

Science
Make soap
Gather and mount leaf specimens
Construct bird feeders and houses
Reproduce feathers and leaves with blueprint paper
Construct chicken and duck pens
Construct weather vane
Build plant flats
Fly homemade kites
Devise supports for pulleys
Set up aquarium or terrarium
Observe child-made sundial
Plant bulbs
Display many varieties of seeds
Photograph with box camera
Observe wild life in parks
Care for plants

Music and the Arts
Use child-made rhythm instruments
Make gifts for holidays
Make album for snapshots
Spatter-print leaves, torn paper
Compile scrapbook

Social Studies
Build models of houses, churches, roads, vehicles
Make movable partitions for housekeeping corner
Construct crate furniture
Build playhouses
Assemble stores
Construct child-size trains, boats, cars, planes
Make play stoves, refrigerators, sinks
Make toys
Visit local markets, stores
Invite fire chief, policeman to classroom

Take walking trips
Visit police station
Shop for needed supplies

SECOND GRADE

Health and Safety
Choose workbench committee
Discuss care of clothing during work
Construct smock racks
Make cookie cutters
Construct and build with miniature and large blocks
Design safety posters
Make first aid kit
Lay out street plans
Observe ambulance and other emergency facilities

Language Arts
Introduce research method for project ideas
Construct felt boards or flannelgrams
Make book holders
Make large lettered blocks
Build child-size shadow frame

Figure 168. Second graders work on model trucks.

Bind books
Construct "movie" box
Typewrite with primer typewriter

Mathematics
Make abaci and counting frames
Build early clocks
Construct stores
Design and use play money
Make flannelgrams
Build post offices, banks
Construct felt boards
Record daily temperatures

Science
Construct weather vane with cardinal directions
Make plant flats and flower boxes
Make simple electrical devices
Use simple machines
Connect telephone and telegraph equipment
Invite electrician to classroom
Set up terrarium
Construct sundial and record readings
Experiment with magnets
Gather various seeds and display
Explore school grounds for unusual plant growth

Music and the Arts
Paint flowerpots
Design and make cookie cutters
Make gifts for holidays
Create torn-paper mosaics
Make simple picture frames

Social Studies
Arrange floor map of neighborhood
Make symbolic boats, planes, cars
Construct child-size stores, boats, planes, trains
Build post office
Visit fire house, telegraph office
Invite policeman to classroom
Visit pet shop, motor vehicle bureau

THIRD GRADE

Health and Safety
Make stilts, shuffleboard, ring toss, bowling games
Make smock racks
Construct dressing table with crates
Display food products
Shine shoes at homemade stand
Prepare first aid kit
Freeze vegetables

Language Arts
Make plans for construction work
Make furniture for library corner
Visit public library
Make book rests and book marks
Read about industries and industrial processes
Design and make puppets

Mathematics
Use simple fractions in measuring
Construct arithmetical games:
   bean bag boards, ring toss, dominoes, bingo, etc.
Make height-measuring devices
Make bank window

Science
Experiment with food preservation
Construct planet boards
Visit airport
Plant seeds
Make "tin" can telephones
Make plant flats
Experiment with sound of many materials
Make usable model water wheels

Music and the Arts
Make rhythm instruments
Use homemade stringed instruments
Construct model boats, cars, planes, trains
Make holiday gifts
Weave with simple homemade looms

Make papier-mâché masks and figures

Social Studies
Construct dioramas of city and suburban life
Make models of homes of other lands
Visit farm, bank, gas station
Make relief maps of other lands
Make maps and models of communities
Build model airport or railroad terminal
Visit water pumping station

FOURTH GRADE

Health and Safety
Repair bicycles
Make stilts
Make first aid kit
Record weights and heights of class members
Make aprons and smocks

Language Arts
Visit backstage and projector room of local theater
Make secenery and props for plays
Design and make book covers
Correspond with commercial houses for information related to studies
Make "movie" boxes
Make puppets

Figure 169. Fourth graders demonstrate musical triangles.

Mathematics
Construct advanced abaci
Concentrate on accuracy in measurement
Draw graphs on materials production
Make devices to show: square, circle, rectangle, triangle

Science
Make display boxes for rocks, seeds, insects, minerals, etc.
Construct telegraph sets
Model volcanoes in relief
Plant seeds
Experiment with strength of various building materials
Make paper
Test soils and use fertilizers
Make woodland terrarium

Music and the Arts
Weave with textiles and reed
Use linoleum blocks for printing
Make holiday gifts
Dye materials
Make candles and wax tablets
Make scrapbook covers
Present puppet show with homemade puppets and stages
Use Indian designs for bracelets, conch belts, medallions, etc.
Construct model and life-size totem poles
Visit jeweler at work
Darn socks and press clothing
Use coils and slabs in making pottery

Social Studies
Make dioramas and models of Indian and early settler life
Construct life-size teepees, igloos, wigwams
Make community maps
Visit lumberyard
Cast bricks of clay, plaster, cement
Lay out and construct model roads, bridges, canals, airports
Build walls of many materials
Visit museum

FIFTH GRADE

Health and Safety

Build traffic signs for bicycle safety programs
Repair bicycles
Make home plates, bases, bat stands
Make first aid kits and shoe shine boxes
Build snowball target

Language Arts

Give reports on work
Make pigeonhole mailbox
Use school office duplicating machine
Construct scenery and props for dramatics
Make book rests and book ends
Use recording machines
Read about industries and industrial processes

Mathematics

Make scale drawings of homes and classroom
Construct advanced abaci for decimals
Measure materials with a good degree of accuracy
Visit architect or engineer

Science

Construct devices to show erosion, cross section of earth
Wire bells
Design mock-ups of electrical devices

Figure 170. Fifth graders work on model to demonstrate lightning.

Build models of dams, reservoirs
Fly homemade model gliders
Build simple apparatus for levers, gears, inclined planes
Collect and mount specimens of rocks, soils
Graft plants
Experiment with strength of textile materials

Music and the Arts
Make quilting frame and patchwork quilt
Work with various media typical of our country's craftwork
Embroider samplers and make frames
Make good reproductions of boats, planes, cars
Make holiday gifts
Construct file for art work
Experiment with color mixing
Visit cabinetmaker
Make camping equipment
Fire and glaze clay work
Mend clothing

Social Studies
Make contour maps of U.S. and neighboring countries
Mass-produce objects
Make models of oil fields, coal mines, lumber camps
Display various types of wood and pictorialize their uses
Make relief maps of rivers and products of the U.S.
Visit print shop
Collect and test building materials
Construct models to show conservation of land
Make models of early American homes and furnishings
Collect and draw pictures of clothing styles
Make flags and holders
Assemble diorama of frontier life
Collect and compare textile samples
Test minerals for chemical make-up

SIXTH GRADE

Health and Safety
Conduct bicycle safety programs
Approach electricity from safety aspect

Construct batting tees
Draw plan of activity areas on playground
Construct first aid kit
Identify substances by taste and smell

Language Arts
Compile school newspaper
Construct magazine racks and book carts
Make scenery and props
Make pigeonhole mailbox
File materials in homemade files
Design and make scrapbook covers
Operate movie projector
Read about industries and industrial processes

Mathematics
Prepare bill of materials for construction
Plan dream houses
Construct balance scale and weigh materials
Make liquid, dry, and square measure devices
Read scale drawings and plans
Make circular and linear fraction boards
Construct decimal divider

Science
Make weather vane, anemometer, and rain gauge
Construct crystal radio sets
Visit telegraph office
Dig raw clay
Make periscopes and wind tunnels
Develop photographic film
Model fossils in plaster
Make models of windmills, gristmills, and canal locks
Construct an observatory
Design machines to illustrate levers
Experiment with models of aircraft control surfaces (rudder, aileron, elevator)
Construct devices to show erosion
Make electromagnets and electrical quiz board
Make rocket ship models

Music and the Arts
Make gifts using various crafts of the world

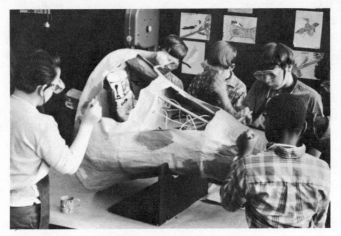

Figure 171. Sixth grade rocket ship model.

Embroider samplers
Construct service equipment for lower grades
Make tiles and mosaics
Experiment with glazes
Make camping equipment
Use linoleum blocks for printing programs for school plays
Print with silk screen and stencils

Social Studies
Make relief maps showing land formations
Assemble dioramas of rice fields, jungles, harbors
Reproduce significant inventions
Operate model of canal locks
Make hunting, fishing, trapping devices
Chart industries of states
Make commerce charts
Visit newspaper plant
Visit governmental offices

EMPHASES BY AREAS OF LEARNING

Choices among possible activities are governed by the goals and the curriculum of the entire elementary school. The following overview indicates some of the interrelationships between industrial arts and the more common areas of learning.

Health and Physical Education

One of the tasks of the modern elementary school is to deal with the health and safety needs of children from the very beginning of school, continuing to do so as students mature. The construction of traffic signs and related traffic films help pupils to fulfill some of these needs. A field trip, whether it be a walk or a ride, provides an excellent opportunity to concentrate on traffic safety. The playground, cafeteria, workshop, workbench, and gymnasium act as proving grounds for safety discussions and practices. Here, and later on at appropriate intervals, there are discussions, experiments, and construction activities pertaining to fire safety and electrical safety.

Handwork also provides the necessary practice and training in hand-eye co-ordination, and large- and small-muscle development essential to safe living. From time to time there is need for deviation from the academic routine. Working with the hands provides this relaxation and contributes to health objectives. For the older child, industrial arts provides many experiences that are carried over to the home in the form of avocational interests.

Children sometimes are encouraged to make scale drawings of the school and the playground. These drawings point out the particular safety considerations of these areas. Here, too, children participate in making their own safety rules, form committees to patrol areas and to supervise work areas, and participate in cleanup routines. Objects such as first aid kits, shoe shine boxes, and smock racks, are constructed to emphasize organization, neatness, and cleanliness.

Later, children begin to use equipment for individual physical activity and noncompetitive group games. They can construct most of such equipment: stilts, snowball targets, shuffleboard, jump ropes, and similar toys and games.

When the children begin to ride bicycles, there is the opportunity for lessons and re-emphasis on bicycle safety and maintenance. Children construct imitation traffic signs and take drivers' tests. Many films and other aids are available in this area.

In the upper grades of the elementary school, children need other types of play equipment: scoreboards, bases, equipment boxes, and kicking tees, to name a few. These again are child-constructed. Of greatest importance is the fact that all of these activities make health and safety instruction much more meaningful than they otherwise would be.

Language Arts

Communicating experiences for children begin with listening to stories, read and told, and participating in simple conversations with the teacher. The teacher helps to prepare children for reading experiences by making labels for articles in model stores and various other things constructed by the children. Later on, the children themselves make the labels.

As children are introduced to text and library books, they begin to realize that these are the sources of ideas for much of their construction work and for many other activity projects. Objects such as chart stands, book display stands, book marks, and book ends, are constructed by the children, and all of these, in turn, tend to aid and stimulate the reading program.

Many reading, creative writing, and public speaking experiences stem from the preparation and presentation of dramatic activities. As an aid to mastering this phase of the curriculum, children construct puppets, stages, scenery, and props.

Letters of inquiry and appreciation to people within or outside of the school are always effective in relating the language arts to other areas of learning. Throughout all of the activity work, there are countless opportunities for children to discuss and plan their work both in written and oral form.

Mathematics

Throughout the grades, many opportunities are provided for children to use numbers. Efforts in early grades are directed toward readying children for number work by seizing concrete opportunities to make numbers important. Working with wood and other materials helps children gain concepts of size. Lumber, for example, is "thin," "long," "in two pieces," "half of," "too big." Children find that two people need two saws, one for each, that nails have numerals and that higher numerals indicate larger nails. These simple, well-directed experiences prepare children for their later applications of these concepts.

Soon children perceive definite needs for measuring. A store, constructed for other arithmetical situations, must be a certain size to fit in the shopping corner. Then rulers become important and the reasons for mathematical computation become evident.

As number studies progress, subtraction and addition bring children to three-place numerals. The construction of an abacus helps clear up doubts in children's minds regarding the evolution of these higher numerals. If

Figure 172. Scale model buildings.

the abacus has eight blocks of wood, two more blocks must be made for the first row of ten blocks.

Not only is the level of abstraction reduced through the use of such arithmetical devices, but the actual construction processes also present valuable learning experiences.

As children work with numbers, fractions receive attention. Many opportunities arise here: measuring objects in terms of sixteenths of an inch, constructing fraction boards, measuring rooms, and making floor plans to scale. Almost simultaneously with the study of fractions, decimals are considered, and children find that figuring costs of materials for the things they make provides real problem-solving opportunities.

These and many other industrial arts activities grow out of the mathematics part of the curriculum with the result that both types of experience are enriched.

Science

Science is an area of learning that often ties in with industrial and practical arts. From the beginning exploratory stages, children explore devices to use with their magnets, pulleys, weather observations, and classroom pets. They discover that the tools they use frequently are a combination of levers and other simple machines. Children find that tools and materials help them produce flower boxes, collection mounts, weather vanes, and many other items. Since many materials are used for this exploration, children learn that different materials react to similar forces in different ways, that some materials are strong, heavy, or rustproof, and that these qualities help to determine their use.

Children become interested in their natural world, and such child-constructed items as sundials, planet boards, wind tunnels, and weather instruments become important. This leads into man's use of the natural laws as models of canal locks, water wheels, and devices to show the principles of flight, erosion, and air pressure are produced and used.

The child's activities progress in complexity with his growing experiences, and soon he begins to work with electrical apparatus, simple radio sets, and photographic equipment. Through learning-by-doing he becomes familiar with scientific methods of searching for answers and solving problems, and he begins to apply his findings to subsequent activities.

Music and the Arts

Through the arts, the elementary school child finds many and varied opportunities for creative activity. His early rhythm development is reinforced through the use of simple rhythm sticks and sandpaper blocks. Often, this is followed by the addition of percussion and string instruments. Here, child-made xylophones, drums, cigar-box guitars, and harps are appropriate. The presentation of musical programs is vitalized by scenery and props which the children design and construct in the classroom.

Figure 173. Teachers display samples of rhythm instruments constructed in an in-service course.

Figure 174. Examples of origami, the Japanese art of paper folding.

Children are encouraged to express themselves through construction as well as the more traditional art forms. As they progress, the teacher demonstrates better ways to use scissors and hammers, but he rarely dictates the child's end product. The alert teacher realizes that the *child's development* is the end product, and that the tools used and the boats constructed are merely means by which the child can be helped to grow.

Discussions centering around the arts and crafts of other lands become more meaningful when children actually engage in pottery, weaving, and woodworking. Similarly, during the gift-giving seasons, innumerable opportunities present themselves for original designs and creative thinking in terms of the construction of the gifts.

Social Studies

Many industrial and practical arts experiences in the elementary school revolve around and evolve from the social studies. When discussing the problems of shelter in their own country and abroad, children see why homes are constructed differently in various places throughout the world and why some building materials are used more extensively than others. The importance of the industries involved and some of their problems become apparent through such studies. Modes of transportation and communication are investigated, and the construction of models, maps, and panoramas becomes important.

The teacher helps children to compare their lives with those of the early settlers. Children learn through activity programs that though basic human needs have not changed, technological improvements have placed man in a better position to control his environment and provide for his needs.

Children discover that their way of living is influenced by the location of natural resources and by other geographical conditions of the regions in which they live. Such studies are made more meaningful by the construction of contour maps and panoramas of rice fields, wheat farms, or lumber mills. Children are encouraged to collect, mount, and display items of historical significance, clothing of other countries, and samples of minerals and other raw materials.

What one single feature of man's material existence today is more significant than the industries which man has fashioned? How could one describe the social order of his country without placing heavy emphasis on the part played by man's industrial and technological inventiveness? Some of the most awesome social forces in the world today are the result of industrial capacity. At every juncture, if children are to understand the industrial society and feel its exciting tempo, they must participate in industrial enterprises firsthand.

Through construction activities and observations, the child sees his life and his environment, as well as those of his ancestors and his neighbors, by intimate, firsthand contact. Better learning inevitably results.

Figure 175. Toy animals cut from felt and stuffed.

*Figure 176. Planning
a model house.*

DECIDING ON WHAT TO DO

Teachers know only too well that good programs for children's learning do not just happen. Although plans must remain flexible where young children are concerned, teachers can nevertheless plan ahead for most of the learning experiences that should occur. Certainly, the modern teacher does not give pupils detailed directions and expect them merely to be carried out. But he does think through many possibilities for each phase of the curriculum framework, and he pre-plans broadly for maximum educational efficiency.

To illustrate the kind of thinking which goes into this planning stage, the following example is offered for a third-grade study of neighborhood facilities.

What does the teacher hope to achieve? First, he wants his children to see the importance of the relationships that exist in all phases of life in the neighborhood. Second, the teacher wants to stress the dignity and social significance of all kinds of work. Third, since this is the start of the year, the teacher feels that it is important to acquaint his children with some of the necessary classroom routines regarding the location and use of materials which they will encounter throughout the year. Next, it is important for the children to know something about the location of their neighborhood, in relation to other neighborhoods. Finally, the teacher would like all these goals to develop smoothly into a coherent, integrated unit of study.

How does the teacher proceed in pursuing these goals? As a starting point he thinks about what *could* be done: *a*. A small group of children could construct a child-size store for use in the classroom; *b*. The class could visit a farm; *c*. A large map of the community might be constructed by a group; *d*. Each child could construct a truck or some other vehicle or implement characteristic of some occupation.

Each possibility is now given careful consideration: *a*. If a decision were made in favor of the classroom store, it would have to be constructed by a small group, since there would not be enough work to permit all children to participate simultaneously. If a small group did the work, the teacher would like the same children to participate each time work took place so that these children would gain a sense of following through to the completion of the entire project. Involving the same children would hasten the completion of the store, since time would not be lost bringing a new group up to date on the progress whenever a work period occurred. On the other hand, it would be difficult to convince the nonworking children that they should wait for this type of experience until another project was ready for construction. Also, there might be the disadvantage of having the store completed so early that the experiences with money, which should develop from the use of the store, would precede the necessary preparatory work with numbers.

b. How about the visit to the farm? Certainly the bus trip to the farm would be profitable since the class could talk about roads, the community helper—the bus driver—and the time factor involved in travel. The tour of the farm would provide good background knowledge of another occupation. Children would gain a better insight into how food is grown, and how it gets to the table. However, the entire unit, even with the preparation and evaluation, would be brief, taking only a few days. The teacher is interested in a smooth flowing approach to the curriculum, rather than a series of short choppy experiences. The teacher must also consider that because it is early in the year, the children have not really come to know one another, and this lack of experience in working together might not be conducive to leaving the classroom in a group at this time.

c. The large community map project would help to acquaint the children with other parts of their community and with the cardinal directions. This project, however, has little else to offer with regard to community helpers and other neighborhood facilities.

d. Finally, the teacher considers the construction of model trucks, and other vehicles and implements that are used by important community helpers. This approach has the advantage of including all the children, since the possibilities of projects are endless—trains, all kinds of trucks, buses, planes, boats, advertising circulars, nurses' kits, farm implements, telephones, television sets, etc. Since all of the children would be working from time to time, there would be opportunities to teach the skills and uses of certain basic tools and materials to the entire class at one time. This would establish routines and understandings early in the year. The work would carry over for a considerable period of time, creating desirable continuity. Individual interests would be more likely to be satisfied, since there would be fewer limitations on the choice of projects. With all of the construction completed, this unit could very well lead into the large community map previously considered, and the objects produced could be placed on the map and moved from place to place as a play feature. And last, all of the children would have something of which they could be proud, and which they could take home.

The teacher now looks over all the possibilities and, in this case, decides on the last alternative, as it seems to have so many advantages when compared with the others.

A decision has been made; how does the teacher present the idea to the children, and yet have them take a real part in the project? A good approach is to lead up to a discussion by centering reading experiences around some of these community helpers and tools of their trades. Having children bring in some of their toys that relate to this study is also helpful. Showing films on topics, such as airports and policemen, also will help prepare the class. Finally, the teacher presents the construction plan in a very general way, and then invites suggestions for things to make.

It is unwise for the teacher to come to this teacher-pupil planning session with detailed plans in mind. Many choices should be made by the children. There is no reason why some children could not work on the community map and relate this to the construction of the other objects. Some might even construct models of public buildings or stores for the community. The teacher uses this teacher-pupil planning session to help children learn democratic processes and also to stimulate constructive thinking. Soon the children feel that they are taking a real part in this project, and often good ideas the teacher had not considered come out of the discussions.

Figure 177. Constructing models for a transportation unit.

The work begins (Figure 177). Since the teacher can foresee that each child will have to use the try square, saw, hammer, file, sandpaper, and paints, he plans to give demonstrations to the entire class, a little at a time, and progressively as the needs arise. Most children will need advice on methods of attaching wheels to vehicles, for example.

As the work progresses in a series of work periods, the teacher and children sit down periodically to evaluate the progress and attempt to solve some of the problems that have arisen. Time is set aside to discuss the things that have been learned and to plan subsequent steps.

Bringing the unit to a conclusion (culminating the experience) is a vital part of the total experience. Time is provided for the whole group to go back over some of the problems and evaluate the methods of solution. The teacher brings out the important things learned and helps children to tie together all of their experiences in the unit. Finally, the facts which became known stimulate conclusions and generalizations under the teacher's careful guidance.

One good way to complete this unit would be to invite other classes to see the work and hear oral reports pertaining to the unit. Another way would be to display the entire project in the library and to display along with the project children's written reports about all phases of the unit. Many other summing-up methods are possible, varying in character with the nature of the particular situation.

The industrial arts experiences are but a small part of this total unit on community facilities. There have been other concomitant learning experiences which have made their contributions to the total unit. But the part played in the learning process by the industrial arts activities has been substantial. The whole unit has been made more meaningful, more enjoyable, and more productive because of the kinds of activities that were used. Careful planning has made the important difference.

FIELD TRIPS

Field trips are so widely used in the modern school as a part of the activity program that it seems appropriate to discuss them briefly. The use of the field trip is in close alignment with the concept of reducing the level of abstraction. Through such experiences children gain deeper insights into all areas of learning. It is one thing to talk about erosion and another actually to see rain-ravaged sections of terrain. It is one thing to talk about newspapers, and it is quite another to visit a newspaper plant with the distinctive smells of ink and paper, the unique sounds of the roaring presses, and the busy bustling about of newspapermen and printers.

Why and when should a teacher decide to take his class on a field trip? One of the unique purposes of a field trip is to stimulate child interest in certain phases of classroom study. Many times this method of extending child interests is most effective if it is used prior to the introduction of a new unit of classroom study. The occurrence of the excursion at this time

Figure 178. Skin shed from a living snake.

helps to provide children with the necessary background information for meaningful subsequent learnings.

Again, a trip can add reality to classroom experiences during a unit of study. A trip provides opportunities for children to verify some of the conclusions that have been drawn. At the same time, many of the questions arising in the course of classroom work are cleared up through the gathering of additional information. Here the children experience a new and completely different method of assimilating facts.

The field trip also helps to break down the barrier that sometimes exists between life in school and life outside the school. Children are helped to realize that learning does not cease as they leave the school building. The teacher, of course, helps here, but the trip itself stimulates further outside learning quite apart from school and teacher. Closely allied to this aim is the hope that the school field trip will encourage family field trips.

Frequently, the field trip is used as the culminating activity for a unit of study. In this case, the teacher familiarizes the children with many of the ramifications of the topic that will be discussed. The class then sets out on the trip with definite ideas in mind regarding their points of observation or things to look for. In actuality, this again is a method for verification of facts, but now it acts to clarify any misconceptions that might possibly have developed in the classroom.

The fact that the trip is a proving ground for classroom citizenship education cannot be overlooked. During the course of the trip, the children more readily see the need for cooperation, leadership, good manners, and respect for other people's property. The teacher takes advantage of this opportunity to emphasize these needs.

Because of the informality of this type of learning, the trip offers rare opportunities for the teacher to see his children in a different environment. Many times latent talents and interests blossom, and the teacher returns to the classroom with new insights into child needs and clues to how they can be met.

How does the teacher go about planning and arranging the field trip? After he considers his goals, the teacher must investigate some of the possibilities for field trips related to the study at hand. If the request for a trip must go through administrative channels, the person in charge of audio-visual aids may be able to answer some of these questions: a. Will a certain company permit a class visit? b. Will there be a guide available? c. Will the school system honor the request? d. Are there other recommended trips related to this topic?

In schools where an industrial arts consultant is available, he has this information and will assist in preparing and conducting trips.

Figure 179. Field trips add reality
to classroom experiences.

When the teacher has a number of alternative trips in mind, he discusses them with the children and together they decide on a final destination. It is advisable for the teacher to pre-visit any given destination to determine its educative value. This also will aid the teacher in preparing the children for the trip. In the event that other classes have taken the trip, consultation with teachers who have made the trip previously may make the pre-visit less vital.

The requisition of a bus through the main office is quite often a procedure that must be followed, and there may be office forms which will help the teacher do this. To insure a completely successful trip, the teacher should also look into school policy with reference to: parental permission, liability, use of parents as chaperons, and provision for expenses.

In advance of the trip, the teacher conducts discussions pertaining to types of clothing to be worn by the children; attire for a farm visit would be quite different from the appropriate dress for a museum. Youngsters should also be aware of opportunities to take notes, if that seems appropriate to the teacher, or to use cameras.

En route to the place of observation, children find enjoyment and learning in noting the sights and also in discussing the anticipated observations. At the destination a maximum of learning takes place if the group pursues its goals with efficiency. If time permits, unanticipated sidelights can be discussed and noted, adding to the enjoyment of the trip. On the return trip, the group discusses the excursion freely and exchanges reactions, ideas, and notes.

The trip takes on greater import when the teacher plans for a thorough follow-up. Providing time for reports on the trip encourages children to evaluate the trip. Writing letters of appreciation and sharing the experiences of the trip with other classes are invaluable for children. Reading and displaying material from the trip provide rich experiences, too. These, and other summing-up techniques, will help to bring the unit to a climax and will insure that maximum educational gain results.

CONSTRUCTION PROJECTS

The construction of various objects constitutes a large part of the industrial arts program of the modern elementary school. Since the selection of these objects to be constructed is determined by the units of study and the needs of a given classroom, it is normal to find great variety in the work undertaken. Most of the work, however, falls into the following broad categories: packing-crate construction, gifts, toys, equipment, illustrative devices, and props for dramatizing activities.

On the following pages are shown a number of things found to be highly successful. Although the ideas presented may meet specific needs, they should also provide suggestions for other projects. The last section of this chapter lists books that contain additional construction-project ideas.

Packing-Crate Construction

Many objects can be constructed by using various types of packing-crates as the basic material. Crates that are constructed flimsily or are made of extremely hard wood are not satisfactory for use with children. The best crates to use are made of soft, straight-grained, reasonably thick wood.

NOTE: As a safety measure, all bent nails, staples, wire, and other hazardous materials should be removed from the crates before work begins.

BANK WINDOW

Two 1" x 2" strips are used for the vertical pieces of the bank window (Figure 180). These strips should be sawed to a length equal to the height of an average child plus 6 inches. One of the strips cut to that length should be nailed on the right side of the crate; the other strip should be nailed on the left side of the crate. The nails should be driven into the thicker parts of the crate, not just into the thin side pieces. Cardboard or soft wallboard is used for the lower panel and tacked to the 1" x 2" strips. The same procedure is followed for the upper panel and for the supporting middle panel, leaving an opening large enough for convenient vision. The entire assembly is laid down with the front panel on the floor. Then, the two narrow strips are glued in place for the window bars. The bank window can be painted.

DRESSING TABLE

After the crates for the dressing table (Figure 181) are spaced at the appropriate distance, the wallboard is cut to fit and nailed in place on top of the crates. A number of narrow boards nailed next to one another would serve the same purpose. Now the entire unit is placed on the floor with the open side of the crates down. A strip, 1" x 2", is nailed to the lower back edges of the crates to give the table rigidity.

The crate partitions serve as shelves, and these openings can be covered with cloth for a draw curtain. A small standing mirror adds the finishing touch after painting.

STORE I

The store (Figure 182), which also could be used as a post office or carnival booth, is really a combination of the bank window and the dressing table previously described. Here the crates may be turned in or out, de-

Figure 180. Bank window.

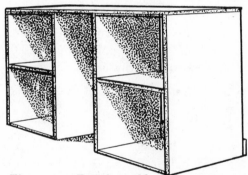

Figure 181. Dressing table.

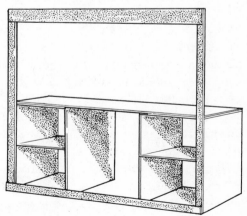

Figure 182. Store.

pending on whether or not this will be a self-service store. The height of the vertical 1″ x 2″ strips depends on the height of the children, and the spacing of the crates depends on the room space available. A third crate may be used in the center for additional shelving area.

STORE II

After the four rear crates for the store (Figure 183) are placed open-side down on the floor, 1″ x 2″ strips are nailed horizontally across the top and bottom of the crates, joining them together. Now the 1″ x 2″ vertical strips are nailed on the two outside boxes so that they extend high enough to be above a child's head. Two other single crates are placed open side up on the floor and vertical 1″ x 2″ strips are nailed to them for the front corner posts. All of the crates are placed in their upright positions and horizontal 1″ x 2″ strips are nailed to them to join the front crates to the rear ones. The front lift-up counter top can be made from a piece of wood, 1″ x 12″, or a piece of wallboard. If a piece of wood is used, the hinges are fastened with wood screws. If wallboard is used, the hinges are fastened with wood screws on the crate side and stove bolts on the wallboard side. Before tacking the large piece of mural paper for the roof, sagging is eliminated by nailing horizontal strips around all corner posts as supports for the mural paper. The entire unit is sanded and painted for a finished appearance.

CHAIR

Crates with center partitions are most desirable for chairs (Figures 184 and 185), but smaller crates without partitions may also be used. If center-partition crates are used, lines are drawn (for sawing) across the sides at a desirable height for the arms. If the chair is to be armless, the lines are drawn at a point even with the top of the center partition. Note that both ends of the crate are left on for this operation; this gives better support for the sawing operation. After the sides are sawed through, the crate end is removed for the top of the chair. For the armchair, horizonal 1″ x 2″ strips are nailed at the top of the arms and back rest. The armless chair requires only a 1″ x 2″ strip at the top of the back rest. In both cases, as indicated in the illustration, two 1″ x 2″ vertical braces are nailed to the back of the crate to give additional support.

If crates that do not have center partitions are used, the same procedure is followed, but after one end is removed, it is nailed back at a desirable sitting height. In all cases, the 1″ x 2″ strips are nailed on the outside of the crates

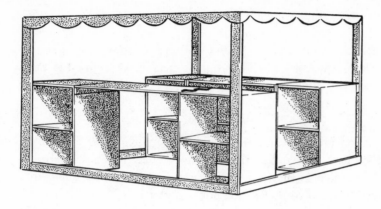

Figure 183. Store.

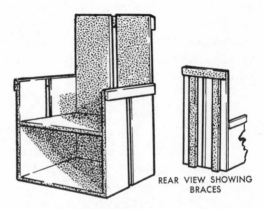

REAR VIEW SHOWING
BRACES

Figure 185. Packing-crate chairs.

Figure 184. Chair.

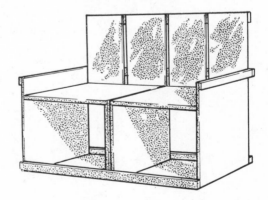

Figure 186. Double seat.

with the nails piercing the thin crate wood first and then the thicker 1″ x 2″ strips.

The chair can be upholstered by placing cotton batting, or a number of layers of soft cloth, where desired. Then upholsterers' tacks are used to tack a suitable material over the padding.

DOUBLE SEAT

The construction procedure for the double seat (Figure 186) is similar to that for the chairs. After the arms are sawed and the ends removed, 1″ x 2″ strips are nailed to the top of each arm on the outside. Then, the crates are placed on the floor, open side down, and a 1″ x 2″ strip is nailed at the bottom of the back to join the crates together. A horizontal 1″ x 2″ strip is nailed to the ends of the strips on the arms. This will brace the back rest. The crates are turned over with the back resting on the floor and a 1″ x 2″ strip is nailed to the bottom of the front. (A piece of wallboard can be nailed across the entire lower front section to serve the same purpose and also enclose this section.) Next, the 1″ x 2″ strip is nailed at the top of the back rest.

After the seat is sanded and painted, it can be upholstered as previously described for the chairs.

TABLE

The top for the table in Figure 187 can be made from one piece of plywood, firm wallboard, or two pieces of narrower wood. The size of the top is determined by the space available in the room and the purpose for which it is intended. If a one-piece top is to be used, the material is centered on top of the crate and nailed from the top. If two narrow pieces are used, they are joined together with corrugated fasteners and then 1″ x 2″ strips (cleats) are nailed at the ends for additional strength. Now the top is centered on the crate and nailed. The surface and edges are sanded and painted.

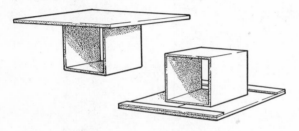

Figure 187. Table.

SHELVING UNIT

The crates are assembled into an attractive unit (Figures 188 and 189), and then nailed together wherever the thick pieces of wood adjoin. If the unit does not seem to be sturdy, 1″ x 2″ strips are nailed to the thick pieces in the back. The entire unit is sanded and painted.

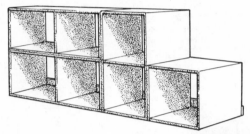

Figure 188. Shelving unit.

Figure 189. Painting a shelving unit.

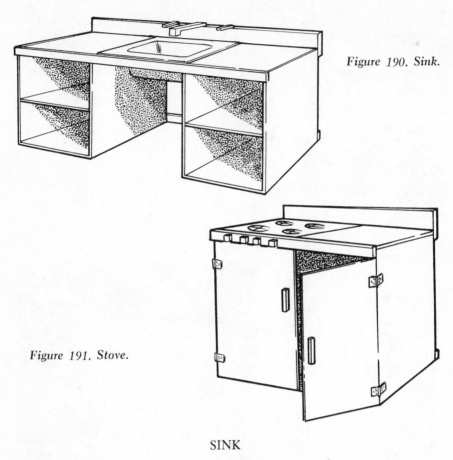

Figure 190. Sink.

Figure 191. Stove.

SINK

The metal or plastic pan that forms the basin for the sink (Figure 190) can be purchased in most hardware and department stores. The pan should not be wider than the top of the crates to be used. The crates are stood on end and the pan is set in position so that the side lips of the pan rest on top of the crate tops. Now a strip of wood 1″ x 2″ is cut to a length equal to that of the entire unit and nailed in place across the top of the front of the crates. Another strip of 1″ x 2″ is cut to the same length, and nailed to the back of the crates at the bottom. A strip of wood, 1″ x 4″, is nailed to the top back of the crates to serve as a splash board. Now odd pieces of scrap wood are nailed to the top of the splash board for faucets. Only one nail is used in each faucet so that it can pivot.

The sink is sanded and painted. The top of the sink can be covered with oilcloth to protect it from the water. The front of the unit can be curtained or covered with wallboard.

STOVE

The crates for the stove in Figure 191 are placed open side down on the floor and a 1" x 2" strip is nailed to the back at the bottom of the crates. Then a 1" x 4" piece is nailed to the back at the top of the crates to serve as a splash board. The unit is turned over and a 1" x 2" strip is nailed to the front at the top of the crates. The doors are cut from pieces of plywood or firm wallboard and fastened with hinges and stove bolts. Pieces of scrap wood are glued or nailed in place for the burner controls, and the burners are painted on top of the stove. The entire unit is sanded and painted.

Gifts

Most school programs include gift-making and gift-giving experiences. Children quickly realize that a gift takes on greater significance when it is one to which thought and effort have been given. Furthermore, gift construction lends itself to the introduction of new ideas and media.

Teachers are fully aware of the benefits derived from activities that provide creative opportunities. Gift-making programs provide unlimited avenues for the use of original ideas and designs which lead to habits of attacking larger problems methodically and purposefully.

Children have great interest in gift-making as an opportunity for individual expression. They work on objects that have particular interest to them. Teacher guidance certainly is still a legitimate part of the whole experience.

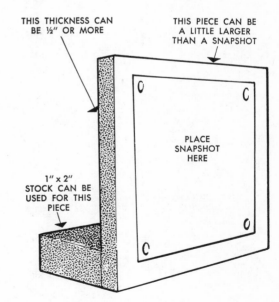

Figure 192. Snapshot holder.

The ideas presented on the following pages (Figures 192 to 206) are offered as starting points for gift-making activities. They have been found to hold a great deal of interest for children, and in many cases, have come directly from them. In addition, the ideas are quite simple and the objects can be constructed with little difficulty by most elementary school children. The teacher's knowledge of child development will help to guide children in selecting and designing objects that are appropriate to the level of their maturity.

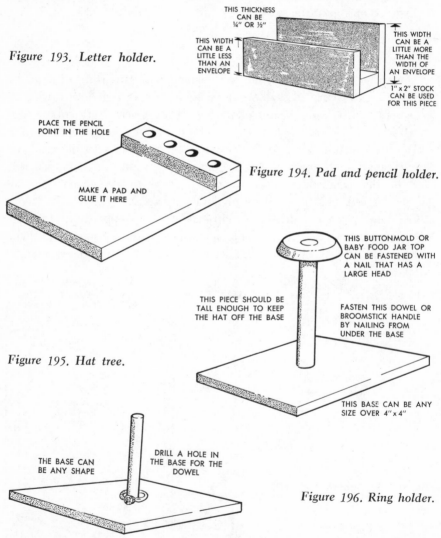

THIS THICKNESS CAN BE ¼" OR ½"

THIS WIDTH CAN BE A LITTLE LESS THAN AN ENVELOPE

THIS WIDTH CAN BE A LITTLE MORE THAN THE WIDTH OF AN ENVELOPE

1" x 2" STOCK CAN BE USED FOR THIS PIECE

Figure 193. Letter holder.

PLACE THE PENCIL POINT IN THE HOLE

MAKE A PAD AND GLUE IT HERE

Figure 194. Pad and pencil holder.

THIS BUTTONMOLD OR BABY FOOD JAR TOP CAN BE FASTENED WITH A NAIL THAT HAS A LARGE HEAD

THIS PIECE SHOULD BE TALL ENOUGH TO KEEP THE HAT OFF THE BASE

FASTEN THIS DOWEL OR BROOMSTICK HANDLE BY NAILING FROM UNDER THE BASE

Figure 195. Hat tree.

THIS BASE CAN BE ANY SIZE OVER 4" x 4"

THE BASE CAN BE ANY SHAPE

DRILL A HOLE IN THE BASE FOR THE DOWEL

Figure 196. Ring holder.

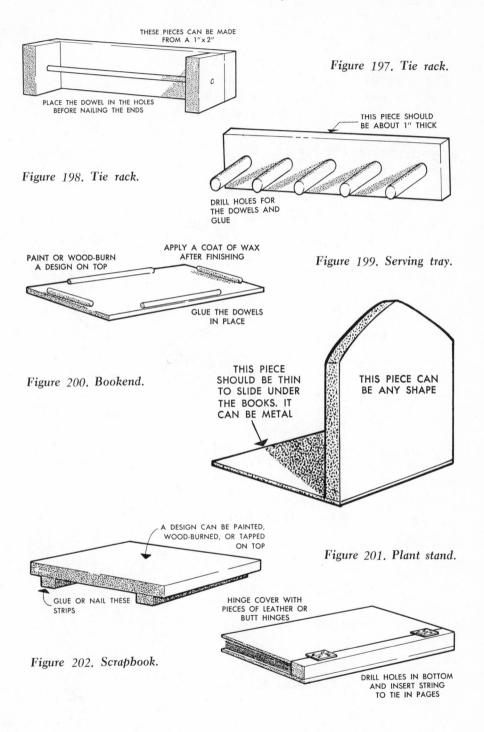

THESE PIECES CAN BE MADE
FROM A 1" x 2"

PLACE THE DOWEL IN THE HOLES
BEFORE NAILING THE ENDS

Figure 197. Tie rack.

THIS PIECE SHOULD
BE ABOUT 1" THICK

Figure 198. Tie rack.

DRILL HOLES FOR
THE DOWELS AND
GLUE

PAINT OR WOOD-BURN
A DESIGN ON TOP

APPLY A COAT OF WAX
AFTER FINISHING

Figure 199. Serving tray.

GLUE THE DOWELS
IN PLACE

Figure 200. Bookend.

THIS PIECE
SHOULD BE THIN
TO SLIDE UNDER
THE BOOKS. IT
CAN BE METAL

THIS PIECE CAN
BE ANY SHAPE

A DESIGN CAN BE PAINTED,
WOOD-BURNED, OR TAPPED
ON TOP

Figure 201. Plant stand.

GLUE OR NAIL THESE
STRIPS

HINGE COVER WITH
PIECES OF LEATHER OR
BUTT HINGES

Figure 202. Scrapbook.

DRILL HOLES IN BOTTOM
AND INSERT STRING
TO TIE IN PAGES

Toys

Toy construction is a popular activity for children in all grades. Children enjoy using the toys, and teachers find that this activity helps supply the ever-present need for additional classroom equipment. Many times toy-making is used in upper grade programs to provide gifts for younger brothers

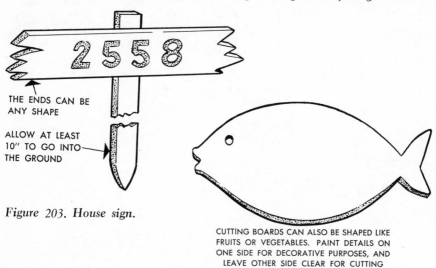

THE ENDS CAN BE ANY SHAPE

ALLOW AT LEAST 10" TO GO INTO THE GROUND

Figure 203. House sign.

CUTTING BOARDS CAN ALSO BE SHAPED LIKE FRUITS OR VEGETABLES. PAINT DETAILS ON ONE SIDE FOR DECORATIVE PURPOSES, AND LEAVE OTHER SIDE CLEAR FOR CUTTING

Figure 204. Cutting board.

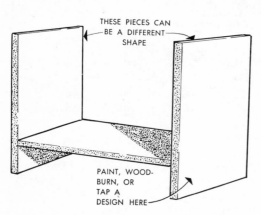

THESE PIECES CAN BE A DIFFERENT SHAPE

PAINT, WOOD-BURN, OR TAP A DESIGN HERE

Figure 205. Book rack.

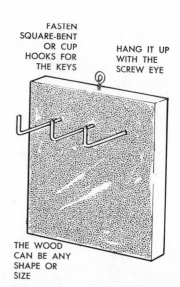

FASTEN SQUARE-BENT OR CUP HOOKS FOR THE KEYS

HANG IT UP WITH THE SCREW EYE

THE WOOD CAN BE ANY SHAPE OR SIZE

Figure 206. Key holder.

and sisters, or as a service to charitable organizations. The construction of many toys of similar design can be the center of an assembly line experience for upper grades that study our country's industries (Figure 207).

Children construct toys on all grade levels, but as they mature, teachers provide the guidance which helps to improve the construction quality and the design. The kindergarten pupil, very happy with his three-piece airplane, adds a propeller and a rudder in the first grade, and soon he is concerned about wheels and cockpits. This moving from the symbolic stage to the representational stage is a process which teachers should encourage.

Wood glue is desirable for many of the small toy parts. Nails often split the thin wood required in making many of these toys.

The ideas presented on the following pages (Figures 208–215) are a cross section of the many toys that can be made by children. Few dimensions are given since the drawings are not meant to be restrictive. The toys can be constructed on any scale, and ideas from one toy can be applied to others. The toys shown with wheels can be constructed without wheels in lower grades. It has been found that young children have the same enthusiastic response to playing with toys—with wheels or not.

Figure 207. Results of an assembly line experience.

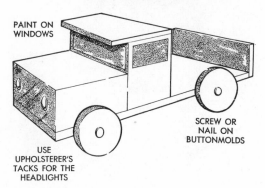

PAINT ON
WINDOWS

SCREW OR
NAIL ON
BUTTONMOLDS

USE
UPHOLSTERER'S
TACKS FOR THE
HEADLIGHTS

Figure 208. Truck.

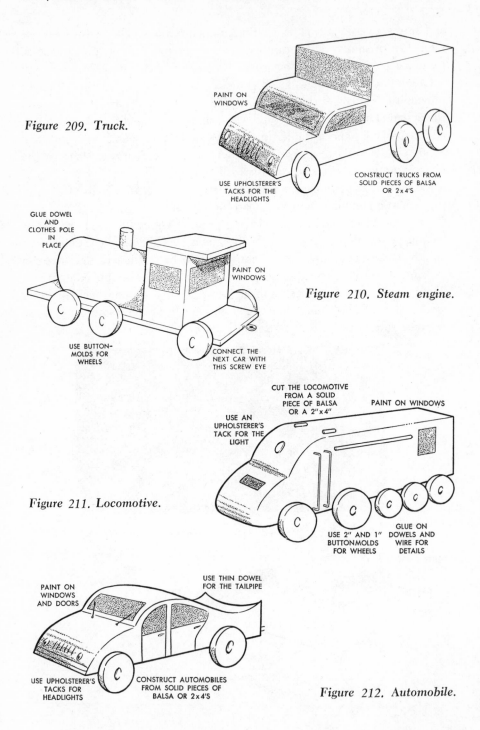

PAINT ON WINDOWS

Figure 209. Truck.

USE UPHOLSTERER'S TACKS FOR THE HEADLIGHTS

CONSTRUCT TRUCKS FROM SOLID PIECES OF BALSA OR 2 x 4'S

GLUE DOWEL AND CLOTHES POLE IN PLACE

PAINT ON WINDOWS

Figure 210. Steam engine.

USE BUTTON-MOLDS FOR WHEELS

CONNECT THE NEXT CAR WITH THIS SCREW EYE

CUT THE LOCOMOTIVE FROM A SOLID PIECE OF BALSA OR A 2" x 4"

PAINT ON WINDOWS

USE AN UPHOLSTERER'S TACK FOR THE LIGHT

Figure 211. Locomotive.

USE 2" AND 1" BUTTONMOLDS FOR WHEELS

GLUE ON DOWELS AND WIRE FOR DETAILS

PAINT ON WINDOWS AND DOORS

USE THIN DOWEL FOR THE TAILPIPE

USE UPHOLSTERER'S TACKS FOR HEADLIGHTS

CONSTRUCT AUTOMOBILES FROM SOLID PIECES OF BALSA OR 2 x 4'S

Figure 212. Automobile.

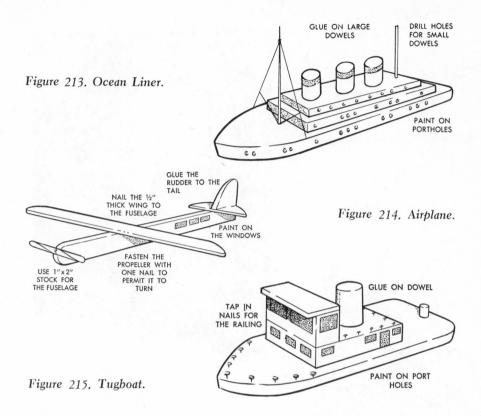

Figure 213. Ocean Liner.

GLUE ON LARGE DOWELS

DRILL HOLES FOR SMALL DOWELS

PAINT ON PORTHOLES

GLUE THE RUDDER TO THE TAIL

NAIL THE ½" THICK WING TO THE FUSELAGE

Figure 214. Airplane.

PAINT ON THE WINDOWS

USE 1" x 2" STOCK FOR THE FUSELAGE

FASTEN THE PROPELLER WITH ONE NAIL TO PERMIT IT TO TURN

GLUE ON DOWEL

TAP IN NAILS FOR THE RAILING

Figure 215. Tugboat.

PAINT ON PORT HOLES

Equipment

Some of the objects which can be constructed are pieces of equipment that aid the program in general. Sometimes equipment of this sort is not commercially available and sometimes the available commercial equipment does not meet specific needs. Furthermore, considerable learning results from the experience of constructing some of these items.

The objects shown on the following pages can be constructed by teachers in in-service industrial arts courses conducted by industrial arts consultants and teacher educators, and much of this equipment also can be made by the children.

The dimensions of the articles should vary depending on the height of the children, and the purposes for which the pieces are intended. When there is doubt, it is best to follow the dimensions given. The reading and interpreting of sketches and plans of this type result in many valuable learning experiences for children.

Figure 216. Smock rack.

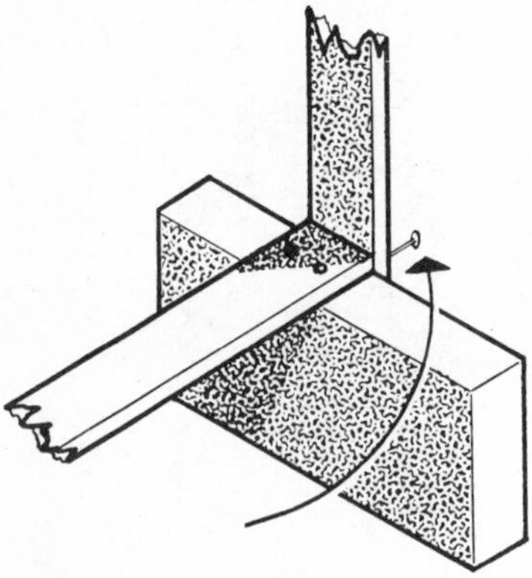

Figure 217. Nailing 6 or 8-penny nails into lower section of smock rack.

SMOCK RACK

The smock rack shown in Figure 216 is one that teachers find helpful in the development of neat living habits. It can be constructed easily and can be made to fit any corner of the classroom. If the rack is placed against a wall, the hooks are placed on one side; if it is placed away from the wall, hooks can be placed on both sides.

After the vertical 1″ x 2″ strips are sawed to a desirable height for the children, they are nailed to the thick pieces that serve as feet for the rack. These feet are approximately 2″ x 6″ x 8″. The length of the rack is determined by the number of children in the class, allowing about 2 or 3 inches between the hooks for the smocks. After sawing a 1″ x 2″ strip to this length, the strip is nailed on top of the vertical pieces so that the thick feet are on the inside of the vertical strips. Now the distance under the horizontal strip is measured from the inside of one vertical strip to the inside of the other vertical strip. A piece of 1″ x 2″ is sawed to this length and nailed on top of the thick stands, joining the lower part of the rack.

Now a fairly long nail, a 6 or 8 penny, is driven through the vertical strips into the ends of the lower horizontal strip as illustrated in Figure 217. The wood is then sandpapered and painted and the square-bent screw hooks are put in place.

CHART STAND

The chart stand (Figure 218) often is used for reading-experience charts in the lower grades, but it can also be used for a bulletin board or painting easel.

The over-all dimensions are determined by taking into account the size of the paper to be used and the height of the children. Then, all of the 1″ x 2″ strips are cut and placed on the floor in their proper positions. Now all pieces are fastened together with two corrugated fasteners at each joint (Figure 219). A piece of soft wallboard is nailed to each section. The sections are stood up, back to back, and hinges fastened at the top to join them. In the lower grades, pieces of leather can be used, rather than hinges.

Figure 218. Chart stand.

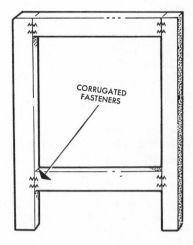

Figure 219. Fastening chart stand frame with corrugated fasteners.

CORRUGATED FASTENERS

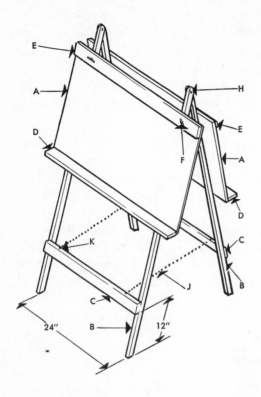

Figure 220. Easel.

Now the lower parts are spread, and a piece of safety chain or heavy cord fastened to each side so that the stand does not spread apart.

EASEL

This multi-purpose easel (Figure 220) can be constructed by teachers in in-service courses, or by children as part of the regular program. It can be folded easily for convenient storage.

Materials Needed

Plywood panels, ¼" x 24" x 32" (two)
Legs, ¾" x 1" x 60" (four)
Braces, ¾" x 2½" x 24" (two)
Trays, ¾" x 2½" x 32" (two)
Holding bars, ¾" x 2½" x 32" (two)
Carriage bolts, washers, wing nuts, ¼" x 1½" (four carriage bolts and wing nuts, four washers)

Wood screws, F.H. steel (1½", No. 10) eighteen
Wood screws, R.H. blue (1½", No. 14) two
Wood screws, F.H. steel (1", No. 8) twelve
Safety chain, 24" long (two)
Screw eyes, small, to fit ends of chain (four)

Assembly Procedure

1. Fasten trays D to panels A using five 1½", No. 10 screws for each.
2. Fasten holding bars E to panels A using two bolts and wing nuts on each bar with one washer on each bolt.
3. Fasten panels A to legs B with three 1", No. 8 screws for each leg. Adjust the position of the panels to suit the grade level.
4. Fasten braces C to legs B using two 1½", No. 10 screws at each joint.
5. Fasten the back leg assembly to the front leg assembly with the two R.H. screws. Screws should be left loose enough to permit folding the easel.
6. Fasten chains J with the screw eyes.

BOOK TRUCK

Although the book truck (Figure 221) might appear to be a difficult object to construct, closer inspection will reveal its simplicity. The truck is an

Figure 221. Book truck.

Figure 222. Dado joint.

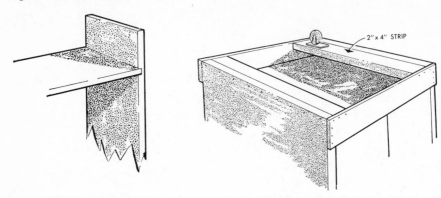

Figure 223. Fastening casters on inverted book truck.

invaluable aid for sharing sets of books between classrooms as well as for housing a set of encyclopedias for one classroom.

Lumber measuring 1″ x 12″ is most suitable. The other dimensions are determined by the books for which the truck is used.

The lumber is cut to size and the shelves are fastened in position. Dado joints can be used for the shelves, together with glue and screws (Figure 222). Lower grade children can fasten the shelves with shelf supports as shown in Figure 221.

Now the lower panels are fastened in place with nails or screws to give additional strength and improved appearance.

The book truck is inverted, and strips 1″ x 2″, or preferably, pieces of 2″ x 4″ are nailed in place so that they extend from one lower panel to the other, as illustrated. The 1″ x 2″ strips or pieces of 2″ x 4″ will be firm if nails are driven into them from the lower part of the sides and panels. Now plate-type casters are fastened to the 1″ x 2″ strips, or better, to pieces of 2″ x 4″ at all four corners (Figure 223).

SCISSORS HOLDER

The scissors holder (Figure 224) is made from a one-pound coffee can. The cover should be taped on securely with cellulose or masking tape. Now a beverage can opener is used to cut a series of "V" cuts around the edge of the can. The can labels are painted for an attractive finish.

When using the can opener to make the "V" cuts, be sure to raise the

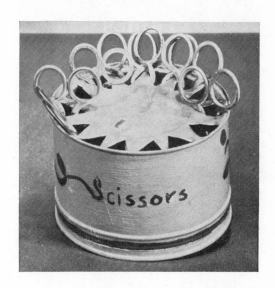

Figure 224. Scissors holder.

handle far enough to press the cut metal against the can so that inquisitive fingers will not be cut by the extremely sharp point of the "V."

PORTABLE TOOL PANEL

This tool panel (Figure 225) is excellent where tools are shared by a number of classrooms, where portability is desirable for sweeping, or to provide for other classroom activities.

Materials Needed

Plywood, good both sides, ¾" x 24" x 32"
Pine, ¾" x 11" x 33½"
Pine, ¾" x 5½" x 11" (two) top corners rounded with 2½" radius
Pine, ¾" x 2½" x 33½" (two)
Pine, 2" x 4", 12½" long (two)
Casters (four, plate-type)

Assembly Procedure

1. Attach braces C to the plywood panel A with glue and F.H. steel wood screws (1¼", No. 6).
2. Attach the floor B to braces C and panel A with F.H. steel wood screws (1½", No. 8).
3. Attach floor B to plates E with F.H. steel wood screws (1¾", No. 10).

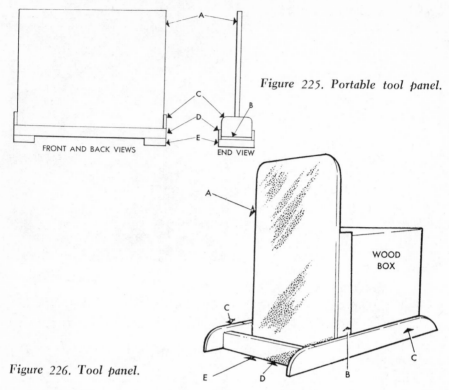

Figure 225. Portable tool panel.

Figure 226. Tool panel.

4. Attach box sides D to braces C and floor B with F.H. steel wood screws (1½", No. 8).
5. Attach the casters.

The tools are hung on screw hooks or blocks of wood that are fastened to both sides of the panel. A 2" x 4" block can be nailed in place as shown in Figure 42, page 79, for holding such tools as screw drivers and scratch awls.

TOOL PANEL

This stationary tool panel (Figure 226) is simple to construct and inexpensive.

Materials Needed

Plywood, ½" (or ¾") x 24" x 48"
Uprights, pine, 1" x 2" x 24" (two)
Braces, pine, 1" x 6" x 24" (two)
Floor, pine, 1" x 4" x 24" (one)
Tray front, pine, 1" x 4" x 24" (one)

Assembly Procedure

1. Nail uprights B to panel A with 8-penny box nails.

Figure 227. Portable tool rack.

2. Nail floor *D* to panel *A* with 6-penny nails.
3. Nail braces *C* to the edge of panel *A* and uprights *B* with 4-penny nails and to floor *D* with 6-penny nails.
4. Nail the tray front *E* to braces *C* and the edge of tray *D* with 6-penny nails.

The tools are hung on screw hooks or blocks of wood that are fastened to the front of the panel. A box for wood can be placed in the rear if desired.

PORTABLE TOOL RACK

Tools are hung on both sides of this portable tool rack (Figure 227), and supplies are placed on the center shelves.

Materials Needed

Plywood, ¾″ x 15″ x 28″ (two)
Pine, 2″ x 2″ x 17½″ (two), crosscut the ends to 80°
Pine, 1″ x 2″ x 16¾″ (two), crosscut the ends to 80°
Plywood, ¾″ x 15″ x 17″ (one), bevel the ends 80°
Pine, 1″ x 2″ x 9¾″ (two), crosscut the ends to 80°
Plywood, ¾″ x 10″ x 15″ (one), bevel the edges 80°
Plate casters

Assembly Procedure

1. Attach the caster blocks *B* to shelf *D* with 6-penny nails.
2. Attach sides *C* to shelf *D* with wood glue.
3. Attach sides *E* to shelf *F* with 4-penny nails.

4. Attach shelf D to panels A wth F.H. steel wood screws (1¾″, No. 6).
5. Attach shelf F to panels A with F.H. steel wood screws (1¾″, No. 6).
6. Fasten casters G to caster blocks B.

ROOM DIVIDER

On all grade levels, room dividers of this type are useful for library corners, work areas, playhouses, and the like (Figure 228).

The wallboard is cut to the desired size and framed with 1″ x 2″ strips. The 1″ x 2″ strips are joined with corrugated fasteners and the wallboard nailed to the frame. Staves measuring 1″ x 6″ x 8″ are attached to the bottom by nailing them to the edges of the 1″ x 2″ strips and reinforcing the joint with metal corner braces or homemade plywood triangles.

Figure 228. Room divider.

Figure 229. In-out box.

IN-OUT BOX

The in-out box (Figure 229) is convenient for collecting, storing, and distributing such items as assignments, workbooks, and paper.

The dimensions of the box are determined by the papers or books for which the box is intended. All the pieces are made with ½" wood, except the bottom of each box, which is made of wallboard. After sawing out the radius for each box front, the boxes are assembled. Then the boxes are joined with ½" x 2" strips, and sanded, painted, or shellacked.

BIRDHOUSE

Birdhouses are excellent for use in connection with nature studies. They are made with many different materials and in various shapes.

The birdhouse in Figure 230 is made with ¾" wood, a large can with the ends removed, and a dowel. Two wooden disks are cut to fit the ends of the can, and a hole is bored in one of the disks for the entrance. Then a smaller hole is drilled for the perch below the entrance. Both disks are fastened in place by driving tacks through the metal. The roof is nailed on by driving box nails through the roof, through the metal, and into the wooden disks. The perch is fitted in place and a screw eye fastened in the roof for hanging. Holes punched in the bottom of the house will act as a drain.

BIRD FEEDER

The sides and back of the bird feeder in Figure 231 are fastened to the floor with box nails. Then the uprights are nailed to the sides at each corner.

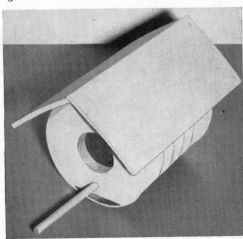

Figure 230. Birdhouse.

Figure 231. Bird feeder.

Figure 232. Storage-display panel.

After the roof is nailed to the uprights, small holes are drilled in the center of the roof and floor to receive the wire for hanging. The bird feeder is then sanded and painted with exterior paint.

STORAGE-DISPLAY PANEL

Panels of this type are used for displays, bulletin boards, and many other purposes (Figure 232). This particular panel is used to store rhythm instruments on one side, and the other side is used for a book display.

The pegboard is cut to size and framed with 1″ x 2″ strips. The pieces of the frame are joined with corrugated fasteners and the wallboard attached to the frame with small box nails. The tops of the panels are hinged together with pieces of leather, or butt hinges. The panels are spread apart at the base and joined with pieces of chain or table leg brackets.

The display panel in the photograph is made with perforated hardboard (pegboard). The instruments are hung on stove bolts, which are fastened to the hardboard with nuts, two washers and two nuts for each bolt. This is a sturdier hanger than some commercial ones that tend to pull away when items are removed.

PAINT CARRIER

Empty one-half pint or pint-size milk cartons, obtained from the school lunch program, make ideal containers for small quantities of water paint (Figure 233). This paint carrier holds a group of the cartons so that a number of colors are readily available. The carrier may also be used for crayons and similar materials that are moved about in a classroom.

The number of empty milk cartons to be used is decided on, and they are assembled in the proper position. Now the dimensions of the carrier are determined from the group of milk cartons. Strips measuring 1″ x 2″ are

Figure 233. Paint carried.

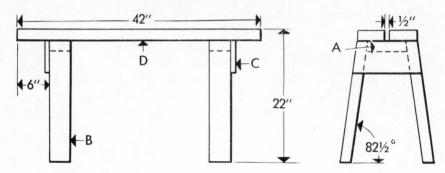

Figure 234. Sawhorse-type workbench.

used for the handles and nailed on the appropriate sides. After the box frame has been assembled, the bottom is nailed to the frame.

SAWHORSE TYPE WORKBENCH

When floor space is at a premium, a small bench of this type will serve very well (Figure 234). C-clamps can be used as holding devices for sawing and for other operations.

Materials Needed

Cleats, 2" x 4" x 8⅝" (two), ends beveled 82½°
Legs, 2" x 4" x 20⅞" (four), ends beveled 82½°
Braces, 1" x 6" x 12¾" (two), ends crosscut 82½°
Tops, 2" x 6" x 42" (two)

Assembly Procedure

1. Attach cleats A to tops D with F.H. steel wood screws (2¾", No. 14).
2. Attach legs B to the ends of cleats A with F.H. steel wood screws (2¾", No. 14).
3. Attach braces C to legs B with F.H. steel wood screws (1¾", No. 12).

WORKBENCH

A workbench like the one in Figure 235 can be constructed from fairly inexpensive materials. It is sturdy and heavy enough to hold two woodworkers' vises.

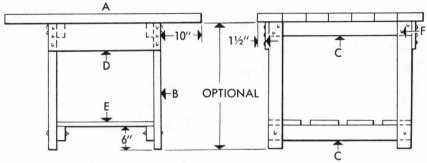

Figure 235. Workbench.

Materials Needed

Top, 2″ x 6″ x 48″ (seven)
Legs, 2″ x 4″ x optional length (four)
Rails, 2″ x 4″ x 35½″ (four)
Apron, 1″ x 8″ x 27¼″ (two)
Shelf, 1″ x 8″ x 24″ (four)
Carriage bolts, ⅜″ x 3½″ with washers (twelve)
Wood screws, F.H. steel, 1¾″, No. 10 (thirty-six)
Wood screws, F.H. steel, 3″, No. 14 (twenty-eight)

Assembly Procedure

1. Fasten rails C to legs B with one carriage bolt in each bottom corner and two in each top corner.
2. Fasten shelf pieces E to lower rails C with F.H. steel wood screws (1¾″, No. 10). Use three screws at each end of each shelf piece.
3. Fasten top boards A to the top rails with F.H. steel wood screws (3″, No. 14). Countersink two screws in each end of each board.
4. Fasten apron boards D to legs B with F.H. steel wood screws (1¾″, No. 10). Use three screws in the ends of each board.
5. Attach the vises.

ANIMAL CAGE

The dimensions of this guinea pig or rabbit cage are determined by the animal's living habits and the room space available (Figure 236).

After the 1″ x 2″ strips are sawed to the desired lengths, the front and back of the cage are assembled and fastened with corrugated fasteners. The completed front and back sections are joined by nailing 1″ x 2″ strips be-

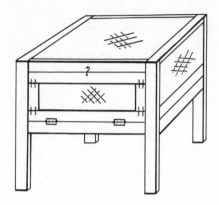

Figure 236. Animal cage.

tween them with 6-penny box nails. Strips measuring 1" x 2" are used for the door frame and fastened to one another with corrugated fasteners. The door is then hinged to one side of the cage and a hook and eye are installed on the other side. The cage is inverted and a panel of exterior plywood with 1" x 2" notches cut out of the corners is nailed to the bottom of the cage for a floor. Double-pointed tacks are used to fasten screening, hardware cloth, or poultry wire to the sides, top, and door of the cage.

Smaller cages can be constructed by removing one or two sides from a packing crate. A door can be hinged on one side and screening, hardware cloth, or poultry wire fastened to the other side.

RHYTHM INSTRUMENTS

The construction of rhythm instruments (Figures 237 and 238) enhances rhythmic development and music appreciation. The instruments shown are constructed with materials that are readily available.

Broom sticks, chair rungs, or wooden dowels are easily converted into rhythm sticks. Sandpaper blocks are constructed by tacking coarse sandpaper on pieces of scrap wood, and then smaller pieces of scrap wood are glued or nailed to the blocks for handles. A rattle is constructed by nailing a thin strip of wood to the cover of a small cardboard box. Then a few pebbles are placed in the box bottom. The box is assembled and taped closed. A large nail suspended on a string will produce a chimelike sound when tapped with another nail. Discarded drum skins, chamois, pieces of

Figure 237. Rhythm instruments.

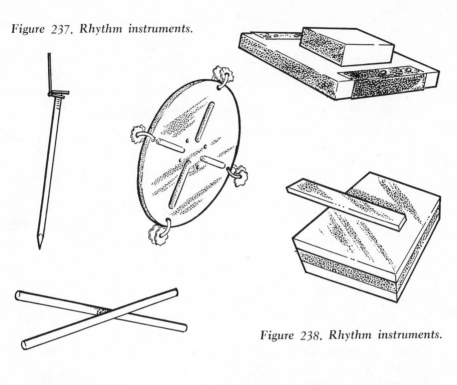

Figure 238. Rhythm instruments.

DRUM

Figure 239. Fourth grader and his drum.

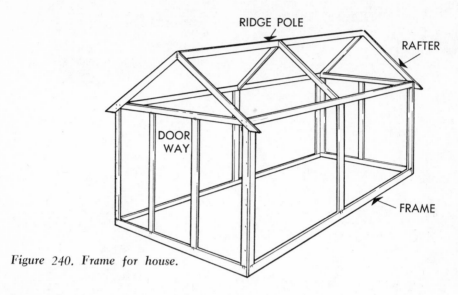

Figure 240. Frame for house.

inner tube rubber, or shellacked fabrics make ideal drum heads when nailed on nail kegs or round cheese crates. A paper plate or a circular piece of wallboard is suitable for the base of a tambourine. The rattles, which are wired to the tambourine, are constructed by flattening bottle caps and removing the cork pieces.

These are but a few ideas for rhythm instruments. Teachers can encourage children to design and create many others.

PLAYHOUSE

A classroom playhouse (Figure 240) can be the center of number and reading experiences as well as a training ground for wholesome living habits. The dimensions of the playhouse are determined by individual needs and available room space. There should be many windows to assure good air circulation in the house. It is sometimes best to omit the roof to be sure of adequate ventilation. However, if a roof is desirable, the modern flat type is easiest for children to construct. In all cases, it is best if the walls are prefabricated, and then fastened together.

If a peaked-roof house is to be constructed, the following procedure is suggested:

First, the frame for the front and the frame for the back walls of the house are assembled, using 1″ x 2″ strips and corrugated fasteners. The end roof rafters are nailed to the 1″ x 2″ strips that form the front and back wall frames. Next, the side wall frames are assembled in the same manner. Then short box nails are used to fasten heavy cardboard or wallboard to all the frames, and the windows and doorways are cut out. All the sides are then placed upright and fastened together with 6-penny box nails. A 1" x 2" strip is used for the ridge pole; this is nailed, front and back, to the peak of the roof. One or two additional roof rafters are put in place, and then wallboard is fastened on top of the rafters for the roof. It is best to leave the doorway and windows open for good air circulation and proper teacher supervision.

The entire house is painted with water-soluble latex-base paints.

Illustrative Devices

All objects constructed in an elementary industrial arts program are, in a sense, illustrative devices, since they all help to present practical illustrations for various areas of learning. The objects discussed here, however, differ somewhat because they are constructed as teaching aids for specific subject areas. The teacher makes use of these devices in lessons that involve skills and concepts that are difficult for children to acquire through merely verbal instruction.

The devices shown on the following pages are some that have been used often. They came about as the result of extensive experimentation by teachers and children. Certainly, there are many other possibilities. Teachers sometimes construct these devices in in-service courses, and children often construct them as a part of their normal classroom work.

Figure 241. Teacher in in-service course puts finishing touches on clock mock-up.

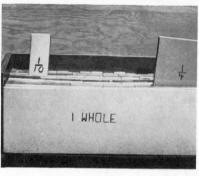

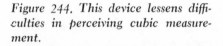

Figure 242. Square inches, feet and yards become more meaningful through such devices.

Figure 243. Observation and handling of the various pieces help children understand and compare fractions.

Figure 244. This device lessens difficulties in perceiving cubic measurement.

Figure 245. Children compare weights of many substances with balance scale.

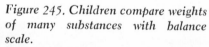

TRAFFIC LIGHT

A traffic light (Figure 250) aids in the development of safety practices. Colored cellophane is taped behind the openings, and bulbs, batteries, and switches are used to light the device. Or, the lights can be merely painted on the surface of the wood.

WEATHER INSTRUMENTS

Weather vanes and anemometers help in forecasting the weather (Figure 251).

Sheet aluminum or wallboard is used for the pointer and fin of the weather vane and nailed to the crosspiece. Halves of rubber balls or formed aluminum disks are used for the anemometer cups and nailed to the crosspieces. The anemometer crosspieces are nailed to a 1" x 6" x 6" block which turns around on a dowel.

Figure 246. Children measure themselves with the aid of yard-sticks nailed to the vertical board.

Figure 247. Since both materials adhere, well, either flannel or felt may be used on the surface of the board.

Figure 248. Counters help to ease the transition from one-place to two-place numerals.

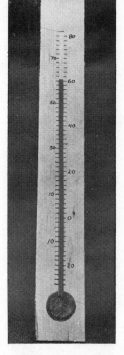

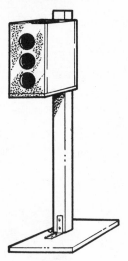

Figure 249. Traffic light.

Figure 250. Tape ends are sewed together in the back to permit children to regulate thermometer reading.

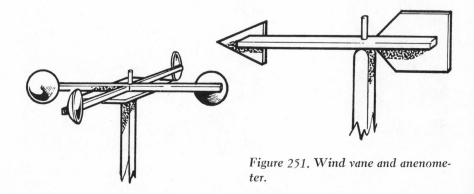

Figure 251. Wind vane and anenometer.

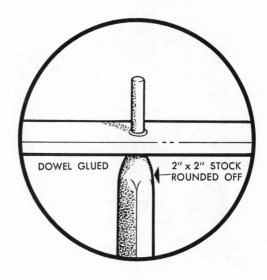

DOWEL GLUED

2" x 2" STOCK
ROUNDED OFF

*Figure 252. Dowel glued in
rounded-off 2" x 2" upright.*

The instruments will turn freely if a ¼" hole is drilled in the end of the
2" x 2" upright. Then the end of the 2" x 2" is rounded off as shown in the
illustration, and a ¼" dowel is glued in the hole (Figure 252). A ⁵⁄₁₆"
hole is drilled in the crosspiece and block, and the whole unit is placed
over the dowel. The hole in the weather vane crosspiece is drilled at the
balancing point.

Both instruments are supported by 2" x 2" strips of wood nailed to packing crates. Cement blocks or other weights can be placed in the crates for
sturdiness.

PANORAMAS AND DIORAMAS

A panorama (Figure 253) is usually constructed on a piece of wallboard
or directly on a table. The reproduced objects are placed on the wallboard
or table so that they become the center of interest. Panoramas may be set
up to show transportation methods, Indian villages, waterfront activities,
and similar scenes.

The diorama (Figure 254) differs from the panorama in that the background of the scene is as important as the objects in the foreground. To

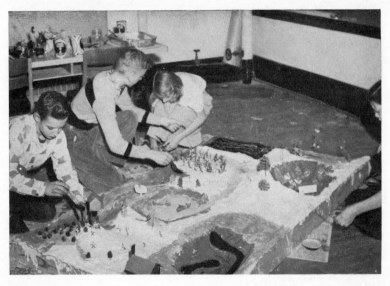

Figure 253. Sixth graders working on panorama related to study of soil conservation.

accomplish this, the scene must have a back and sides. A cardboard box, with the top and one side removed, serves very well for this type of project. Other times, depending on the size of the project, the setting is constructed from pieces of wallboard and wood. A city skyline and road intersection, or a tree-lined horizon and lumber camp might be subjects for dioramas.

RELIEF MAPS

The construction of various types of relief maps helps to enrich studies in land formations, topography, elevations, and natural resources. The base for the maps is usually a soft wallboard which will absorb some of the plastic mixture used and produce better adhesion. The outline is drawn on the wallboard either by projecting an actual map with the use of an opaque projector, or by drawing it freehand. The plastic mixture is then applied on the board and modeled to desirable shapes and elevations.

Many materials can be used for this purpose. Some that have been used are plaster, sawdust and glue, Portland cement and powdered asbestos, oil clay, flour and salt, and papier-mâché. The materials may be used independently but often desirable results are obtained when one material is mixed with another. Water is added to those materials which require it until a claylike consistency is reached. Experimentation with many mixtures will prove helpful in discovering the best material for a given need.

After the modeling is completed and the mixture has dried, other features are added by gluing on labels or signs, weeds for vegetation, samples of products, and paint. Keys are also added for further identification.

MODELS

The construction of models (Figures 255 and 256) is often a part of various classroom learning experiences. Most models of this type are larger in scale than those used for panoramas. More detail is possible in this type of construction and possibilities for subjects are unlimited. Some models that have been constructed are ships of early days, buildings, castles, machines, and landmarks.

Figure 254. Dioramas of life in Southwest desert and Northwest rain forest.

Figure 255. Sixth grader and medieval castle.

Figure 256. Model of Mexican cart.

Balsa wood and wallboard are excellent materials for model making although there are others. Whenever possible windows and doors are painted on models, and other more pronounced details can be made three dimensionally and glued on the exterior of the models.

COLLECTIONS

Some collections, such as Indian arrowheads, Mexican jewelry, and miniature flags, may consist of pupil-made reproductions. Other collections include actual specimens like coins, butterflies, wood samples, stamps, rocks, and soils (Figure 257). In any case, the collections are enhanced when mounts or display frames are constructed.

The nature of the mounts will depend on the size of the display. Butterflies, for example, can be attractively displayed on cotton in a thin box bottom. A window can be cut from the box top and celluloid fastened on the inside of the window cutout. The box top is placed over the bottom, taped together and painted.

Other collections which have considerable weight, such as rocks, are displayed in wood-constructed frames with celluloid tacked on top. Most specimens will adhere well to the backing if cellulose cement is used.

Props for Dramatizing Activities

The dramatization of stories, reports, compositions, and other pupil efforts is always an effective stimulant for all areas of learning. Whether the presentation is a one-child impromptu affair or a large-cast production, the stage and settings should receive attention. In the elementary school, the end result is usually more effective when the properties are simple.

a. Stage flats are constructed with 1″ x 2″ strips and are fastened with triangles of wallboard at the joints, as illustrated (Figure 258).

Any number of sections are joined together with butt hinges. If loose-pin hinges are used, the sections can be taken apart for storage. The flats are covered with mural paper on which the scenes are painted.

b. All types of buildings are constructed in much the same manner as the flats. Buildings usually consist of only two sides, situated on the stage so that only that much of a building is in view. The edge of the roof can be painted in perspective on the upper edge of the flat or a triangular frame can be constructed for some peaked roofs. Doorways can be left completely open and situated on the stage so that this is not too obvious. If a movable door is essential, the frame is constructed to fit the doorway, covered with

Figure 257. Collection of rocks, shell-fish and butterflies.

Figure 258. Stage flat frame; joints are strengthened with wallboard triangles.

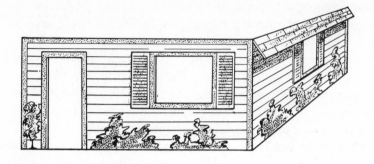

Figure 259. Special effects painted on stage scenery.

Figure 260. Child-made stage flats.

mural paper, and fastened to the doorway with butt hinges. Windows are merely cut out of the mural paper. Shutters, shrubs, house frame, and other details are painted on the mural paper (Figure 259).

c. Vehicles are painted on small flats or pieces of wallboard. Through a system of braces, the units can be strapped to a custodian's dolly or to an express wagon and pulled across the stage.

d. Foliage of all types is painted on stiff cardboard or wallboard and tacked to braces and stands. Sometimes cardboard boxes will suffice as stands, with stove bolts, nuts, and washers used to fasten the wallboard to the boxes.

e. Other props, such as utensils, tools, containers, and objects which are carried by the actors, are either actual representations or facsimilies constructed with wood, paper, and cardboard. The outlines can be cut out and the details illustrated with paint.

f. Shadow frames are constructed with 1" x 2" strips and fastened at the joints with triangles of wallboard as described for the stage flats. Right triangles measuring 24″ x 24″ are cut from plywood for the stands and fastened to the lower parts of the vertical strips with butt hinges. Now an old bed sheet or a piece of muslin is tacked on the frame. An opaque projector or some other light source, in the rear, will produce well-defined shadows.

g. The dimensions of puppet stages are determined in part by the number of characters needed on stage at one time. Some small hand-puppet stages are constructed with cardboard boxes, and others are assembled with wood and wallboard, as illustrated (Figure 261).

The scenery for this stage is tacked on the strips that extend beyond the sides in the rear. This type of stage is placed on a table for presentations. This same construction can be used for string-puppet stages by increasing the distance from the top of the stage opening to the top of the front and side panels.

Larger puppet stages (Figure 262) are constructed in a manner similar to that used for stage flats with 1″ x 2″ strips and hinged wings. The dimensions are determined by the height of the children and also by the number of performers on stage at once. The joints can be fastened with corrugated fasteners before the wallboard or unbleached muslin is nailed to the frames.

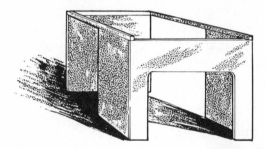

Figure 261. Small hand-puppet stage placed on table.

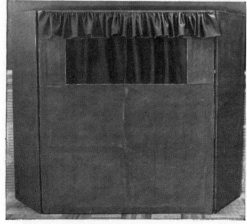

Figure 262. Hand-puppet stage.

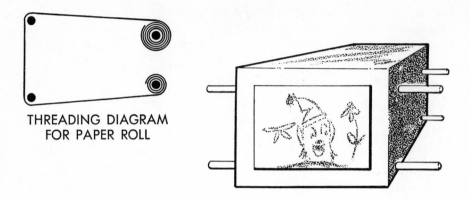

THREADING DIAGRAM
FOR PAPER ROLL

Figure 263. Roller movie box with threading diagram.

h. To show sequential learning experiences or stories, a continuous roll of mural or craft paper frequently is effective (Figure 263). The illustrations can be drawn directly on the paper roll or on individual sheets of paper taped to the roll. The roller movie box can be made with a large cardboard box. The "stage" opening is cut from the bottom of the box, and holes are pierced in the sides of the box for the soft wooden dowels. Two dowels are placed toward the back of the sides for winding and two dowels forward to keep the paper roll tight for easy viewing. The paper roll is fastened to the dowels with thumbtacks or tape.

SELECTED REFERENCES

BOOKS FOR CHILDREN

The references listed here describe *things to make and do.* Those listed at the end of Chapter 4 describe processes. References which do both are listed in both places. The numerals in parentheses following each reference indicate the grade levels for which each book is appropriate as specified in *The Children's Catalog,* 11th ed., 1966, published by H. W. Wilson Company, New York. These grade-level recommendations are included with the permission of the H. W. Wilson Company.

Drama Activities

Berk, Barbara, *The First Book of Stage Costume and Make Up* (New York: F. Watts, 1954), 45 pp. (4–8).

Bufano, Remo, *Remo Bufano's Book of Puppetry* (New York: Macmillan Co., 1950), 232 pp. (5–8).

Jagendorf, Moritz A., *The First Book of Puppets* (New York: F. Watts, 1952), 66 pp. (4–6).

Parish, Peggy, *Let's Be Indians* (New York: Harper & Row Publishers, 1962), 96 pp. (2–5).

Pels, Gertrude J., *Easy Puppets* (New York: T. Y. Crowell, 1951, 104 pp. (3–6).

Science Activities

Adler, Irving, *Machines* (New York: John Day Co., Inc., 1964), 47 pp. (4–6).

Bendick, Jeanne, *The First Book of Space Travel* (New York: F. Watts, 1963), 93 pp. (4–7).

Bergoust, Erik, *Birth of a Rocket* (New York: G. P. Putnam & Sons, 1961), 48 pp. (5–7).

Buehr, Walter, *The First Book of Machines* (New York: F. Watts, 1962), 53 pp. (4–6).

Cooke, David C., *How Helicopters Are Made* (New York: Dodd, Mead Co., 1961), 64 pp. (4–6).

Corbett, Scott, *What Makes a Car Go* (Boston: Little, Brown and Co., 1963), 43 pp. (3–6).

———, *What Makes TV Work?* (Boston: Little, Brown and Co., 1965), 46 pp. (4–7).

David, Eugene, *Television and How It Works* (Englewood, N.J.: Prentice-Hall, Inc., 1962), 72 pp. (3–5).

Epstein, Sam, *All About Engines and Power* (New York: Random House, Inc., 1962) 144 pp. (5–7).

Gould, Jack, *All About Radio and Television* (New York: Random House, Inc., 1958), 144 pp. (5–7).

Hoke, John, *The First Book of Photography* (New York: F. Watts, 1954), 69 pp. (5–8).

Meyer, Jerome S., *Picture Book of Radio and Television and How They Work* (New York: Lothrop, Lee & Shepard Co., Inc., 1951), 40 pp. (5–7).

Pine, Tillie S., *Simple Machines and How We Use Them* (New York: McGraw-Hill, Inc., 1965), 48 pp. (2–4).

Roberson, Paul, *Engines* (New York: John Day Co., Inc., 1965), 48 pp. (4–6).

Schneider, Herman, *Everyday Weather and How It Works* (New York: McGraw-Hill, Inc., 1951), 189 pp. (5–8).

———, *More Power To You* (W. R. Scott, 1953), 128 pp. (5–7).

———, and Nina, *Science Fun With Milk Cartons* (New York: McGraw-Hill, Inc., 1953), 159 pp. (5–8).

———, *Your Telephone and How It Works* (New York: McGraw-Hill, Inc., 1965), 117 pp. (5–7).

Spilhaus, Athelstan Frederick, *Weathercraft* (New York: Viking Press, Inc., 1951), 64 pp. (6–9).

Zim, Herbert S., *Things Around the House* (New York: Wm. Morrow and Co., Inc., 1954), 32 pp. (1–4).

————, *What's Inside of Engines?* (New York: Wm. Morrow and Co., Inc., 1953), 32 pp. (3–6).

Toy Activities

Downer, Marion, *Kites: How to Make and Fly Them* (New York: Lothrop, Lee & Shepard Co., Inc., 1959), 64 pp. (4–7).

Gilmore, H. H., *Model Boats for Beginners* (New York: Harper & Row Publishers, 1959), 97 pp. (4–7).

————, *Model Rockets for Beginners* (New York: Harper & Row Publishers, 1961), 117 pp. (4–7).

————, *Model Submarines for Beginners* (New York: Harper & Row Publishers, 1962), 122 pp. (4–7).

Neal, Harry Edward, *Story of the Kite* (New York: Vanguard Press, Inc., 1954), 61 pp. (4–8).

Waltner, Willard, *Hobbycraft Toys and Games* (Lantern Press, 1965), 138 pp. (4–7).

Wood Activities

Beim, Jerrold, *Tim and the Tool Chest* (New York: Wm. Morrow and Co., Inc., 1951), (1–3).

Cracker, Constance Homer, *Creative Carpentry* (Boston: Houghton Mifflin Co., 1951), 39 pp. (4–8).

Zarchy, Roger Lewis, *Woodworking* (New York: Alfred A. Knopf, Inc., 1952), 44 pp. (4–6).

Other Activities or a Variety of Activities

Adler, Irving, *Tools in Your Life* (New York: John Day Co., Inc., 1956), 128 pp. (5–7).

Barr, Donald, *The How and Why Wonder Book of Building* (New York: Grosset & Dunlap, Inc., Publishers, 1964), 48 pp. (4–7).

Carlson, Bernice Wells, *Make It and Use It* (Nashville: Abingdon Press, 1958), 160 pp. (3–6).

————, *Make It Yourself* (Nashville: Abingdon Press, 1950), 160 pp. (3–6).

Chapman, Jane, *Girl's Book of Sewing* (Greenberg, 1952), 88 pp. (4–9).

Cooke, David C., *How Superhighways Are Made* (New York: Dodd, Mead & Co., 1958), 64 pp. (4–7).

Dean, Elizabeth, *Printing: Tool of Freedom* (Englewood Cliffs, N.J.: Prentice-Hall, Inc., 1964), 64 pp. (4–6).

Hirsch, S. Carl, *This is Automation* (New York: Viking Press, Inc., 1964), 128 pp. (5–7).

Hunt, W. Ben, *Golden Book of Indian Crafts and Lore* (New York: Simon and Schuster, Inc., 1954), 112 pp. (4–6).

Kettelkamp, Larry, *Drum, Rattles and Bells* (New York: Wm. Morrow and Co., Inc., 1960), 47 pp. (4–6).

——, *Flutes, Whistles and Reeds* (New York: Wm. Morrow and Co., Inc., 1962), 48 pp. (4–6).

——, *Horns* (New York: Wm. Morrow and Co., Inc., 1964), 48 pp. (4–7).

——, *Singing Strings* (New York: Wm. Morrow and Co., Inc., 1958), 48 pp. (4–6).

Lee, Tina, *Things to Do* (Garden City, N.Y.: Doubleday & Co., Inc., 1965), 64 pp. (3–5).

Leeming, Joseph, *Fun With Wire* (Philadelphia: J. B. Lippincott Co., 1956), 96 pp. (5–7).

Mandell, Muriel, *Make Your Own Musical Instruments* (New York: Sterling Co., Inc., 1957), 126 pp. (4–7).

Russell, Solveig Paulson, *Wonderful Stuff, The Story of Clay* (Chicago: Rand McNally & Co., 1963), 64 pp. (3–5).

Weiss, Harvey, *Sticks, Spools and Feathers* (New York: Scott, W. R., 1962), 64 pp. (5–7).

Zarchy, Harry, *Leathercraft* (New York: Alfred A. Knopf, Inc., 1953), 44 pp. 5–9).

——, *Weaving* (New York: Alfred A. Knopf, Inc., 1953), 44 pp. (5–9).

BOOKS FOR TEACHERS

Game, Model, and Toy Activities

Champion, Paul V., *Games You Can Make and Play* (Milwaukee: Bruce Publishing Co., 1950), 128 pp.

La Berge, A. J., *Boats, Airplanes, and Kites* (Peoria, Ill.: Chas. A. Bennett, 1950), 135 pp.

Lawson, Arthur, *Homemade Toys for Fun and Profit* (New York: David McKay, 1953), 178 pp.

Yates, Raymond F., *How To Improve Your Model Railroad* (New York: Harper & Row Publishers, 1953), 98 pp.

Zarchy, Harry, *Model Railroading* (New York: Alfred A. Knopf, Inc., 1955), 172 pp.

Textile Activities

Alexander, Marthann, *Weaving Handcraft* (Peoria, Ill.: Chas. A. Bennett, 1950), 290 pp.

Buehr, Walter, *Cloth From Fiber to Fabric* (New York: Wm. Morrow and Co., Inc., 1965), 96 pp.

Gallinger, Osma (Palmer) Couch, *Joy of Hand Weaving* (Scranton, Pa.: International Textbook, 1950), 306 pp.

Joy, Edith, *Child's Book of Knitting* (Greenberg, 1952), 92 pp.

Picken, Mary (Brooks), *Singer Sewing Book* (New York: McGraw-Hill, Inc. rev. 1953), 244 pp.

Science Activities

Bendick, Jeanne, *Electronics for Young People* (New York: McGraw-Hill, Inc., 1960), 190 pp.

Mann, Martin, *How Things Work* (New York: T. Y. Crowell, 1960), 146 pp.

Meyer, Jerome S., *World Book of Great Inventions* (Cleveland: World Publishing Co., 1956), 270 pp.

Nagle, Avery, *Fun With Naturecraft* (Philadelphia: J. B. Lippincott, Co., 1964), 80 pp.

Smith, Joseph Albert, *Fun-Time Radio Building* (Chicago: Children's Press, Inc., 1961), 63 pp.

Other Activities or a Variety of Activities

Araki, Chiyo, *Origami in the Classroom* (Rutland, Vt.: Chas. E. Tuttle, 1965), 40 pp.

Association for Childhood Education International, *Children Can Make It*, 1954.

Bank-Jensen, Thea, *Play With Paper* (New York: Macmillan Co., 1962), 48 pp.

Brown, Mamie E., *Elementary Handcrafts for Elementary Schools* (Exposition Press, 1956), Chapters 2–8.

Champion, Paul V., *Creative Crate Craft* (Milwaukee: Bruce Publishing Co., 1951), 110 pp.

Cook, Sherman R., *Tin Things We Like To Make* (Milwaukee: Bruce Publishing Co., 1952), 105 pp.

Cooke, David C., *How Books Are Made* (New York: Dodd, Mead & Co., 1963), 63 pp.

Cummings, Richard, *101 Hand Puppets* (New York: David McKay, 1962), 147 pp.

Dow, Emily R., *Crafts for Fun & Fairs* (New York: M. Barrows, 1964), 271 pp.

Gilbert, Harold, *Children Study American Industry* (Dubuque, Iowa: W. C. Brown Co., 1966), 211 pp.

Granit, Inga, *Cardboard Crafting* (New York: Sterling Publishing Co., Inc., 1965), 96 pp.

Houtzig, Esther, *Let's Make Presents* (New York: T. Y. Crowell, 1962), 191 pp.

Hunt, W. Ben, *The Golden Book of Crafts and Hobbies* (New York: Golden Press, 1957), 111 pp.

Johnson, Pauline, *Creating With Paper* (Seattle: University of Washington Press, 1958), 207 pp.

Lincoln, Martha, *The Workshop Book for Parents and Children* (Boston: Houghton Mifflin Co., 1955).

McCall's Book of Paper, Wood and Paint Crafts (New York: Golden Press, 1965), 48 pp.

Moore, Frank C., Carl H. Hamburger, and Anna-Laura Kingzett, *Handcrafts for Elementary Schools* (Boston: D. C. Heath and Co., 1953), Chapters 5–12.

Nagle, Avery, *Kitchen Table Fun* (Philadelphia: J. B. Lippincott Co., 1961), 95 pp.

Newkirk, Louis V., and La Vada Zutter, *Crafts for Everyone* (Princeton, N.J.: D. Van Nostrand Co., Inc., 1950), 210 pp.

Ota, Koshi, *Printing for Fun* (New York: Astor-Honor, 1960), 53 pp.

Sarasas, Claude, *The ABC's of Origami; Paper Folding for Children* (Rutland, Vt.: Chas. E. Tuttle, 1964), 55 pp.

Snook, Barbara, *Costumes for School Plays* (Newton Center, Mass.: Chas. T. Branford, 1965), 96 pp.

Wagner, Glenn A., *Hobbycraft for Everybody* (New York: Dodd, Mead & Co., 1954), 96 pp.

Weiss, Harvey, *Clay, Wood and Wire* (New York: W. R. Scott, 1956), 48 pp.

————, *Paper, Ink and Roller; Printmaking for Beginners* (New York: W. R. Scott, 1958), 64 pp.

Wills, Royal Barry, *Tree Houses* (Boston: Houghton Mifflin Co., 1957), 66 pp.

appendix / THE INDUSTRIAL ARTS SPECIALIST-CONSULTANT

The following pages include items which industrial arts specialist-consultants may find helpful. Included are notes dealing with: a. The Consultant's function; b. Getting the program underway; c. Notes for a talk to the P.T.A.; and d. An outline for an industrial arts course for in-service classroom teachers.

THE CONSULTANT'S FUNCTION

1. To serve as protagonist, co-ordinator, and explainer of the program.

2. To make himself available for consultation. It seems reasonable that a full-time consultant should service between twenty to twenty-five classrooms. When more than twenty-five classrooms are involved, programs too often degenerate into pure craft activities because of time pressures.

It is important that time be provided for consultation sessions, either before or after regular school hours or, if the curriculum organization of the school permits, during the school day. A sign-up schedule posted on the faculty bulletin board may be useful.

Consultation sessions should be characterized by a spirit of cooperative endeavor between the consultant and the classroom teacher. The classroom teacher may sometimes be able to tell the consultant exactly what service is needed. At other times, the teacher may only acquaint the consultant with the area of learning under consideration and ask for activity suggestions. Since the consultant should be familiar with the subject of the conference beforehand, as indicated on the sign-up schedule, he can come to the session prepared with suggestions, resource materials, and ideas.

It is important that these teacher-consultant conferences precede the pupil activities, so that everyone concerned may have an understanding of the goals and the proposed procedures. Many times, the only business transacted at a conference is the scheduling of a planning time for teacher, class, and consultant.

3. To maintain a daily schedule which permits providing help when and where it is needed. Such help may be in the form of:

a. Demonstrating to a class, either in the classroom or in the laboratory.
b. Arranging for or accompanying a group on a field trip.
c. Discussing with a class a topic related to classroom work.
d. Assisting during a class work period.
e. Providing supplies and materials.
f. Helping to evaluate work in progress or a unit just completed.

4. To provide the stimulation of idea sheets to classroom teachers. These may be in the form of:

a. Process or operation descriptions, illustrated.
b. Project ideas.
c. Newsletters concerning industrial arts activities within the school.
d. Descriptions and order blanks for materials available from the laboratory.
e. Leaflets on specific phases of the curriculum.
f. Reprints of appropriate magazine articles.
g. Listings of field-trip possibilities.
h. Listings of new teaching resources available.
i. General announcements concerning the industrial arts activity program.

5. To oversee the laboratory.

6. To provide in-service instruction for classroom teachers on an informal basis or as an organized course.

7. To keep appropriate records, including:

a. Diary of services the consultant performed.
b. Equipment inventory.
c. Tool inventory.
d. Supplies and materials inventory.
e. Current classroom curriculum emphases.
f. Budget items.
g. Lists of books and other appropriate resources, including audio-visual aids available.

INDUSTRIAL ARTS CONFERENCES

(in your classroom)

Week of ....

Day	Time	Teacher	Subject of Conference
Monday	8:30		
	8:45		
Tuesday	8:30		
	8:45		
	3:00		
	3:30		
Wednesday	8:30		
	8:45		
Thursday	8:30		
	8:45		
	3:00		
	3:30		
Friday	8:30		
	8:45		

Figure 264. Consultant's conference sign-up schedule.

8. To keep himself informed of conditions and trends in his own school system and community, and of professional trends in his field and in elementary education generally.

SPECIAL NOTE: In addition to the functions listed above, a substantial part of the consultant's work is to deal effectively with all of the people in the school community. The consultant must have frequent, pleasant contacts with a wide variety of people if his program is to be successful. His program will be an effective one if he can maintain harmonious relationships with his co-workers. Vital personality traits for the consultant include a sense of humor, sincerity, dedication, resourcefulness, and efficiency.

Further, the industrial arts consultant is concerned with, and actively participates in, many areas of the school's total program directly or indirectly related to his field. He utilizes his special talents and skills to augment the work of curriculum-area committees, school building committees, teachers' associations, schedule committees, and the like. The industrial arts consultant, who possesses the traits, interests, and abilities outlined, is a valuable asset to the total educational program of a community.

GETTING THE PROGRAM UNDER WAY

The following suggestions are especially appropriate where the industrial-arts activity program is new to a school and the school year is just beginning. It is assumed that tools, materials, and other physical facilities are at hand.

1. The school administrator and the industrial arts consultant share responsibility for informing classroom teachers of the new industrial arts consultant services available.

2. Through general faculty meetings, grade-level meetings, and idea sheets, the consultant acquaints teachers with possibilities for getting the program started. The consultant constantly invites suggestions from classroom teachers.

3. The consultant keeps in mind that the program must be flexible, and that teacher requests can be expected to differ in approach and scope, even on similar grade levels. Often classroom teachers look to the consultant for his evaluation of their requests for services.

4. The consultant observes that some teachers want or require more help than others. He is efficient in providing that help.

5. The consultant permits the program to progress at a rate set chiefly by the classroom teachers. He realizes that the success of the program depends on the extent to which real teacher-child needs are met, and on the wholehearted support of the classroom teachers.

6. The consultant sometimes finds it desirable to work first where his services are most welcome. He depends on "word-of-mouth salesmanship," but he also "advertises" the activities of outstanding classes and enthusiastic teachers.

7. The consultant helps to set up displays and exhibits, and he distributes idea sheets to provide stimulation and interest in the program.

8. The consultant is tactful and considerate in visiting classrooms and offering his services.

9. As the program progresses, the need for a workshop for teachers may

Figure 265. Historical model enlivens a social studies lesson.

become apparent; then, the consultant makes the necessary preliminary arrangements. Here again the success of the workshop will depend upon the fullest possible cooperation by classroom teachers. The consultant should proceed only when he has reason to expect enthusiastic support of the idea. Classroom teachers should have a part in the planning and conducting of the workshop.

10. At all times, the consultant attempts to define his role as that of a helping teacher rather than a supervisor or critic.

11. The program in one specific classroom may get under way in the following way:

a. The classroom teacher signs up for a conference with the consultant.

b. The teacher and consultant discuss the needs and decide upon a plan of procedure.

c. The teacher and consultant schedule a series of class-teacher-consultant planning and working sessions.

d. After the planning session with the entire class, the consultant may work with a committee of children in the classroom or in the laboratory, in a series of work sessions.

e. The consultant points out certain phases of the work to the teacher and children that may be accomplished between his visits, perhaps providing a short memorandum to remind the classroom teacher of next steps to be taken.

f. The consultant gradually withdraws from the activity, as the classroom teacher and children feel that they can carry on unaided.

g. From time to time, the consultant may "drop in" to see if he is needed and to help evaluate the progress.

NOTES FOR A TALK TO THE P.T.A.

As a protagonist or salesman, the industrial arts consultant is anxious to have other people understand his program fully. He welcomes all opportunities to tell his story publicly. The parent-teacher meeting is an ideal vehicle for the dissemination of these ideas, and the industrial arts consultant makes (or fills) requests frequently for this type of a discussion. The suggestions below, modified to suit the occasion, might be appropriate for a large general meeting, a smaller grade-level, or single-classroom meeting, or a workshop for parents.

1. Introduction.

a. Expression of gratitude for the opportunity presented.

b. Humorous anecdote to fit the occasion.

c. Brief recall of an industrial arts (or "manual training") program in which parents might have participated when they were in school.

2. Function of the Current Industrial Arts Activity Program (use *and illustrate* these points as time and circumstances permit).

a. Develop adequate meanings by reducing levels of abstraction and enriching the curriculum.

b. Provide for individual differences.

c. Make children enjoy learning.

d. Provide the beginnings of occupational information.

e. Provide socializing experiences.

f. Develop a desirable personality.

g. Motivate learning.

h. Establish learning readiness.

i. Teach fundamental skills.

3. How the Program Operates.

a. Cite examples of science projects, mathematics projects, language arts projects, and others.

b. Display examples of work done by children.

c. Use slides, tape recordings, and the like, which illustrate the work in progress.

4. What Can Parents Do?

a. Encourage children in their work.

b. Avoid deprecating practical arts work.

c. Avoid applying adult standards to child efforts.

d. Display sincere interest in child's activities.

5. Conclusion.

a. Industrial arts is tailor-made for the elementary school child; it is a highly significant part of his total education.

b. None of this program would be possible without the enlightened, enthusiastic contributions of classroom teachers.

c. Conferences with parents are highly desirable in planning for the child's total development.

OUTLINE FOR AN INDUSTRIAL ARTS COURSE FOR IN-SERVICE CLASSROOM TEACHERS

Plans for a good course must take into account the local situation: past experiences and goals of the people involved, time and facilities available, and the like. Therefore, this outline is only suggestive.

Figure 266. Model ship building.

Here it is assumed that the classroom teachers enrolled have had virtually no formal instruction in shopwork, that the class numbers twenty enrollees, and that the course meets once a week, for three hours, for twenty weeks. It is further assumed that the course meets for credit. A noncredit course might be less demanding. If it is possible, you may wish to give the students preliminary notice. They should bring to class a notebook and pen or pencil, the prescribed textbook for the course, and some protective garment like a shop coat, smock, or large, serviceable apron.

First Meeting

1. See that the class is seated comfortably.
2. Introduce yourself and identify the course.
3. Take roll and have the people introduce themselves briefly.
4. Describe the course and distribute an abbreviated course outline, including a summary of course requirements.
5. Indicate the textbook to be used and alert the class to additional references available.
6. Have examples of between four and six projects of classroom industrial arts equipment available for viewing—workbench, sawhorse, easel, portable tool panel, flannelgram, all attractively finished, preferably using a good deal of color.
7. Explain that students will divide themselves into groups of approximately four, and that each group will work on any one of the above projects. It is not necessary that all projects be chosen, and more than one group can choose to work on the same kind of item.
8. Have a short break while students examine items, and choices are made of items and group mates.
9. After the break, record the names of group members and their project choices.
10. Distribute duplicated plan sheets of any equipment items not included in the textbook. Sheets should show: a drawing in perspective or simplified orthographic projection, a list of materials needed, and a list of major steps or operations. (One hour.)
11. Move to the work area and demonstrate the process of "getting out stock," using a rule, try square, framing square, and panel saw as appropriate to work. Suggest the possibility of practicing sawing on rough lumber first. Refer the students to Chapter 4, the section on *Cutting and Sawing* in the textbook. Suggest that they might refer to appropriate pages while waiting for tools. (Fifteen minutes.)
12. Have the students work as groups under the instructor's supervision, getting out their stock. Work continues until thirty minutes before the end of the class session.

13. Call the group together and explain the clean-up procedure. Put one person in charge of cleanup for his group.
14. Assign lockers and designate storage places.
15. Assemble the group in their seats, make appropriate encouraging remarks, and solicit questions and comments.
16. Assign Chapter 1 of the text, and suggest scanning entire text.
17. Dismiss the class.

Second Meeting

1. Have the class take their seats and call the roll.
2. Discuss the material covered by Chapter 1. (Fifty minutes.)
3. Call attention to the TOOL USE RECORD at the end of this section and explain its use.
4. Have the students work until one group has all necessary stock cut out.
5. Assemble in the work area and demonstrate "making things smooth" using the block plane, half-round cabinet file, and sandpaper as appropriate to the work. Refer the students to the text, Chapter 4, the section titled *Making Things Smooth*. (Twenty minutes.)
6. Demonstrate, only to the group concerned, any other tool needed for a particular item being made, such as the coping saw or jig saw for the portable tool panel.
7. Have the students continue with their work until one group has all stock ready for assembly.
8. Assemble the group and demonstrate "making holes" and appropriate fastening processes. Call attention to the text, Chapter 4, sections titled *Making Holes* and *Fastening Pieces Together*. (Fifteen minutes.)
9. Work continues until cleanup.
10. Have the class seat themselves: assign Chapter 4, in the textbook.
11. Assign students the task of deciding what they would like to make after the group project has been completed. The second project, which is normally individual work, will be started next time, so it will be necessary for them to bring a sketch of what will be made. This should be a device to illustrate something they will be teaching in their own classes five or six weeks hence, preferably an illustrative device of some sort. Refer to Chapter 5, the section titled *Construction Projects*.
12. Dismiss the class.

Third Meeting

1. After the class is seated, call the roll. (Do this at the beginning of each session; this step will not be repeated in the notes from here on.)
2. Discuss the material covered in Chapter 4, explain that processes described

there, but not yet demonstrated, will be demonstrated in due course. (Thirty minutes.)

3. Have three or four people describe their plans for their next project (select these people beforehand if possible). Discuss the relative merits of the proposed projects. (Fifteen minutes.)

4. Work continues until one group is ready to apply a finish to the group project.

5. Have the students assemble in the work area and demonstrate the appropriate finishing processes, limiting the explanation to surface preparation and the application of shellac on these equipment items. Call attention to Chapter 4, the section titled *Painting and Finishing Processes*. (Ten minutes.)

6. While part of any one group is performing finishing operations, check plans for the next project with other members of group; then discuss plans with the people who were doing the finishing so that all members of the group have an opportunity to participate in the finishing steps.

7. In the course of the class session, check all project plans. Designate the materials which must be brought to the class next time, if they are not available in shop.

8. Work continues until cleanup, with the students starting new projects as soon as the group project has been given the first coat of finish.

9. After the class is seated, assign Chapter 5, the first three sections titled: *Starting With the Curriculum; Possible Industrial Arts Activities;* and *Emphases by Areas of Learning.*

Fourth Meeting

1. Discuss Chapter 5, the sections titled: *Starting With the Curriculum; Possible Industrial Arts Activities;* and *Emphasis by Areas of Learning.* (Twenty minutes.)

2. Assemble in the work area, and demonstrate sanding a shellac finish and preparing and applying oil paints and brush cleaning. (Twenty minutes.)

3. Informal individual demonstrations may be needed as people begin working on their individual second projects.

4. About midway through the session, assemble the group and demonstrate the cutting and sawing processes not previously covered. (Twenty minutes.)

5. Work continues until cleanup, but allow for a short discussion of items 6 and 7 below.

6. After the class is seated, assign Chapter 5, the sections titled *Deciding on What To Do, Field Trips* and *Construction Projects*, and a review of Chapter 4, *Planning Processes*. Point out the necessity of planning ahead on items to be constructed as the course progresses. These items may be individual projects, or they may be projects to be constructed by groups constituted by the mutual agreement of the students concerned. There is

a considerable difference of opinion as to the nature of these projects. Some feel that the projects should be useful to the people making them. Others want them to be appropriate to the elementary school program. Course instructors must use their own judgment here. Probably the decision will have to be adjusted to individual requirements.

7. Have each student bring to the next session a suggestion for a field trip, which the entire group might take. These suggestions should reflect the worthwhile purpose that a proposed trip ought to fulfill. Point out that the question of a class field trip will be resolved at the next meeting. The nature of the trip will vary with local situations, but, in general, one should look for a mechanized industry with a fair amount of automation.

Fifth Meeting

1. If not covered previously, the matter of disposing of the equipment items made by the groups should be taken up, and the local policy on paying for materials should be explained.
2. Discuss Chapter 5, the sections titled *Deciding What to Do, Field Trips* and *Construction Projects,* and Chapter 4, the section titled *Planning Processes.* (Twenty minutes.)
3. Discuss the field trip, having people indicate and justify their suggestions. Decide, as a class, whether a field trip would be worthwhile and, if so, what the nature of the trip should be. Set a date, possibly the class meeting two weeks hence; appoint a committee on arrangements and have them meet with the instructor at some convenient time. (Ten minutes.)
4. The work continues under the instructor's supervision; individual demonstrations are given as needed.
5. About midway through the session, assemble the group and demonstrate processes of making holes, not previously discussed. (Fifteen minutes.)
6. Work continues until cleanup.

Figure 267. Building a model rocket brings the space age into the laboratory.

7. Have the class seated; promise a report by the committee on field-trip arrangements next time; inform the students of next week's forty-five minute quiz on Chapter 1 and Chapter 5.

Sixth Meeting
1. Discuss the suggestions of the committee on field-trip arrangements and make final plans for the trip, making sure that the purposes to be achieved are understood. (Fifteen minutes.)
2. Conduct a quiz on Chapter 1 and Chapter 5. (Forty-five minutes.) Students who finish early may go to work.
3. Work continues until about midway through the session.
4. Assemble the group and demonstrate processes of smoothing surfaces not previously covered. (Ten minutes.)
5. Work continues until cleanup.
6. After the class is seated, remind students of field-trip procedure.

Seventh Meeting
1. Take the field trip.
2. If the trip is not taken, or if it was taken at some time other than class time, use the notes for the "Eighth Meeting" and move up each succeeding meeting.

Eighth Meeting
1. Discuss the field trip if this was not possible at the conclusion of the trip; discuss the quiz. (Ten to twenty minutes.)
2. Work continues until cleanup time. Assemble the class for the next step.
3. Have the class take their seats and demonstrate the planning processes, including sketching and drawing. Opinion varies considerably on this matter. Some specialists feel that sketching is adequate, and others introduce the basic drawing instruments, T square, triangles, and scale. Sketching styles vary also, with greatest emphasis given to perspective sketching. Some instructors include cabinet and/or isometric projection, and some insist that simple orthographic projection is also appropriate, even though it will not be used in the elementary grades as a rule. (Fifteen to thirty minutes.)
4. Assign homework preparation of project plans, as appropriate.

Ninth Meeting
1. Discuss planning processes and homework project plans. (Fifteen minutes.)
2. Work continues until about midway through session.
3. Assemble the group and demonstrate processes of fastening pieces together not previously covered. (Fifteen minutes.)
4. Work continues until cleanup.
5. Assemble the class and assign Chapter 3, the first four sections titled *A Place to Work, Classroom Work Areas, Specialized Industrial Arts Shops,*

and *Equipment and Its Arrangement*. Make appropriate observations concerning the projects being chosen and designed by students. Indicate possibilities of introducing greater inventiveness and variety in media, projects, and processes.

Tenth Meeting

1. Discuss Chapter 3, the first four sections, utilizing available pictures and examples.
2. Work continues until midway through session.
3. Assemble and demonstrate finishing processes not yet covered. (Twenty minutes.)
4. Work continues until cleanup.
5. Assemble the class, assign Chapter 3, the last four sections titled *Basic Tools for Use in a Classroom, Basic Tools for Industrial Arts Workroom, Supplies for a Typical Industrial Arts Classroom Program*, and *Supplies for Industrial Arts Workrooms*.

Eleventh Meeting

1. Discuss Chapter 3, the last three sections. (Thirty minutes.)
2. Work continues until it is time to clean up and assemble for item 3 below.
3. Show film: "A B C's of Hand Tools," available from General Motors Corporation, Department of Public Relations, 1775 Broadway, New York, New York. Call attention to the availability of industrial films, and indicate some of the film possibilities.
4. Inform students of next week's one-hour quiz on Chapters 3 and 4.

Twelfth Meeting

1. Conduct a quiz on Chapters 3 and 4. (Sixty minutes.)
2. Work continues until midway through the session.
3. Assemble the group and demonstrate some process not covered by the textbook, possibly a ceramics process, and indicate appropriate references. Encourage project designing making use of a new process.
4. Work continues until cleanup.

Thirteenth Meeting

1. Review the quiz on Chapters 3 and 4. (Ten to twenty minutes.)
2. Work continues until midway through session.
3. Assemble the group and demonstrate some process not covered by the textbook, possibly a textiles process, and indicate appropriate references and project possibilities.
4. Work continues until cleanup.
5. Have the class take their seats, ask the students to think about accepting one of these four assignments: 1. Read some of the references listed at the end of Chapters 4 and 5 and report on them briefly in class; 2. Read one or

more of the other references listed at the end of each of the chapters in the text and report on them briefly in class; 3. Prepare a short demonstration on some new process for presentation to the class; 4. Prepare some project idea sheets for distribution to the entire class. Indicate that choices should be made by next class, but that choices should be discussed with the instructor before too much detail work is done on these assignments.

Fourteenth Meeting
1. Make final decisions on the individual assignments discussed at the end of the last meeting. Ask the students to check with the instructor during the period to complete plans. Try to provide for two short student demonstrations and three of the other kinds of student presentations during the next meeting.
2. About midway through the session, assemble the group and demonstrate some new process, possibly a craft process like kite-making, fishing-fly-tying, basketry, or gimp braiding.
3. Work continues until cleanup and dismissal.

Fifteenth Meeting
1. Have presentations by three people who have accepted individual assignments other than demonstrations, each person to be limited to ten minutes' time. (Thirty minutes.)
2. About midway through session have presentations by two people who have prepared demonstrations. (Twenty minutes.)
3. Work continues until cleanup.
4. Assign Chapter 2.

Sixteenth Meeting
1. Have reports from people about their individual assignments. Distribute this activity throughout the class session as conditions warrant. (Fifty minutes.)
2. At the close of the meeting assign a term paper to be prepared by each student on: "How I Will Use Industrial Arts Activities in My Teaching." Explain that reference should be made to programs for any exceptional students for whom the teachers might be responsible. These are to be submitted at the eighteenth meeting.

Seventeenth Meeting
1. Listen to five people as they present reports of their individual assignments; distribute throughout the class session as conditions warrant. (Fifty minutes.)
2. Work continues.
3. At the close of the session remind students of the paper due for the next meeting.

Eighteenth Meeting
1. Have five people present reports of their individual assignments; distribute throughout the class session as conditions warrant. (Fifty minutes.)
2. Collect term papers.
3. At the close of the meeting plan for an open-house display to be held at the twentieth meeting, displaying work class has done. Encourage students to invite their school administrators and other colleagues.
4. Remind the class that a final examination will be held at the nineteenth meeting.

Nineteenth Meeting
1. Conduct the final examination. (Sixty minutes.)
2. Return the student papers submitted during the previous week.
3. Complete plans for the open-house display of the students' work. The open house should begin one hour after class normally meets.
4. Work continues.

Twentieth Meeting
1. Return final examination papers.
2. Prepare for the open house.
3. Conduct the open house.
4. Work continues as conditions permit.
5. Conduct closing "ceremonies" as appropriate.

TOOL USE RECORD

Figure 268 lists the common tools with which classroom teachers should become familiar. It may be desirable to add other tools to the list, but these are basic. Teachers may wish to place a check in one of the small boxes following the name of a tool, each time they have occasion to use the tool. This will provide teachers with an easy method of checking on the extent of their experiences with tools. It should be remembered that one can achieve a degree of skill with these tools, even if they are used only to practice on scrap material.

Tools	Number of times used							Principal uses of tools
Jig saw								
Panel saw								
Compass saw								
Backsaw								
Coping saw								
Try square								
C clamp								
Tin snips								
Pliers								
Hand drill								
Bit brace								
File								
Claw hammer								
Screw driver								
Wrench								
Block plane								
Nail set								
Scratch awl								

Figure 268. Tool use record.

INDEX